# Eastern Sierra and Death Valley Camping With Privacy

Your Guide To Finding the Most Private Campsites
Near Mammoth Lakes, Tuolumne Meadows, Death
Valley, and Beyond

## Kimberly and Patrick Wilkes

ISBN 978-1515196204

Nature can be beautiful, but on rare occasions it can also be dangerous. By reading this book you agree that the author and photographer assume no liability for any accidents, injuries, or property damage that may occur when camping, hiking, or taking part in any activity mentioned in this book.

This book is dedicated to Kim's older brother Lance, who taught her the joys of camping in the Sierra, and to Patrick's family and Native American friends of the Eastern Sierra.

# Table of Contents

# Introduction
## How To Use This Book To Find Peaceful Campsites with the Most Privacy

Do you like camping where your neighbors are out of sight behind vegetation or far enough away to give you lots of elbow room? Even though we enjoy meeting new people when we're camping, we still like to return to a sheltered campsite that's away from the crowds.

The problem is, when you're making reservations on recreation.gov, you can't always tell which sites have the most privacy. Some sites look like they're spaced far apart when in fact they're located across an open meadow in full sight of each other. Other spaces might have trees or a big hill between them, giving them lots of privacy — but you would never know that by looking at the maps on recreation.gov.

Even if you prefer to choose the first-come, first-served spaces when you arrive at a campground, it's handy to know which campgrounds in a particular canyon or area have the best selection of campsites with privacy. That way, especially if you're arriving on a busy Friday, you'll know which campground to visit first, and possibly beat the other campers to the choice spots. In a place like Death Valley, where campgrounds are located long distances apart, it's especially helpful to know which sites in which campgrounds are the best so you can plan your trip accordingly.

In order to help you know exactly which spaces have the most privacy, we looked at a whopping 3,416 campsites in 91 campgrounds between Hope Valley and Lone Pine and everything in between as well as campsites in Death Valley and near the Ancient Bristlecone Pine Forest. Then we critiqued each of the privacy-worthy spaces in this book.

By using this *Eastern Sierra And Death Valley Camping With Privacy* book, you'll know exactly which campsites to choose and which campgrounds have the most spaces with privacy. You'll be one step ahead of other campers. And you'll have a better chance of grabbing the perfect campsite that's surrounded by a cushion of privacy.

In addition to describing the spots with the most privacy, we also provide a description of each campground along with some basic facts. And we let you know what activities are near where you set up camp.

**What Do We Mean By Campsites with Privacy?**

In order for a campsite to be included in this book it had to meet one of several qualifications. The campsite had to:

1) Be far enough away from neighboring sites so that they didn't feel intrusive, and/or
2) Be surrounded by vegetation on one or more sides, which blocked the view of any neighbors, and/or
3) Have some sort of natural feature obscuring the view of one or more neighbors such as a hill or rocks, and/or
4) Feel private and peaceful, especially compared to other sites in the campground.

**How Did We Rate the Campsites?**

In addition to describing each of the campsites, we gave the campsites the following ratings in order to give you a good idea about their privacy factor.

When rating the campsites, some of the factors we took into consideration were: 1) How close is the site to its neighbors? 2) How many nearby neighbors does it have? 3) Is there thick vegetation, completely hiding the site from view of neighbors? 4) If the neighbors are closer, is there some vegetation filtering them from view? 5) Is there a hill or giant boulder intervening between two campsites?

Some of this was subjective, because we rated each campsite based on how it felt when we were standing in the campsite or standing near the campsite looking into it if someone was staying in the site during our visit.

Here are general guidelines as to what each ranking means:

**A+**
This means a campsite is either surrounded completely by vegetation or is so far away from its neighbors that it provides the ultimate in camping privacy. These are the cream of the camping with privacy crop. Often, but not always, A+ spaces are pushed back from the campground road.

**A**
Slightly less private than an A+ site, it may have a minor flaw that prevents it from reaching A+ status. For example, the fire pit and picnic table might be close to the campground road, even if the tent pad is hidden away behind vegetation. Maybe there's vegetation on only two sides instead of three. Maybe most of the neighbors are far away with one neighbor that's just close enough to make the site less than A+ worthy. Or maybe the site is located in a meadow, in full view of the campground road even if it has no neighbors on any side.

**A-**
Still a very private campsite, it may have a couple of minor flaws. Maybe neighboring spaces are absent on three sides, but on the other side, there's a neighbor. The neighbor isn't so close as to make it a deal breaker, but there's not as much space between campsites as there might be in an A+ spot.

## B+

In a B+ site, you'll have good privacy, but the neighbors might be a bit closer compared to an A or A+ site. Maybe vegetation partially blocks the view of the neighbors, but you have a filtered view of them.

## B

This type of campsite may have a more exposed feel to it. Maybe the space is in the pines and the neighbors aren't too close, but there's not much understory and you can see them really well. Or perhaps the campsite is located in the sagebrush and rabbitbrush and it has a neighbor on one side so that it doesn't have a complete cushion of privacy. Yet, it still isn't a bad campsite and still feels reasonably private.

## B-

For us to rank a campsite as B-, usually it had to have at least one or two neighbors that were clearly visible. In some cases, perhaps the driveway of the neighboring site was located close enough that if an RV parked there it might feel intrusive—but yet the campsite had neighbors on no other sides.

## C+

We did not include very many C+ campsites in this book because most C+ campsites lacked the privacy level we like. If we did include a C+ site it was for good reason, such as the campsite had a spectacular view and still had a slightly above average level of privacy. Or perhaps the C+ site was located in a busy area of the campground or next to a stream or lake and we wanted to give you at least one option in case you had your heart set on staying in that location.

Anything below a C+ we didn't include in the book, because we felt as if people who enjoy privacy while camping would not appreciate those campsites.

## Our Descriptions of the Campsites

In the book, we refer to some feature as being to the left, right, behind, or in front of a campsite. Usually, these directions refer to when you are standing in the driveway of the campsite facing the campsite. In this case, in front of the campsite would be across the campground road. However, in a campsite where you had to take a short trail to reach it and that trail was perpendicular to the driveway, we measured left, right, behind, and in front from the place where the trail entered the camp space.

## Which Campgrounds Are Featured in the Book?

We looked at 3,416 campsites throughout the Eastern Sierra and Death Valley from Hope Valley to Lone Pine including Grandview Campground in the White Mountains. Campgrounds we did NOT include in the book were campgrounds run by Inyo County such as Independence

Creek, Diaz Lake, Portagee Joe, Taboose Creek, and Baker Creek because we felt as if those campgrounds did not offer any campsites with privacy — they felt more like parking lots than campgrounds. We did, however, include BLM-operated Tuttle Creek in the book. We did NOT include Goodale Creek or Horton Creek, also BLM campgrounds, but at some point we may write about them in the campground updates page on our website at **www.ilovetheeasternsierra.com**.

Most of the campgrounds we included were National Forest Service Campgrounds or National Park Campgrounds, but we did include some privately operated campgrounds such as Hope Valley Resort and Panamint Springs Resort.

Whenever possible we tried to actually stand in a campsite to see how private it felt. However, if a space was occupied we could only do this if the person or persons staying there invited us into their campsite. We also attempted to talk to a camp host of the campground, but a camp host was not always there at the time of our visit.

## What Do We Mean By Takes Reservations?

When we say a campsite is reservable or that a campground takes reservations, we mean during peak season. There are some campgrounds, such as East Fork, that make all their campsites first-come, first-served in the fall. Furnace Creek Campground in Death Valley takes reservations from October 15 – April 15, but the rest of the year it is first-come, first-served.

## Create Your Own Slice of Serenity

We invite you to find the most beautiful and peaceful campsites in the Eastern Sierra and Death Valley by using this book as your guide. We love to camp and we hope this book will help others find peace and rejuvenation in nature.

# HOPE VALLEY

# Crystal Springs Campground

**Directions From Nevada:** From Highway 395 in Minden, Nevada, drive up Highway 88 approximately 15 miles. About half mile past the Highway 4/89 turnoff in Woodfords, California, turn left on to Crystal Springs Road. The campground entrance is approximately a half mile on the south side of the road.

**Directions from Sacramento/San Francisco:** Take Highway 50 East toward South Lake Tahoe. After descending into the Tahoe basin, take a right on State Route 89. Go over Luther Pass and turn left where SR 89 dead ends at State Route 88. Drive past Sorensen's Resort and follow SR 88 downhill through Woodfords Canyon. Take a right on Crystal Springs Road. (If you reach the intersection of Highways 4/89 you've gone too far.) The campground will be immediately visible on your right.

## What's It Like?

At the bottom of Woodford's Canyon, near the Carson River, this campground sits under a canopy of pines. It doesn't have much understory between spaces, and some of the sites are too close together. Plus, in the neighborhood next to the campground there are houses, which intrusively peer over at some of the spaces. It's also near Highway 88, so many of the campsites are plagued by road noise. But we found three spaces here we liked. And this is a lightly used campground during the week, which means that despite the proximity of other campsites, you might have few if any neighbors mid-week. It's a great home away from home for anglers, with the Carson River a short walk away from the campsites.

**Words of Warning:** Because of its lower elevation, Crystal Springs Campground may roast during the hottest days of summer, especially when the temperature is near 100 in nearby Gardnerville. During heat waves, it could be in the low 90s here in the daytime. Luckily, it's rare for the temperatures to hover that high and you can always drive a half hour up the road to Carson Pass to escape the heat of the day.

**What's It Near?**

• Fishing for rainbow, brown, and Lahontan cutthroat trout in the West Fork of the Carson River.

• Twenty minutes to Grover Hot Springs State Park. In addition to a soak in the spring-fed pool at the state park, take an easy, 2.7-mile, round-trip hike to Grover Waterfall.

• Hiking in Hope Valley, on the Pacific Crest Trail, on the Tahoe Rim Trail, and by Carson Pass. The trail to Winnemucca Lake, which puts on a spectacular wildflower display in July, is about 25 minutes away.

• Hiking and fishing are at Indian Creek Reservoir, and there's also some great bird watching here. We saw white pelicans, a beautiful yellow and black bird, and a parade of baby Canadian geese trailing along behind their mother.

• Grab a bowl of soup or chili or nibble on a Panini sandwich at Woodford's Station a mile or so away from the campground.

• Breakfast, lunch, and homemade pies with deliciously flakey crust are less than 10 minutes away at Hope Valley Resort. A little ways beyond is Sorensen's Resort where you can feast on their famous beef bourguignon or quiche, sandwiches, steaks, pasta, and seafood. I don't know which I'm more addicted to, their berry cobbler, served with a scoop of ice cream, or the French toast with berry compote. Sorensen's is open for breakfast, lunch, and dinner.

**Elevation:** 6,000 feet

**Toilets:** Vault

**Verizon Cell Service?** No

**Takes Reservations?** No. First come, first served.

**Number of Campsites:** 20

**Bear Boxes?** Newly installed the fall of 2014

## Campsites with the Most Privacy

**#3 Privacy Rating: A**
**Reservable?** No. First-come, first served.

A spacious spot studded with lichen-speckled boulders, #3 backs up against a hill and features a view of a rocky outcropping. This site has lots of elbow room, thanks to the lack of nearby neighbors on the left, right, and behind. Plenty of pines shade the site and the water spigot is conveniently close. A giant boulder rises up in front of the campsite across the street, erasing the picnic table from view. Definitely the best site in the campground from a privacy perspective. And it has the least amount of road noise from Highway 88, due to its location at the rear of the campground.

**#9 Privacy Rating: B-**
**Reservable?** No. First-come, first served.

This space has some advantages that make it worthy of this book. It's nestled under the pines and features a spectacular view of the rocky spires rising up on the other side of Woodfords Canyon. Plus, no neighbors are visible on the left, right, or behind. Set your chair in the grassy areas surrounding the site and listen to the Carson River, which flows behind the campsite on the other side of Crystal Springs Road. The bathrooms are across the campground road from #9, so there are no immediate neighbors on that side, although facing that direction, you'll have a distant view of a lot of the other campers in the campground.

The site also has some disadvantages. The fire pit and picnic table are close to the campground road. It's also a small campsite with bushes pushing their way into the grassy border, not leaving a lot of room for a large tent. And you'll hear road noise drifting over from Highway 88, where cars whoosh by on the other side of the Carson River. Despite the disadvantages, its location near the river makes it a good choice for anglers. It's also a good choice for campers with a small trailer, pickup truck with a camper top, or camper van. Or, if you have a tent and you think the road noise will bother you, bring earplugs.

**#17 Privacy Rating: B+**
**Reservable?** No. First-come, first served.

The only thing between you and the Carson River is Crystal Springs Road, which parallels Highway 88 and passes behind this campsite. No neighbors interfere with your privacy on the right and trees hide the view of the houses that peer out over the campground in that direction. The space on the left is far enough away and hidden by bushes and manzanita, so it won't intrude upon your privacy. #17 is tucked back to make the across-the-road neighbor a non-issue. This site also has a view of the impressive cliffs towering over the other side of Woodford's Canyon. The one flaw? Road noise from Highway 88. Tent campers bring your earplugs.

## Kit Carson Campground

**Directions from Nevada:** From Highway 395, follow Highway 88 for about 16 miles. Kit Carson Campground is on your right. If you reach Sorensen's Resort you've gone too far.

**Directions from Sacramento and San Francisco:** Take U.S. Highway 50 to the Lake Tahoe Basin. Immediately after descending into the Basin, take a right on Highway 89. Follow it up over Luther Pass and where the road intersects with Highway 88 take a left. The campground is just past Sorensen's Resort on the left, across from Hope Valley Resort.

## What's It Like?

Resting under a grove of aspens and Jeffrey pines with the West Fork of the Carson River flowing by peacefully, the sites in this campground are well spaced, and many (but not all) offer good privacy. It's a tranquil setting, but depending on which site you choose, you'll have to put up with some road noise from Highway 88. In the early summer, the Carson River might muffle some of the road noise when the water is flowing at its strongest. Due to the small parking spaces, this campground is best for tents and small motorhomes, trailers, pickup trucks with a camper top, and camper vans.

## What's It Near?

• Fishing for rainbow, brown, and Lahontan cutthroat trout in the West Fork of the Carson River.

• Lake Tahoe is about 20 miles away.

• Less than a half hour to Grover Hot Springs State Park. In addition to a soak in the spring-fed pool at the state park, take a 2.7-mile round-trip hike to Grover Waterfall.

• Hiking in Hope Valley, on the Pacific Crest Trail and Tahoe Rim Trail, and by Carson Pass. The trail to Winnemucca Lake, which puts on a spectacular wildflower display in July, is about 20 minutes away.

• Hiking and fishing are at Indian Creek Reservoir, and there's also some great bird watching here. We saw white pelicans, a beautiful yellow and black bird, and a parade of baby Canadian geese trailing along behind their mother.

• Grab a bowl of soup or chili or nibble on a Panini sandwich at Woodford's Station a few miles away from the campground at the bottom of Woodford's Canyon.

• Breakfast, lunch, and homemade pies with deliciously flakey crust are across Highway 88 from the campground at Hope Valley Resort. A little ways beyond is Sorensen's Resort where you can feast on their famous beef bourguignon or quiche, sandwiches, steaks, and seafood. I don't know which I'm more addicted to, their berry cobbler, served with a scoop of ice cream, or the French toast with berry compote. Sorensen's is open for breakfast, lunch, and dinner.

**Elevation:** 6,900 feet

**Toilets:** Vault

**Verizon Cell Service?** No

**Takes Reservations?** Yes. Visit **www.recreation.gov** for reservations. Some sites are first-come, first-served.

**Number of Campsites:** 12

**Bear Boxes?** Yes.

# Campsites with the Most Privacy

**#2 Privacy Rating: B-**
**Reservable?** Yes. Visit **www.recreation.gov** for reservations.

It's always peaceful to set up camp next to a stream. This site is perched above the Carson River, which flows behind it. Sit on the large boulder overlooking the river and watch the water begin its journey toward the Carson Valley. The space is more out in the open than many in the campground, but it's set back from the campground road, so it doesn't feel too exposed, even to the neighbors across the street. Plus, the only company you'll have on either side are aspens. Some pines provide shade. Its biggest flaw? The only thing between you and Highway 88 is the river, meaning you'll have to put up with some road noise.

**#3 Privacy Rating: B**
**Reservable?** No. First-come, first served.

Trees surround this site on three sides creating a lot of privacy from adjoining neighbors, although it's a sunny, grassy spot, visible from the campground road. The site is across the campground road from the stream, which means it's also within hearing distance of cars zipping along Highway 88 on the other side of the river.

**#5 Privacy Rating: B+**
**Reservable?** Yes. Visit **www.recreation.gov** for reservations.

Located on an aspen-lined cul de sac, this space has no neighbors on the left or right and the river marches along behind it. Jeffrey pines shade some of the campsite. The bathroom is across the street. The good news? This space has a ton of privacy. The bad news? You'll hear some road noise from Highway 88 so tent campers bring your earplugs.

**#8 Privacy Rating: A+**
**Reservable?** Yes. Visit **www.recreation.gov** for reservations.

This campsite is the most private in the campground and one of the coolest campsites we saw on our travels. At first glance, it seems too close to the camp host site on the right. But a short path leads from the parking spot to the campsite, where the picnic table and fire pit sit on the edge of a clearing surrounded by aspens and are completely hidden from the campground road. In fact, you can't see them until you're almost upon them. Aspens and a large boulder block the view of the campground host and aspens completely hide the view of the camp space to the left.

Behind the site, aspens and conifers are your only neighbors. A little path leads from the clearing where the picnic table and fire pit are located into a small circular arena surrounded by aspens, a cozy location for your tent. There's room for another tent in the main part of the campsite, too. Another short path leads to a rock outcropping with a view of Woodfords Canyon to the east. Like the other spaces on this side of the campground, #8 is located farther from Highway 88 and the road noise is minimized (although not gone altogether).

## #9 Privacy Rating: B+
**Reservable?** Yes. Visit **www.recreation.gov** for reservations.

A big hunk of a boulder to the right of this space eliminates the view of any neighbors on that side. Aspens to the left partially filter the view of the neighboring space in that direction. No neighbors intrude on your privacy across the street or behind. A big conifer shades the picnic table. This space is also farther from Highway 88, so the road noise here is less than spaces closer to the river.

## #10 Privacy Rating: B+
**Reservable?** Yes. Visit **www.recreation.gov** for reservations.

Aspens to the right of this space partially filter out the views of #9. The neighbor to the left is a good distance away and plenty of aspens grow in between the two sites, erasing that spot from view. To the rear of the campsite, a pine forest sprinkled with some aspens makes for a tranquil backdrop. Tall pines shade the picnic table. Based on this site's location, you'll escape much of the road noise from Highway 88.

## #11 Privacy Rating: A
**Reservable?** Yes. Visit **www.recreation.gov** for reservations.

This space sits on a loop at the rear of the campground. A boulder the size of a small trailer parked to the right of the campsite partially screens the site from view of the road. The nearest campsite to the right (#10) is a good distance away anyway, but the boulder doubly ensures that #11 will escape any prying eyes from that direction. A conifer-covered hill rises up to the left. Low-growing aspen trees mingle with the pine trees surrounding the campsite. Across the street there are no neighbors. A row of aspens in front of #11 partially shelters it from view of the street on one side.

Like most of the sites in this campground, the space is partially shaded by evergreens and aspens, although the sun will spotlight the picnic table throughout parts of the day. Less road noise here, too, but it's not gone completely.

**#12 Privacy Rating: A**
**Reservable?** No. First-come, first-served.

This site was closed for repairs when we were visiting. We're presuming it will be open by the time you read this book, although we make no guarantees. Aspens almost completely encircle #12, on the cul de sac at the rear of the campground. Slightly closer to Highway 88 than #11, this site has a bit more road noise. Even so, it's in a tranquil setting where you can watch the aspens quiver in the breeze.

## Hope Valley Resort Campground

**Directions from Sacramento and San Francisco:** From Highway 50 in South Lake Tahoe, soon after the road descends from Echo Summit, take a right on Highway 89 and follow it over Luther Pass. At the intersection of Highways 88 and 89, take a left and travel about 1¼ miles to the campground on the right.

**Directions from Nevada:** From Highway 395 in Minden, take a right on Highway 88. Follow the road up into the mountains for about 16 miles. Hope Valley Resort is on the left at the top of Woodford's Canyon. If you reach Sorensen's Resort, you've gone too far.

**What's It Like?**

Operated by Sorensen's Resort, Hope Valley Resort Campground sits under a grove of aspens next to the West Fork of the Carson River. The campground is nestled in the river canyon below Highway 88, so the one disadvantage is you'll hear road noise. Still, the canopy of aspens overhead adds a touch of tranquility, and because most of the sites are located far below the highway the road noise is smothered in many locations. Many of the sites have electrical hookups for trailers. Hot showers offer a luxury absent at many campgrounds.

**Words of Warning:** There are no bear boxes.

**What's It Near?**

• Fishing for rainbow, brown, and Lahontan cutthroat trout in the West Fork of the Carson River.

• Lake Tahoe is about 20 miles away.

• Hiking in Hope Valley, on the Pacific Crest Trail, on the Tahoe Rim Trail, and by Carson Pass. The trail to Winnemucca Lake, which puts on a spectacular wildflower display in July, is about 20 minutes away.

• Less than a half hour to Grover Hot Springs State Park. In addition to a soak in the spring-fed pool at the state park, take an easy, 2.7-mile, round-trip hike to Grover Waterfall.

• Sweet-toothed campers will love pitching a tent or parking a trailer steps away from some of the best homemade pie in the Eastern Sierra served at Hope Valley Resort Café. Manager Leesa Lopazanski also bakes up some of the best homemade scones I've ever tasted. Stop by the resort for breakfast and lunch.

• At Sorensen's Resort, about a quarter mile away from the campground, feast on beef bourguignon, quiche, sandwiches, steaks, pasta, seafood and much more. I don't know which I'm more addicted to, their berry cobbler, served with a scoop of ice cream, or the French toast with berry compote. Sorensen's is open for breakfast, lunch, and dinner.

**Elevation:** 6,900 feet

**Toilets:** Flush

**Verizon Cell Service?** No

**Takes Reservations?** Yes. Call (530) 694-2629 or e-mail info@hopevalleyresort.com

**Number of Campsites:** 22

**Bear Boxes?** No

## Campsites with the Most Privacy

**#3 Privacy Rating: A**
**Reservable?** Yes. Call (530) 694-2629 or e-mail info@hopevalleyresort.com

Perched in the boulders above the rest of the campground, this walk-in site comes with a spectacular view of Woodfords Canyon and not a glimpse of your nearest neighbors, walk-in sites 1 and 2. The space is out in the open with only some small conifers and junipers, allowing you to admire an unobstructed view of the stars or the full moon at night. Along with the spectacular view of Woodford's Canyon, you have a bird's eye view of Highway 88 off to the left across the Carson River.

However, #3 also has some flaws that you may or may not be able to live with. To reach the site, you'll have to trek about 54 feet up a hill from where you park your car (bring a wheeled cart to load your stuff). Plus, the bathrooms are a hike away down and back up a steep hill, an estimated 1/8 mile between the campsite and the bathrooms. During the day, you can use the restrooms at Hope Valley Café and Store, which are closer to the campsite.

The road noise also is particularly noticeable in this spot and the other two walk-in sites since they're raised up from the rest of the campground and closer to Highway 88. Even so, if you bring earplugs and don't mind getting some exercise, this is a sweet spot.

**#11 Privacy Rating: A+**
**Reservable?** Yes. Call (530) 694-2629 or e-mail **info@hopevalleyresort.com**

With no other spaces visible behind, to the right, or across the street, #11 is the campsite equivalent of a loner sitting off by itself. To the left, conifers and aspens hide the view of the campground road. A rocky cliff rises up in the distance behind the site, adding an element of interest. There's some road noise from Highway 88, but it's not as noticeable as in the walk-in sites.

**#14 Privacy Rating: B+**
**Reservable?** Yes.
Call (530) 694-2629 or e-mail **info@hopevalleyresort.com**

Behind #14, the Carson River, which you can hear but not see from the campsite, begins its descent down Woodford's Canyon. The site is tucked back far from the campground road, so you won't see your neighbor across the way. It has no other spaces behind it or to the right. Space #13 to the left is a stone's throw away, but aspens and evergreens, and a small hill partially filter out the view of your neighbors. In fact, the people staying in site 13 will have a better view of you than you will of them due to their location uphill. A path leads from #14 to #13, making these sites ideal for families and friends who want to camp next to each other. #14 also is near the bathrooms. If #11 and #15 are available, we'd choose those first, but if someone has snatched them up, #14 isn't a bad spot.

**#15 Privacy Rating: A+**
**Reservable?** Yes.
Call (530) 694-2629 or e-mail **info@hopevalleyresort.com**

Dubbed the "honeymoon site" by the camp host, this cozy spot is surrounded on three sides by aspens. The closest neighbor is site #14 across the street, and that camp space is so far back from the campground road, its existence is a non-issue. #15 even comes with its own private seasonal waterfall tumbling down the aspen-covered hillside to the left. This site is small and the fire pit is fairly close to the road. Even so, the space still feels private due to its lack of close neighbors. Plus, your parked car will hide much of the site from the road.

**#17 and #18 Privacy Rating: C+**
**Reservable?**
Yes. Call (530) 694-2629 or e-mail **info@hopevalleyresort.com**

These two twin sites are both embedded in an aspen forest. They wouldn't be our first choice because the sites are small, the fire pit is close to the road, and they're very close together, but a wall of aspens and wooden fences built between the two sites partially screen the view of your neighbors. Across the street and behind grows an aspen forest, so you won't have any company on those sides. These sites are more suited for a camper van or a pickup with a camper top than they are for a tent.

**#22 Privacy Rating: B-**
**Reservable?** Yes.
Call (530) 694-2629 or e-mail **info@hopevalleyresort.com**

#22 hides immediately behind #21. Aspens and low-growing foliage conceals most of the view of #21, but the two sites are close together and you'll probably hear your neighbor talking. The bathroom is immediately to the left and you have no neighbors to your right, so the space in front is your only neighbor. The Carson River babbles over the rocks behind #22 — although you can't see the water, you can hear it. You'll have to squeeze your tent in here since it's not a big spot. In fact, it might be more suited to pickup trucks with camper tops, camper vans, and small trailers.

## Hope Valley Campground

**Directions:** From South Lake Tahoe, take Highway 89 over Luther Pass. At the intersection of Highways 88 and 89, turn right and drive 2.5 miles west on Highway 88. Turn left on Blue Lakes Road and proceed to the campground, approximately 1 ¼ miles on the right.

## What's It Like?

Unlike the other two campgrounds located in Hope Valley, this one has no road noise, given that it's off of Highway 88 on Blue Lakes Road. Unfortunately, it also has the least amount of privacy. It sits under Jeffrey and lodgepole pines with very little understory. Plus, many of the camp spaces are squeezed together. However, we found three sites that meet our privacy qualifications (see description below).

## What's It Near?

• Fishing, boating, and hiking at Blue Lakes. Good hikes to choose from include Meadow Lake (4 miles round trip), Granite Lake (4 miles round trip), and Grouse Lake (10 miles round trip).

• Fishing, boating, and hiking near Caples Lake (about 20 minutes away, West on Highway 88).

• Hiking on the Pacific Crest Trail and the Tahoe Rim Trail and admiring the wildflowers near Winnemucca Lake in July.

• Fishing in the West Fork of the Carson River for rainbow, brown, and Lahontan cutthroat trout, across Blue Lakes Road from the campground.

• Hiking to Thunder Ridge, where you have an Eagle's eye view of Silver Lake.

• Exploring the back roads on an off-road vehicle, all-terrain vehicle, or mountain bike.

• A 40-minute drive to Lake Tahoe.

• Breakfast, lunch, and homemade pies with deliciously flakey crust are a few miles away from the campground, east on Highway 88 at Hope Valley Resort.

• At nearby Sorensen's Resort (go east on Highway 88), feast on beef bourguignon or quiche, sandwiches, steaks, and seafood. I don't know which I'm more addicted to, their berry cobbler, served with a scoop of ice cream, or the French toast with berry compote. Sorensen's is open for breakfast, lunch, and dinner.

**Elevation:** 7,300 feet

**Toilets:** Vault

**Verizon Cell Service?** No

**Takes Reservations?** Yes. Visit **www.recreation.gov** for reservations. A limited number of sites are first-come, first-served.

**Number of Campsites:** 21

**Bear Boxes?** Yes

### Campsites with the Most Privacy

**#5 Privacy Rating: B**
**Reservable?** Yes. Visit **www.recreation.gov** for reservations.

This campsite isn't as private as #8 (below) but it's one of the best in the campground. Four stairs lead from the driveway to a platform with the picnic table, bear box, and fire pit. The trees gather around a clearing for the campsite, meaning there's plenty of shade all around although the sun sneaks through at certain parts of the day.

Mother Nature conveniently placed a giant boulder across the campground road to interfere with your view of the campsites there. The campsite to the right of #5 is far enough away to not feel intrusive. To the left is a space visible about 24 feet away, but conifers between the two spaces partially filter out the view of your neighbor. Behind #5 the campground ends and the forest begins. A nice spot for either a small trailer (no more than 18 feet) or a tent.

**#8 Privacy Rating: A-**
**Reservable?** Yes. Visit **www.recreation.gov** for reservations.

On a quiet loop of the campground road, this is by far the best space in the campground, as far as privacy is concerned. It's also a great tent spot.

To the left, aspens stand guard over a patch of greenery and beyond that is a conifer-covered hill. The tent pad—located in partial shade—is pushed back against a grove of trees. Another space sits behind this one, but it's far enough away that your rearview neighbors aren't in your face. Plus, a large rock and some pines partially block your view of those neighbors. The space to your right nudges up nearby, but a patch of greenery and your vehicle will hide it from view. Even better, there are no spaces across the street and it's near a bathroom.

**#20 Privacy Rating: C+**
**Reservable?** No. First-come, first-served.

We would have given this a higher privacy rating, but it's right across from the campground host with a partial view of the host's campsite. And the tent pad is closer to the campground road than we like to see. Yet, compared to most of the sites in this campground, you've got plenty of elbow room. There are no spaces to the left or right. Blue Lakes Road runs behind the campsite, but at night there's very little traffic on the road. Conifers surround the site on three sides, providing lots of shade, partially filtering out views of Blue Lakes Road, and creating at least a partial barrier between you and the camp host. This site also provides peekaboo views of the meadow across from the campground and the mountains beyond.

# BLUE LAKES

## Lower Blue Lake Campground

**Directions:** From Sacramento, follow Highway 50 east over Echo Summit. Not long after descending into the Tahoe Basin, turn right onto Highway 89 and follow it over Luther Pass. At the intersection of Highways 88 and 89, turn right on Highway 88. Drive about 2.5 miles and then make a left on Blue Lakes Road. Follow Blue Lakes Road for 12 miles to the campground.

**What's It Like?**

In a pine forest along the shore of Lower Blue Lake, this campground is extremely popular on the weekends. Many campers like to stay in one of the lakeside campsites and then park their boat on the water behind their site. This is the first campground in the Blue Lakes area and usually fills up first. To grab the first-come, first-served spots, campers will have to arrive Wednesday or Thursday morning in order to have any hope of finding a campsite for the weekend.

**Words of Warning:** PG&E is taking reservations for some sites in this campground beginning summer 2015.

**What's It Near?**

• Boating, canoeing, and fishing for rainbow and cutthroat trout in Upper and Lower Blue Lakes.

• Hiking near the lakes. Good hikes to choose from include Meadow Lake (4 miles round trip), Granite Lake (4 miles round trip), and Grouse Lake (10 miles round trip). Twin Lake also is a short walk away (1.5 miles round trip) from Lower Blue Lake.

• Access to the Pacific Crest Trail is a short distance from the campground on Blue Lakes Road heading back toward Highway 88.

• Bald eagles visit the lakes in the summer, so keep an eye out.

• Pavement pedaling on Blue Lakes Road with its stunning scenery.

• Fat tire fans will find plenty of scenic dirt roads to explore. One choice: pedal up to Lost Lakes, northeast of Upper Blue.

• All-terrain vehicles can zip along a variety of dirt roads passing through forest and offering views of the lakes and mountains.

**Elevation:** 8,000 feet

**Toilets:** Vault

**Verizon Cell Service?** Can pick up service from some of the pull outs a mile or two away from the campground on Blue Lakes Road heading back out toward Highway 88. Hit or miss.

**Takes Reservations?** Yes. Visit recreation.pge.com for reservations. Some sites are first-come, first-served.

**Number of Campsites:** 17

**Bear Boxes?** Yes

# Campsites with the Most Privacy

**#1 Privacy Rating: A**
**Reservable?** Yes.
Visit www.recreation.pge.com for reservations.

You're steps away from the lake in this conifer-shaded campsite. The view of the water isn't unobstructed — you're looking at the lake through the forest — but you still have refreshing glimpses of sapphire blue between the trees. With no neighbors on the left, behind, or across the street, #1 boasts a fair amount of elbow room. The only visible neighbor is to the right, but that space is a good distance away, and #1 is facing in the opposite direction, so you won't spend a lot of time glancing toward your neighbor anyway.

**#7 Privacy Rating: B+**
**Reservable?** Yes. Visit www.recreation.pge.com for reservations.

This site is less private than #1 but has a better view of the lake. It's still not an unobstructed view since the trees filter it, but you can see more of the sapphire-blue swath of water from here. The nearest campsite sits about 35 feet away to the left. On the right, the neighboring spot is about 45 feet away. On both sides, lots of pines screen out part of the view of the neighbors. There are no campsites immediately across the street or behind.

**#8 Privacy Rating: B+**
**Reservable?** First-come, first-served.

#8 shares its neck of the woods with neighbors to the left and right, but those spots don't feel too intrusive. To the right, the neighboring space is only about 28 feet away, but a big rock partially obscures that site from view along with some well-placed pine trees. The space to the left, about 45 feet away, is on the other side of a lot of conifers. Another spot sits across the street, but it's not directly across from #8 and lots of pines intrude between the two sites. Through the trees, you'll glimpse Lower Blue Lake immediately behind the campsite.

**#17 Privacy Rating: A+**
**Reservable?** Yes. Visit www.recreation.pge.com for reservations.

This site is a dream come true for people who like privacy and great vistas. Lower Blue Lake stretches out immediately behind #17, in view of the campsite. The space to the left is hidden behind a small rocky hill and some conifers. To the right, there are no other campsites, only a view of a rocky point jutting out into the lake, begging anglers to cast their lines. Even though Blue Lakes Road is in front of this campsite, #17 is tucked far enough back that any traffic passing by shouldn't create a distraction. No other camp spaces are directly across the street. It's a sunnier spot than the other sites in the campground, but it has some shade. If you're able to snag this spot you have good camping karma.

# Middle Creek Campground

**Directions:** From Sacramento, follow Highway 50 east over Echo Summit. Not long after descending into the Tahoe Basin, turn right onto Highway 89 and follow it over Luther Pass. At the intersection of Highways 88 and 89, turn right on Highway 88. Go about 2.5 miles and then make a left on Blue Lakes Road. Follow Blue Lakes Road for about 13.5 miles to the campground. It's on the left side of the road about 1.5 miles past Lower Blue Lake Campground.

## What's It Like?

A small campground made up of just a few sites strung out along Blue Lakes Road, Middle Creek Campground feels more like dispersed camping. The sites sit alongside the stream that connects Upper and Lower Blue Lakes.

**Words of Warning:** When we visited in the fall of 2014, there was a sign saying the water is not drinkable.

**You should also know:** Beginning in 2015, PG&E started taking reservations for some sites in this campground.

## What's It Near?

• Boating, canoeing, and fishing for rainbow and cutthroat trout on Upper and Lower Blue Lakes.

• Hiking near the lakes. Good hikes to choose from include Meadow Lake (4 miles round trip), Granite Lake (4 miles round trip), and Grouse Lake (10 miles round trip). Twin Lake also is a short walk away (1.5 miles round trip) from Lower Blue Lake.

• Access to the Pacific Crest Trail is a couple of miles from the campground on Blue Lakes Road heading back toward Highway 88.

• Bald eagles visit the lakes in the summer, so keep an eye out.

• Pavement pedaling on Blue Lakes Road with its stunning scenery.

• All-terrain vehicles can zip along a variety of dirt roads passing through forest and offering views of the lakes and mountains.

• Fat tire fans will find plenty of scenic dirt roads to explore. One choice: pedal up to Lost Lakes, northeast of Upper Blue.

**Elevation:** 8,100 feet

**Toilets:** Vault

**Verizon Cell Service?** Can pick up service from some of the pull outs on Blue Lakes Road heading back out toward Highway 88. Hit or miss. No cell service in the campground itself.

**Takes Reservations?** Yes. Visit www.recreation.pge.com

**Number of Campsites:** 4

**Bear Boxes?** Yes

# Campsites with the Most Privacy

**#18 Privacy Rating: B+**
**Reservable?** Yes.
Visit www.recreation.pge.com for reservations.

An elongated site along Blue Lakes Road, #18 would have been an absolutely perfect spot deserving an A+ rating if it wasn't for the proximity of #18's picnic table to the neighbor on the right, which is why we marked it down to a B+. But some pines intervene between the two campsites so it doesn't feel as if your neighbor is right in your face. Even with the nearby neighbors this site has a lot going for it. The creek flows behind it for one. It has no neighbors to the left or across the street for another. It's a forested spot with ample shade. You could do a lot worse.

**#22 Privacy Rating: A+**
**Reservable?** Yes.
Visit www.recreation.pge.com for reservations.

You've won the campsite jackpot if you land this spacious shady site with room for at least a couple of tents. The stream, which tiptoes past #22 on its way to Lower Blue Lake, has a lot of personality here because it splits and flows around an island. You can see and hear the stream from the campsite, which has no neighbors within view. On the left is a former camp space that is being preserved as a sacred Native American site. Across the street Mother Nature added another creation to her art gallery — an interesting rock formation.

## Middle Creek Expansion Campground

**Directions:** From Sacramento, follow Highway 50 east over Echo Summit. Not long after descending into the Tahoe Basin, turn right onto Highway 89 and follow it over Luther Pass. At the intersection of Highways 88 and 89, turn right on Highway 88. Travel about 2.5 miles and then make a left on Blue Lakes Road. Follow Blue Lakes Road for about 13.5 miles to the campground. It's on the right side of the road about 1.5 miles past Lower Blue Lake Campground.

### What's It Like?

In the forest across Blue Lakes Road from Middle Creek Campground, Middle Creek Expansion Campground sits under the evergreens, but lacks much understory, so you have to search hard to find campsites with privacy — although there are a few. This campground is popular with people who own all-terrain quads, so if you're not a member of this group and you think the sound of all-terrain vehicles buzzing by might bother you, this campground isn't a good choice.

**Words of Warning:** When we visited in the fall of 2014, there was a sign saying the water is not drinkable.

### What's It Near?

• Boating, canoeing, and fishing for rainbow and cutthroat trout on Upper and Lower Blue Lakes.

- Hiking near the lakes. Good hikes to choose from include Meadow Lake (4 miles round trip), Granite Lake (4 miles round trip), and Grouse Lake (10 miles round trip). Twin Lake also is a short walk away (1.5 miles round trip) from Lower Blue Lake.

- Bald eagles visit the lakes in the summer, so keep an eye out.

- Access to the Pacific Crest Trail is a couple miles from the campground on Blue Lakes Road heading back toward Highway 88.

- Pavement pedaling on Blue Lakes Road with its stunning scenery.

- All-terrain vehicles can zip along a variety of dirt roads passing through forest and offering views of the lakes and mountains.

- Fat tire fans will find plenty of scenic dirt roads to explore. One choice: pedal up to Lost Lakes, northeast of Upper Blue.

**Elevation:** 8,100 feet

**Toilets:** Vault

**Verizon Cell Service?** Can pick up service from some of the pull outs on Blue Lakes Road heading back out toward Highway 88, two to three miles from the campground. Hit or miss. No cell service in the campground itself.

**Takes Reservations?** Not as of Spring 2015, but since PG&E just started offering reservations for the other Blue Lakes campgrounds, it would not be surprising if they soon started offering them here as well. For updates, visit our website ilovetheeasternsierra.com

**Number of Campsites:** 34

**Bear Boxes?** Yes

## Campsites with the Most Privacy

**#34 Privacy Rating: B-**
**Reservable?** No. First-come, first served.

This is by no means a perfect site, but it's one of the best in the campground. The woods provide a peaceful backdrop to the campsite and beyond the trees there's a hint of a glimpse of Blue Lakes Road. The nearest space to the left sits about 30 feet away and some conifers partially filter the view. Your neighbor to the right is about 22 feet away, but your vehicle will block some of that site from view, and #34 is facing the opposite direction. Directly across the campground road is another campsite, but #34 is back far enough that the across-the-way site doesn't feel intrusive.

**#51 Privacy Rating: A-**
**Reservable?** No. First-come, first served.

**Note: This site is for people with disabilities.**

Located entirely on a cement platform, making it easy for wheelchairs, #51 is widely spaced from its neighbors with the woods on one side and the bathroom behind it. There's plenty of elbow room between this site and the neighbor to the left and evergreens shoulder their way between the two spaces. Pines also partially hide the view of the neighbor across the street. This shady spot has one big flaw for people who like campfires: there's no fire pit, only a grill.

## #54 Privacy Rating: B+
**Reservable?** No. First-come, first served.

With a forested backdrop and a view of a meadow behind the site, this elongated narrow campsite is a slice of serenity in a campground where many of the spaces are out in the open and a little too close together. A big boulder that looks like a dinosaur head does a good job of screening out the neighboring site to the left. The forest filters the view of the space to the right. Another campsite sits across the street, but a few trees filter it partially from view. The fire pit for this site is closer to the road than we like to see. But compared to many of the sites in this campground, this spot is definitely one of the best.

## #55 Privacy Rating: B
**Reservable?** No. First-come, first served.

We marked this one down to a B rating based on the possibility an RV might park about 18 feet away from you in the driveway for the space next door on the left. On the plus side, though, the picnic table and fire pit for that site are far away from #55 and on the other side of the neighbor's driveway, so the neighbor's vehicle will obscure any view of them eating or sitting by the fire. A big boulder acts like a natural privacy screen from the neighbors to the right—although it doesn't look as much like a dinosaur head as it does from the other side in site #54. Grass sways in the breeze in the meadow behind this shady spot and beyond that tall pines reach for the sky. Evergreens partially hide the view of the site across the street.

## Upper Blue Lake Damsite Campground

**Directions:** From Sacramento, follow Highway 50 east over Echo Summit. Not long after descending into the Tahoe Basin, turn right onto Highway 89 and follow it over Luther Pass. At the intersection of Highways 88 and 89, turn right on Highway 88. Travel about 2.5 miles and then make a left on Blue Lakes Road. Follow Blue Lakes Road for about 13.75 miles to the campground, which is about ¼ mile past Middle Creek Campground on the left.

**What's It Like?**

Rubbing shoulders with Upper Blue Lake, this campground is steps away from fishing and boating. Most of the campsites are shady and located along the shore, with views of the lake through the trees. Like all the campgrounds at Blue Lakes, Upper Blue Lake Damsite Campground is operated by Pacific Gas and Electric Co.

**What's It Near?**

• Boating, canoeing, and fishing for rainbow and cutthroat trout on Upper and Lower Blue Lakes.

• Hiking near the lakes. Good hikes to choose from that are closest to this campground include Granite Lake (4 miles round trip), and Grouse Lake (10 miles round trip).

• Bald eagles visit the lakes in the summer, so keep an eye out.

• Pavement pedaling on Blue Lakes Road with its stunning scenery.

• All-terrain vehicles can zip along a variety of dirt roads passing through forest and offering views of the lakes and mountains.

• Fat tire fans will find plenty of scenic dirt roads to explore. One choice: pedal up to Lost Lakes, northeast of Upper Blue.

**Elevation:** 8,100 feet

**Toilets:** Vault

**Verizon Cell Service?** Can pick up service from some of the pull outs on Blue Lakes Road heading back out toward Highway 88. Hit or miss. No cell service in the campground itself and it's a long drive to the section of Blue Lakes Road where cell service is spotty.

**Takes Reservations?** Yes, beginning in 2015. Visit www.recreation.pge.com for reservations. Some sites are first-come, first-served.

**Words of Warning:** If you search for this campground on recreation.pge.com make sure you spell Dam Site as two words even though the sign at the campground itself lists it as one word, otherwise you won't turn up any results.

**Number of Campsites:** 10

**Bear Boxes?** Yes.

# Campsites with the Most Privacy

**#58 Privacy Rating: A+**
**Reservable?** Yes.
Visit www.recreation.pge.com for reservations.

Off by itself at the beginning of the campground, #58 is one of the best sites for privacy in the Blue Lakes area. The forest envelops this campsite in tranquility. No neighbors are visible to the left or right. Behind the campsite, lodgepole pines grow for as far as the eye can see. To the right, catch glimpses of Upper Blue Lake through the trees. There's a neighbor across the street, but #58 is pushed far back from the road. This is a big camp space with room for at least a couple of tents. It's plenty shady, too, with some dappled sunlight.

**#64 Privacy Rating: B+**
**Reservable?** No. First-come, first-served.

#64 is not as private as site #58, not by a long shot, but it's still better than a lot of the lakeside sites in this campground. Through the evergreens you'll have a filtered view of the lake, which is immediately behind the campsite. The driveway for the neighboring space to the right is only about 20 feet away, but a smattering of trees growing in between the two sites

---

creates some privacy. Pines and your parked vehicle partially screen out the site to the left, but if a travel trailer parks there, you will see it. Bathrooms are across the street so you won't have any neighbors there.

**#65 Privacy Rating: B**
**Reservable?** Yes.
Visit www.recreation.pge.com for reservations.

This isn't a perfect campsite from a privacy perspective, but it still has a lot going for it. It's sandwiched in between spaces on the left and right, but pines partially interfere with the view of the neighbors after you walk down into the campsite. If someone parks a travel trailer in the space to the right, you'll see it from your picnic table, but your eyes will probably be drawn to the view of the sparkling blue water behind the campsite through the trees. There's a nice spot for the tent with a good view of the lake. Plus, no neighbors across the street add to its privacy. Its lakeside location makes up for the closeness of its two neighbors, and it's really one of the best sites in the campground.

## Upper Blue Lake Damsite Expansion Campground

**Directions:** From Sacramento, follow Highway 50 east over Echo Summit. Not long after descending into the Tahoe Basin, turn right onto Highway 89 and follow it over Luther Pass. At the intersection of Highways 88 and 89, turn right on Highway 88. Travel about 2.5 miles and then make a left on Blue Lakes Road. Follow Blue Lakes Road for about 13.75 miles to the campground, which is about ¼ mile past Middle Creek Campground on the right.

**What's It Like?**

Upper Blue Lake Damsite Expansion Campground is across Blue Lakes Road from its sibling, Upper Blue Lake Damsite

Campground. It's farther away from the lake than its sibling, but not by much, and it's still easy walking distance between the campsites and the shoreline. It's a shady campground, but most of the sites are squished together and out in the open under the pines, so we could only find one camp space that fit our privacy requirements (see campsite description below). Like all the campgrounds at Blue Lakes, Upper Blue Lake Damsite Expansion Campground is operated by Pacific Gas and Electric Company.

**What's It Near?**

• Boating, canoeing, and fishing for rainbow and cutthroat trout on Upper and Lower Blue Lakes.

• Hiking near the lakes. Good hikes to choose from that are close to this campground include Granite Lake (4 miles round trip), and Grouse Lake (10 miles round trip).

• Bald eagles visit the lakes in the summer, so keep an eye out.

• Pavement pedaling on Blue Lakes Road with its stunning scenery.

• All-terrain vehicles can zip along a variety of dirt roads passing through forest and offering views of the lakes and mountains.

• Fat tire fans will find plenty of scenic dirt roads to explore. One choice: pedal up to Lost Lakes, northeast of Upper Blue.

**Elevation:** 8,100 feet

**Toilets:** Vault

**Verizon Cell Service?** Can pick up service from some of the pull outs on Blue Lakes Road heading back out toward

Highway 88. Hit or miss. No cell service in the campground itself and it's a long drive to the section of Blue Lakes Road where cell service is spotty.

**Takes Reservations?** Yes, beginning in 2015. Visit www.recreation.pge.com for reservations. Some sites are first come, first served.

**Words of Warning:** If you search for this campground on recreation.pge.com make sure you spell Dam Site as two words even though the sign at the campground itself lists it as one word, otherwise you won't turn up any results.

**Number of Campsites:** 15

**Bear Boxes?** Yes

**Campsites with the Most Privacy**

**#73 Privacy Rating: B+**
**Reservable?** No. First-come, first-served.

With a pull-through driveway, this spot is good for either trailer campers or tent campers. You'll have a glimpse of the bear box in the space to the left, your only nearby neighbor. The space to the right is a good distance away and plenty of pines intervene between the two spaces. Behind the campsite a giant evergreen towers over an outcropping of polished white granite. In front of the campsite through the trees, there's a peek of Upper Blue Lake in the distance. The rest rooms are across the street. This is a spacious campsite, with room for at least a couple of tents.

## Upper Blue Lake Campground

**Directions:** From Sacramento, follow Highway 50 east over Echo Summit. Not long after descending into the Tahoe Basin, turn right onto Highway 89 and follow it over Luther Pass. At the intersection of Highways 88 and 89, turn right on Highway 88. Go about 2.5 miles and then make a left on Blue Lakes Road. Follow Blue Lakes Road for about 14 miles to the campground, which is about a mile past Upper Blue Lake Damsite Campground.

## What's It Like?

Pitch your tent or pull up your trailer at the last campground on Blue Lakes Road, and you won't have far to go to reach the shore of the lake. There's a peek of the water visible through the trees in some of the spaces of the campground. Most of the spaces in this woodsy campground are nudged close together and out in the open. However, there are a few gems that sparkle amid the other lackluster choices (see campsite description below). Like all the campgrounds at Blue Lakes, Upper Blue Lake Campground is operated by Pacific Gas and Electric Company.

## What's It Near?

• Boating, canoeing, and fishing for rainbow and cutthroat trout on Upper and Lower Blue Lakes.

• Hiking near the lakes. Good hikes to choose from that are close to this campground include the easy three-mile hike around Upper Blue Lake, Granite Lake (4 miles round trip), and Grouse Lake (10 miles round trip). Another good choice: trek up the 4WD road to Lost Lakes, northeast of Upper Blue.

• Bald eagles visit the lakes in the summer, so keep an eye out.

• Pavement pedaling on Blue Lakes Road with its stunning scenery.

• All-terrain vehicles can zip along a variety of dirt roads passing through forest and offering views of the lakes and mountains.

• Fat tire fans will find plenty of scenic dirt roads to explore. One choice: pedal up to Lost Lakes, northeast of Upper Blue.

**Elevation:** 8,100 feet

**Toilets:** Vault

**Verizon Cell Service?** Can pick up service from some of the pull outs on Blue Lakes Road heading back out toward Highway 88. Hit or miss. No cell service in the campground itself and it's a long drive to the section of Blue Lakes Road where cell service is spotty.

**Takes Reservations?** Yes, beginning in 2015. Visit recreation.pge.com for reservations. Some sites are first come, first served.

**Number of Campsites:** 32

**Bear Boxes?** Yes

### Campsites with the Most Privacy

**#98 Privacy Rating: B-**
**Reservable?** No. First come, first served.

In a campground where most of the spaces are jammed close together, this one isn't a bad spot. The space on the left is close—about 24 feet away—but evergreens hide some of the view. Plus, the neighbor to the left is closer to the road whereas #98 is back farther. The space to the right is about 18 feet away, but it still feels as if the two sites have enough distance between them because pines filter part of the view of the neighbor. Woods grow behind the campsite, and there are no spaces immediately across the street.

## #112 Privacy Rating: B
**Reservable?** No. First come, first served.

With woods and a tranquil meadow sitting behind it, #112 is definitely one of the best sites in the campground. A small hill rises up to the left of #112, erasing the view of the neighboring site in that direction. The space to the right is visible and not all that far away, but some conifers create a privacy screen and your parked vehicle also will screen out part of the neighbor from view. Through the trees, a hint of a glimpse of the lake in the distance is a bonus. The nearest neighboring spot on the other side of the road isn't directly across the street, although it's not far away. Even so, the woods and meadow behind the site will draw your gaze, so unless the neighbors across the street are having a loud party, their presence won't seem like much of an issue.

## #114 Privacy Rating: A
**Reservable?** No. First come, first served.

This site, the last one on this loop, wins hands down as the most private camp space at this campground. A little hill conceals the view of the space to the right. The trees are your only neighbors on the left. Behind the site, a meadow dotted with willows and beyond that a nice view of a mountain ridge offers a peaceful backdrop. The only visible neighbor is across the street, but #114 is tucked back from the campground road

and some pines intervene between the two sites. This is a large, mostly shady campsite that can fit at least two and probably three tents. One more bonus: It's near the bathrooms.

# MARKLEEVILLE – EBBETT'S PASS

## Turtle Rock Park Campground

**Directions:** From the intersection of Highways 88 and 89 in Woodfords, turn left on Highway 89/4 and travel about four miles to Turtle Rock County Park on the right.

**What's It Like?**

Spread out under a Jeffrey pine forest, Turtle Rock Park Campground sits in a peaceful setting. However, because it lacks a lot of understory, most of the spaces are out in the open and near their neighbors. But a few choice sites are spaced far enough apart to give them good privacy (See below for our description of the best sites). Turtle Rock Campground is operated by Alpine County and has some amenities you won't find in National Forest Service campgrounds such as a tennis court and disc golf course. It also boasts coin-operated showers. It was named for the rock near the campground shaped like — you guessed it — a turtle. Sadly, vandals over the years have destroyed the rock's shape.

**Words of Warning:**

During extremely dry conditions, campfires are not permitted in this campground. When restrictions are in effect, outdoor cooking is allowed only on gas and propane-powered stoves.

Unless you're participating in The Death Ride, avoid staying here the weekend of that event, since this is where the bicycle event begins and the place will hustle and bustle with activity. You can find out the date of The Death Ride each year by visiting deathride.com. In the past it's always taken place in July.

This campground also becomes busier in late May or early June when the adjacent disc golf course holds an annual

---

Pro/Am tournament. Visit **www.discgolfscene.com** to find out the dates for the tournament.

**What's It Near?**

• An 18-hole disc golf course, a tennis and basketball court, and horseshoe pit.

• Hiking and fishing at Indian Creek Reservoir. There's also some great bird watching here. We saw white pelicans, a beautiful yellow and black bird, and a parade of baby Canadian geese trailing along behind their mother.

• Grover Hot Springs State Park is a 10-minute drive away. Soak in the spring-fed pool and take an easy, 2.7-mile, round-trip hike to Grover Waterfall.

• Fishing in the Carson River for rainbow, brown, and Lahontan cutthroat trout.

• Hiking by Monitor Pass, Ebbett's Pass, and Wolf Creek. Some good choices: Nobel Lake by Ebbett's Pass (8 miles round trip, great wildflower displays), Wolf Creek Meadow (3 to 20 miles round trip). Wolf Creek Meadow and areas along this hike may have suffered damage in the Washington Fire in June 2015.

• Dine out at Markleeville, a picturesque little town about two miles away from the campground. Good choices: Stonefly for homemade pizza and Italian food, Ali's Café for breakfast and lunch, or The Deli for great sandwiches.

**Elevation:** 6,100 feet

**Toilets:** Flush

**Verizon Cell Service?** Spotty in the campground but can drive a short ways up the road to the community center to access cell phone service. Also, this campground hopes to have WiFi available beginning the summer of 2015.

**Takes Reservations?** No. First-come, first-served.

**Number of Campsites:** 38

**Bear Boxes?** Yes

## Campsites with the Most Privacy

**#4 Privacy Rating: B+**
**Reservable?** No. First-come, first-served.

This site is well-spaced from its neighbors. The site to the left is far away and to the right the showers ensure there won't be anyone camped immediately next to you on that side. There is a space visible on the other side of the showers, but it's about 90 feet away. Across the street sits another campsite, but a fair amount of space separates the two sites. A backdrop of Jeffrey pines mingled with sagebrush marks the rear boundary of #4. Lots of pines shade #4, but it's bathed by some afternoon sun. A spacious spot that can accommodate three tents.

**#15 Privacy Rating: A**
**Reservable?** No. First-come, first-served.

A peaceful, shady spot under the pines, #15 sits next to a seasonal creek. Behind the site, pines march off into the distance. To the immediate right are the bathrooms. There are no neighbors to the immediate left. The only close company

you'll have is across the street, but #15 is far enough back from the road that you won't feel as if the inhabitants of that site are breathing down your neck.

**#17 Privacy Rating: A-**
**Reservable?** No. First-come, first-served.

Another shady spot, #17 has no neighbors to the immediate right or across the street. Behind the site, Jeffrey pines grow as far as the eye can see. The 48 feet of space between #17 and its neighbor on the left provides ample privacy. Like all the sites in this campground, #17 is forested, but the pines are widely spaced and there's not much understory. Even so, its lack of any nearby neighbors makes it a good choice.

## Markleeville Campground

**Directions:** From Woodfords, turn left on Highway 4/89, and travel for approximately six miles to the Markleeville Campground entrance on the left (north) side of highway. It's about a half mile past Markleeville.

**What's It Like?**

A cluster of camp spaces on the banks of Markleeville Creek, this pleasant little campground settles comfortably in among the Jeffrey pines and cottonwoods. All but one campsite (#7) sit alongside the creek. If you have a large RV this campground isn't for you — trailers are restricted to 24 feet or under.

**What's It Near?**

• Grover Hot Springs State Park is a 5-minute drive away. Soak in the spring-fed pool and take an easy, 2.7-mile, round-trip hike to Grover Waterfall.

• Flycasting for rainbow and brown trout in the East Carson River. Or try your luck in Markleeville Creek or Indian Creek Reservoir.

• Hiking by Monitor Pass, Ebbett's Pass, and Wolf Creek. Some good choices: Nobel Lake by Ebbett's Pass (8 miles round trip, great wildflower displays), Wolf Creek Meadow (3 to 20 miles round trip), or the Carson Confluence where Markleeville Creek collides with the East Carson River (3 miles round trip). Wolf Creek Meadow and areas along this hike may have suffered damage in the Washington Fire in June 2015.

• Dirt roads weaving their way in and out of aspen groves near Monitor Pass are a good option for both mountain bikers and hikers. One of these roads near Monitor Pass leads a short distance up a hill to a spectacular view of Slinkard Valley and the mountains beyond Walker.

• Dine out at Markleeville, a picturesque little town about two miles away from the campground. Good choices: Stonefly for homemade pizza and Italian food, Ali's Café for breakfast and lunch, or The Deli for great sandwiches.

**Elevation:** 5,500 feet

**Toilets:** Vault

**Verizon Cell Service?** No

**Takes Reservations?** No

**Number of Campsites:** 9

**Bear Boxes?** Yes

## Campsites with the Most Privacy

### #1 Privacy Rating: B+
**Reservable?** No. First-come, first-served.

On the banks of Markleeville Creek, #1 sits among the riverside greenery and is shaded by tall Jeffrey pines, including one thick-trunked granddaddy. The stream is clearly visible behind the campsite. To the left and high above the campsite is the day use parking lot. The only visible neighbor is about 42 feet away, across a meadow. A peaceful campsite—the only reason we marked it down to a B+ was because of the space on the right. #1 is considered a walk-in site, but the parking area is just above it, so you won't have to lug your stuff far.

### #5 Privacy Rating: A-
**Reservable?** No. First-come, first-served.

Nicely hidden from the campground road, this streamside campsite is a haven of serenity. The firepit and table sit in a small meadow surrounded by deciduous vegetation and cottonwoods and shaded by a tall conifer. Cottonwoods partially screen out the view of the campsite to the left. The space to the right is visible, but it's about 42 feet away and when you sit by the fire or at the picnic table vegetation partially hides it from view. The creek wanders along behind #5, and although it's easily reachable along a short path, you can't see it from the campsite. There are no neighbors across the street.

**#6 Privacy Rating: A-**
**Reservable?** No. First-come, first-served.

A peaceful site surrounded by cottonwoods, #6 sits in front of the creek, but you can't see the water from the campsite due to a heavy screen of vegetation. To reach the stream, stroll along a short path behind the campsite. A tall, majestic cottonwood spreads its limbs over part of the picnic table, providing a canopy of shade. Bushes partially hide this site from the campground road. No campsites are visible to the right. You can see the site to the left (#5), about 42 feet away across a small meadow, but when you're sitting by the campfire or picnic table vegetation partially filters your view of the neighbors. The day use path is next to this campsite, so you might have fishermen walking past from time to time. However, this day use area doesn't see heavy use, so the disruptions should be minimal.

## Silver Creek Campground

**Directions:** From Markleeville, follow Highway 89/4 to where the two highways separate. Continue straight ahead on Highway 4. The campground is on the left and the right side of Highway 4, about 11.7 miles south of Markleeville.
**What's It Like?**

On the road to Ebbett's Pass in the Humboldt-Toiyabe National Forest, this forested, out-of-the-way campground is much appreciated by those who love its serenity and proximity to scenic hikes and a large selection of lakes and streams for anglers to cast a line. Nestled under the pines and firs above Silver Creek, many — but not all — of the campsites have good privacy. The campground has two loops, one on each side of Highway 4.

**What's It Near?**

• Hiking on the Pacific Crest Trail, 3 miles west of the campground. Be warned it's a very curvy drive to the trailhead. For an easy stroll (2 miles round trip) follow the Pacific Crest Trail North to Upper Kinney Lake.

• Other hikes in the area include one of my favorites: Nobel Lake by Ebbett's Pass (8 miles round trip, great wildflower displays.)

• Fishing in the Carson River for rainbow, brown, and Lahontan cutthroat trout and in Silver Creek for rainbows. Also cast a line in the many alpine lakes in the area.

• History buffs will enjoy exploring the site of Silver Mountain City, a once-booming mining town in the 1860s. When the ore ran out, the buildings were relocated to Markleeville. Today, the only reminder of the town is remnants of the stone jail downstream from the campground.

**Elevation:** 7,100 feet

**Toilets:** Vault

**Verizon Cell Service?** No

**Takes Reservations?** Yes. Visit www.recreation.gov for reservations. A few first-come, first-served sites are also available.

**Number of Campsites:** 22

**Bear Boxes?** Yes

## Campsites with the Most Privacy

**#4 Privacy Rating: A+**
**Reservable?** Yes. Visit www.recreation.gov for reservations.

A shady spot in a conifer forest, #4 is well-spaced from its neighbors. No other campsites are visible to the right. The neighboring space to the left is far away and hidden from view by the trees. Highway 4 is behind the campsite, but a hill hides the road from sight. No neighbors across the campground road further guarantee your privacy.

**#5 Privacy Rating: A+**
**Reservable?** Yes. Visit www.recreation.gov for reservations.

The defining feature of this campsite is the spectacular view from the rock overlook at the rear of the space. Gaze out over a sea of evergreens and beyond that mountains rise up in the distance. As an added advantage, there's lots of shade. With no neighbors visible to the left, conifers concealing the view of the space to the right, and no other spaces across the street, #5 is surrounded by serenity.

**#6 Privacy Rating: A+**
**Reservable:** Yes. Visit www.recreation.gov for reservations.

Another beautiful site, #6 is serenaded by a creek that skips

steeply down a gully far below and behind the campsite. To the left, a manzanita-covered hill mostly hides the view of the nearest neighbor in that direction. There are no neighbors to the immediate right or across the street. Through gaps in the trees there's a glimpse of the cliffs rising up above the canyon.

## #11 Privacy Rating: B-
**Reservable?** Yes. Visit www.recreation.gov for reservations.

This is a good choice for an RV, thanks to the pull-through driveway and the fact that it's closer to the campground road than some of the best sites in the campground, meaning it's

less desirable to tent campers seeking privacy. It's a shady, forested spot under the pines with a smattering of aspens to add a splash of greenery. Highway 4 is up the hill behind the campsite, but there are lots of trees intervening between the road and the campsite.

## #14 Privacy Rating: A+
**Reservable?** Yes. Visit www.recreation.gov for reservations.

A very private and spacious campsite, #14 has no neighbors

on any side. It sits in a sun-dappled conifer forest at the beginning of a cul-de-sac. The main highway is behind the site, but it's up a forested hill about 48 feet away. The unpaved driveway is a bit rocky, but still a site worth grabbing.

## #15 Privacy Rating: A+
**Reservable?** Yes. Visit www.recreation.gov for reservations.

Silver Creek flows to the left of this campsite, too far below #15 to actually see it from most of the space, but you can hear the melodious flow of the water. A trail down to the creek departs from the rear of the campsite. A beauty of a spot located on the end of a cul-de-sac, #15 has no immediate neighbors on any side. It's a forested spot with lots of shade and lots of room to spread out. Deciduous greenery at the back of the campsite adds a touch of tranquility.

## #19 Privacy Rating: A
**Reservable?** Yes. Visit www.recreation.gov for reservations.

This site has a lot of personality and its own water spigot to boot. To the left a grouping of conifers that look like perfectly shaped Christmas trees grow near a small forest of aspens and a meadow. Walk up a little hill behind the site and you'll see Silver Creek gurgling past below. The hill muffles the sound of the creek, though, so you won't hear it from the campsite. There's also a filtered view of the mountains through the trees and a couple of big lichen-covered boulders. A neighboring space (#18) sits nearby on the right. Because #19 is at the end of a long driveway farther from the campground road and #18 is closer to the road, the neighboring site doesn't feel intrusive. And the nearest site across the street is plenty far away.

# WALKER RIVER CANYON

## Bootleg Campground

**Directions:** From Walker, travel south on Highway 395 for 7.7 miles. Campground is on the right in Walker River Canyon in the Humboldt-Toiyabe National Forest.

**What's It Like?**

This lightly used campground in the Walker River Canyon was a pleasant surprise. Resting peacefully under the Jeffrey pines and surrounded by carpets of pine needles, many of the sites are well-spaced apart from each other. It even has flush toilets. This section of the Eastern Sierra doesn't see the number of visitors that flock to locations south of here, so in the past Bootleg has never filled up. Camp hosts Bev and Rusty told us that on Fourth of July 2013 only 16 to 20 of the 63 campsites were filled.

Bev and Rusty do something we've only seen in one or two other campgrounds — they leave a bottle of water on the picnic table to get you started on putting out the fire. Bootleg also has a longer stay limit than most campgrounds in the Eastern Sierra, allowing people to move in for 30 days.

**Words of Warning:** If this campground has a disadvantage it's that it has no bear boxes, but Bev and Rusty said they've only had one bear "cause trouble." Still, you'll want to make certain to put in the trunk of your vehicle your food along with anything odiferous. If your vehicle doesn't have a trunk, cover everything that even looks like food with a blanket.

**Important Note:** The camp hosts told us Bootleg Campground expects to begin offering reservations beginning with the summer 2015 season. However, looking at recreation.gov there is no indication this is happening yet. Perhaps for the

—

2016 season? If this campground begins taking reservations, it may increase the number of people staying here. For updates on this situation, visit the campground updates section of www.ilovetheeasternsierra.com.

**What's It Near?**

• Some of the best BBQ west of Texas at Mountain View Barbecue in nearby Walker, California.

• Hiking to Emma Lake (a beautiful alpine gem at the end of a 1.2 mile, one-way, short, huff and puffer of a hike); Burt Canyon (a mild walk as far as you want to go through a scenic canyon); and Anna Lake (the end point of the Burt Canyon hike, 13.5 miles round trip).

• Trails are also nearby in Little Antelope Valley, accessed by a dirt road north of Walker.

• If you're comfortable hiking cross-country, camp host Rusty said you can reach some beautiful lakes if you trek through the forest near the campground.

• Fishing in the Walker River, across Highway 395 from the campground, and in the nearby Little Walker River and Molybdenite Creek for rainbow and brown trout.

• Devour the burgers and shakes at Walker Burger or grab a picnic lunch, pizza, and baked goods at Walker Country Store. We avoided the temptation of cinnamon rolls when we were there and had sandwiches instead.

• Great breakfasts, lunches, and pie at Meadowcliff Lodge, north of Walker in the Antelope Valley.

• Horseback riding through Little Antelope Pack Station.

**Elevation:** 6,600

**Toilets:** Flush

**Verizon Cell Service?** No

**Takes Reservations?** Not now, but there is talk of this happening in the future. Visit the campground updates page at **www.ilovetheeasternsierra.com** to stay apprised of this situation.

**Number of Campsites:** 63

**Bear Boxes?** No

## Campsites with the Most Privacy

**#8 Privacy Rating: B+**
**Reservable?** No. First-come, first-served. This could change in the future. Visit our campground updates page at **www.ilovetheeasternsierra.com** for the latest information.

A hill rises up behind this partially forested site and the neighbors to the left and right are far away. Jeffrey pines provide some shade. The site is one of a handful away from the hustle and bustle of the main part of the campground. There might be a hint of road noise here from Highway 395, but the highway is far enough away on the other side of a conifer-covered hill to keep road noise to a minimum.

**#11 Privacy Rating: A-**
**Reservable?** No. First-come, first-served. This could change in the future. Visit our campground updates page at **www.ilovetheeasternsierra.com** for the latest information.

This shady site has no neighbors on either side. The forest

stretches out behind it. The only neighbor is site #10 across the street, but it's far enough away that you retain your privacy.

**#12 Privacy Rating: A+**
**Reservable?** No. First-come, first-served. This could change in the future. Visit our campground updates page at **www.ilovetheeasternsierra.com** for the latest information.

In regards to privacy, this space is the clear winner in the campground. It has no neighbors on any side and the only other site you can see from here is just a peek of the camp host's RV far in the distance. Across the campground road, the pines part to reveal a view of a grove of aspens growing on the walls of the Walker River Canyon.

The one disadvantage? The campsite is located up a short but steep hill from the driveway. Since there are no bear boxes here, you'll have to lug your cooler, pots, pans, and dishes up to the picnic table to make meals then lug everything back down to the trunk of your vehicle. But, hey, exercise is a good thing, right? You might hear a hint of road noise from Highway 395, but the breeze sighing through the pines and the fact the campground is set back far from the road means this shouldn't be a deal breaker.

#### #20 Privacy Rating: B+
**Reservable?** No. First-come, first-served. This could change in the future. Visit our campground updates page at **www.ilovetheeasternsierra.com** for the latest information.

Some pines partially filter the view of the only neighboring space. You'll have lots of room in this big campsite and plenty of shade. The bathroom and a water spigot are nearby.

#### #21 Privacy Rating: B+
**Reservable?** No. First-come, first-served.
This could change in the future. Visit our campground updates page at **www.ilovetheeasternsierra.com** for the latest information.

Because it has a pull-through, site #21 is popular with RVs, but it's a fine tent site as well. Lots of greenery behind the space adds tranquility while Jeffrey pines provide shade. There are spaces across the street and to the right and there's a view of the other loop of the campground, so it's not worthy of an A rating, but still a nice campsite. To the left, the neighboring campsite is far away and the forest is your only neighbor to the rear. It is a bit longer of a walk to the bathrooms, but not too far.

#### #23 Privacy Rating: B+
**Reservable?** No. First-come, first-served. This could change in the future. Visit our campground updates page at **www.ilovetheeasternsierra.com** for the latest information.

According to the camp hosts, this is one of the most popular spaces in the campground. A little spring-fed stream makes its way through lush greenery, giving #23 extra personality. This site is close to space #25 on the left, but the two sites are staggered so that they don't crowd each other out. A couple of trees between the sites also help to filter the view. There are no spaces to the right or behind, but you will have a neighbor across the campground road. A nice mixture of shade and sun. Like #21, it's a longer walk to the bathroom from here, but not so far as to make it a deal breaker for most people.

## #31 Privacy Rating: B+
**Reservable?** No. First-come, first-served. This could change in the future. Visit our campground updates page at **www.ilovetheeasternsierra.com** for the latest information.

Well-spaced from its neighbors, this forested site is more suited to a trailer, RV, camper van, or pick up truck with a camper shell. There's no really good place to pitch a tent. Behind the site, your only company is a Jeffrey pine forest. Evergreens provide lots of shade and needles carpet the ground.

## #39 Privacy Rating: A-
**Reservable?** No. First-come, first-served. This could change in the future. Visit our campground updates page at **www.ilovetheeasternsierra.com** for the latest information.

Off by itself, this forested spot is nice for families or anyone who has more than one tent. Big Jeffrey pines with their vanilla-scented bark shade the site. On the other side of a pine forest, Highway 395 runs behind the campsite, but it's far enough away that road noise is virtually nonexistent. This site has easy bathroom access.

## #56: Privacy Rating: A-
**Reservable?** No. First-come, first-served. This could change in the future. Visit our campground updates page at **www.ilovetheeasternsierra.com** for the latest information.

This site is more exposed than the other forested sites in the campground, but its proximity to only one other campsite across the street makes it seem very private. There are no neighbors to the right, the neighboring site on the left is far away, and a large hill rises up behind it.

## #58 Privacy Rating: A
**Reservable?** No. First-come, first-served. This could change in the future. Visit our campground updates page at **www.ilovetheeasternsierra.com** for the latest information.

This camp space has a similar ambiance to its sibling on the right, #56, which is located far enough away to give #58 lots of shoulder room. The two sites share the same hill as a backdrop. A lot of greenery and trees on the left of #58 hide the view of any spaces in that direction and make the site feel less exposed than #56.

## #60 Privacy Rating: B-
**Reservable?** No. First-come, first-served. This could change in the future. Visit our campground updates page at **www.ilovetheeasternsierra.com** for the latest information.

A lush backdrop of wild roses and other greenery are the only neighbor to #60's rear, making for a tranquil backdrop. On the left, two campsites are within view, but one is staggered forward and closer to the campground road, so it doesn't feel too intrusive, and some trees intervene between #60 and the other space. Although it wouldn't be our first choice, if the other sites we've mentioned were taken, we would feel comfortable here.

## Chris Flat Campground

**Directions:** From Walker, CA travel 9.2 miles south on Highway 395. The campground is on the left.

## What's It Like?

A small campground alongside the Walker River, Chris Flat has a few spots with good privacy, many of them set back in the willows. The setting is peaceful, but marred by the fact the campground is so close to Highway 395 that the road noise here is excessive. Still, if you sleep inside a trailer, an RV, a camper van, or a pickup with a camper shell or if you have a tent and bring along earplugs, the campground's location next to the Walker River makes it an ideal spot for anglers. During the spring and early summer of normal snow years, when the Walker River is flowing at its peak, it might drown out some of the road noise.

## What's It Near?

• Some of the best BBQ west of Texas at Mountain View Barbecue in nearby Walker, California.

• Hiking to Emma Lake (a beautiful alpine gem at the end of a 1.2 mile, one-way. short, huff and puffer of a hike); Burt Canyon (a mild walk as far as you want to go through a scenic canyon); and Anna Lake (the end point of the Burt Canyon hike, 13.5 miles round trip).

• Trails are also nearby in Little Antelope Valley, accessed by a dirt road north of Walker.

• If you're comfortable hiking cross-country, camp host Rusty said you can reach some beautiful lakes if you trek through the forest near the campground.

• Fishing in the Walker River next to the campground and in the nearby Little Walker River and Molybdenite Creek for rainbow and brown trout.

• Devour the burgers and shakes at Walker Burger or grab a picnic lunch, pizza, and baked goods at Walker Country Store. We avoided the temptation of cinnamon rolls when we were there and had sandwiches instead.

• Great breakfasts, lunches, and pie at Meadowcliff Lodge, north of Walker in the Antelope Valley.

• Horseback riding through Little Antelope Pack Station.

**Elevation:** 6,740 feet

**Toilets:** Vault

**Verizon Cell Service?** No

**Takes Reservations?** No. First-come, first-served.

**Number of Campsites:** 14

**Bear Boxes?** No

### Campsites with the Most Privacy

**#2 Privacy Rating: B**
**Reservable?** No. First-come, first-served.

You'll have a glimpse of your neighbors in the space to the left (about 24 feet away), but willows and other vegetation provide a partial privacy screen. Willows also do a good job of concealing the view of the space on the right and screen out Highway 395 behind the campsite. A pine shades the picnic table in the afternoon. The only neighbor across the campground road is the Walker River, although you can't see it because willows and junipers interfere with the view.

## #3 Privacy Rating: B+
**Reservable?** No. First-come, first-served.

Seasonal Grouse Creek trickles along to the right of #3 and beyond that you catch a glimpse of site #2 through the vegetation about 24 feet away. Space #4 sits to the left, but you have to look really hard to see it through the willows, small pines, and rabbitbrush. Willows partially block the view of Highway 395 behind the site and beyond the highway a pine-covered hill touches the sky. As with site #2, the Walker River is across the campground road, but willows and trees conceal your view of it. You do have a nice view of the sagebrush-strewn mountains rising up alongside Walker River Canyon. There's very little shade in this site, so bring a canopy.

## #13 Privacy Rating: A
**Reservable?** No. First-come, first-served.

If it wasn't for its proximity to Highway 395, #13 would be the perfect campsite, both for people who like their space when camping and for anglers. It's off by itself at the end of a cul de sac so even though it's a very open campsite in the sagebrush, it has no neighbors to the left or right and behind is nothing but sage, rabbitbrush, and a great view looking down the Walker River Canyon. It also boasts a wonderful view of the Walker River, so anglers can dream about that day's catch while eating breakfast at the picnic table. Beyond the river, the canyon walls rise up toward the sky.

You will have a neighbor across the street in the middle of the cul de sac, but their table and fire pit are a good distance away and screened off behind sagebrush, so they won't pose a threat to your privacy. The picnic table for #13 is in full sun, but you can set a chair under the large pine growing next to the driveway by the river. Highway 395 is completely visible from this site, so at night you might have some headlights shining in your face. Still, this is a very scenic and large camp space, and the highway is at least 30 feet away. It might be worth putting up with the road noise and possible headlights, especially if you have a trailer or some other vehicle to sleep in.

## Obsidian Campground

**Directions:** From Walker, CA, follow Highway 395 south for 13.6 miles. Watch for a sign on the right that announces "campground." It's about 0.7 miles south of the turnoff to Sonora Pass (Highway 108). Turn right at the campground sign onto Little Walker River Road (Forest Service Road 66), and drive 3.4 miles on this dirt road to the campground. Passenger cars can easily make it to the campground, but it will be bumpy.

**What's It Like?**

There's something serene about camping under the aspens and listening to their leaves quiver in the breeze. Two of the three sections of Obsidian Campground allow you to do just that. The first two sections have the largest selection of spaces with privacy. The first section has only three campsites, so you won't have many neighbors if you grab one of those spots. The third section is located under the pines with very little understory; in this section, we found only one space that meets our qualifications. The campground sits on the edge of Hoover Wilderness and near Molybdenite Creek, although the creek isn't visible from any of the spaces.

**Words of Warning**: This campground lacks bear boxes so make sure your food and any fragrant toiletries are locked in your trunk or, if your car has no trunk, toss a blanket or tarp over anything that even looks or smells like food.

---

Obsidian Campground has no water spigots, so make certain to bring your own water if you're camping here.

**What's It Near?**

• Fishing in Molybdenite Creek, the Little Walker River, and West Walker River for rainbow and brown trout.

• Hikes to McMillian Lake (8.8 miles round trip), Emma Lake (a steep 1.2-mile, one-way trek) and Burt Canyon. Emma Lake glimmers like an emerald embedded into a cirque at the base of Mount Emma and Burt Canyon offers more solitude than many hikes in the Eastern Sierra. Keep an eye out for wild irises in Burt Canyon in June. Burt Canyon leads the way to Anna Lake, a 13.5-mile, round-trip trek, but even if you only hike one to three miles into the canyon the scenery is spectacular and the wildflowers and fall foliage here put on a colorful show.

• A scenic drive up to Sonora Pass. Access the Pacific Crest Trail at the Pass.

• Horseback riding through Leavitt Meadows Pack Station.

**Elevation:** 7,800 feet

**Toilets:** Vault

**Verizon Cell Service?** No

**Takes Reservations?** No. First-come, first-served.

**Number of Campsites:** 14

**Bear Boxes?** No

# Campsites with the Most Privacy

**#1 Privacy Rating: A-**
**Reservable?** No. First-come, first-served.

A cozy campsite with room for a small tent, #1 has a different personality than a lot of the other spaces in the first two loops of the campground. Instead of aspens to keep you company, tall pines grow in this site, providing shade to part of the space. You're not deprived of aspens completely, however, thanks to the grove across the road. It feels more exposed than the other two campsites in this section. But since there are only two other spaces in this part of the campground and those spaces are enclosed in aspens and far enough away from #1, camping here still feels as if you're sheltered from the view of neighboring eyes. The lack of neighbors to the left, right, or behind seals the privacy deal here.

**#2 Privacy Rating: A**
**Reservable?** No. First-come, first-served.

Despite having a slight view of space #3 through the aspens to the left, this site gives off good privacy vibes due to its lack of neighbors behind and to the right. Aspens embrace it, but you still have a glimpse of the mountains through a break in the trees to the right—at least until the teenage aspens grow into adults. There's a nice area for the tent here, too.

## #3 Privacy Rating: A-
**Reservable?** No. First-come, first-served.

This campsite has a filtered view of #2 to the right, but it has no neighbors behind it, to the left, or across the street. The big disadvantage is that for some reason this is the only spot in the campground that doesn't have a fire pit. Perhaps that will be fixed at some point in the future.

## #4, #5, #6, and #8 Privacy Rating: A-
**Reservable?** No. First-come, first-served.

Each of these sites are located in an aspen grove in the second loop of the campground. Stay in one of these sites and you're immersed in shimmering green aspen leaves. Each site has a view of at least one neighbor, but it's only a glimpse through a curtain of aspen trunks and branches. #4 also comes with a partial mountain view.

## #7 Privacy Rating: A+
**Reservable?** No. First-come, first-served.

Only a few aspens hover around the edges of the most private site on the loop. Pines reign over the site, providing shade. No neighbors on any side means you have this patch of the campground to yourself. Out of all the sites on this loop, it's the farthest from the bathroom, but the restrooms are still a manageable walk away.

## #10 Privacy Rating: A
**Reservable?** No. First-come, first-served.

This is the only space in the third loop that met our criteria for privacy. The rest of the sites in this section of the campground

---

are like social butterflies, all packed close together. By contrast, #10 sits apart like a shy wallflower. Plenty of pines shade the space, but it's bathed in some afternoon sun. #10 is close to the bathrooms, too.

---

**Are You Enjoying This Book? Write a Review on Amazon.com**

Your input is important to us. Write a review on Amazon and let us know if you like our book and if we've succeeded in helping you find a peaceful campsite.

---

# SONORA PASS

## Sonora Bridge Campground

**Directions:** From Walker, CA, follow Highway 395 south 12.8 miles and take a right on Highway 108 toward Sonora Pass. Drive 1.4 miles to the campground on the left.

**What's It Like?**

This campground surprised me. I'd driven past it a couple of times before but never gave it much thought. Now that I've seen it, I'd really like to stay there. Many of the campsites — although not all — are well-spaced from each other and some have pleasant views of the canyon leading up to Sonora Pass. It's located in the area where the sagebrush flirts with Jeffrey pines and junipers.

Even though it's just a few miles from the marine base up the road, most of the helicopters and planes launching from the base seem to fly over Leavitt Meadows and the nearby campground there — at least the times I have hiked in the area — but there is a chance a helicopter or two might buzz over here.

**Words of Warning:** The closest restaurant is in Walker, a curvy 14-mile drive away. So bring plenty of food. Also, this campground lacks bear boxes so make sure your food and any fragrant toiletries are locked in your trunk or, if your car has no trunk, toss a blanket or tarp over anything that even looks or smells like food.

**What's It Near?**

• Fishing for trout in the West Walker River and Little Walker River.

• The Leavitt Meadows trailhead, with hikes to Roosevelt and Lane Lakes (5 miles round trip) and a loop hike leading to Poore Lake and Secret Lake (6 miles round trip). Roosevelt Lake is a serene little gem with cattails and grass growing on floating logs.

• Horseback riding through Leavitt Meadows Pack Station.

• A scenic drive up to Sonora Pass.

• Hiking on the Pacific Crest Trail. The trailhead is at Sonora Pass.

• Hikes to Emma Lake (a steep 1.2 mile, one-way trek) and Burt Canyon are nearby, accessed by driving back to Highway 395, turning right, traveling 0.7 miles, and then taking another right on Little Walker River Road. Emma Lake glimmers like an emerald embedded into a cirque at the base of Mount Emma, and Burt Canyon offers more solitude than many hikes in the Eastern Sierra. Keep an eye out for wild irises in Burt Canyon in June. Burt Canyon leads the way to Anna Lake, a 13.5 miles round-trip trek, but even if you only hike one to three miles into the canyon the scenery is spectacular and the wildflowers and fall foliage here put on a colorful show.

**Elevation:** 6,800 feet

**Toilets:** Vault

**Verizon Cell Service?** No

**Takes Reservations?** No. First-come, first-served.

**Number of Campsites:** 23

**Bear Boxes?** No

# Campsites with the Most Privacy

**#1 Privacy Rating: B+**
**Reservable?** No. First-come, first-served.

Two tall, Siamese twin Jeffrey pines greet you as you pull into the driveway of this spacious site. It's in the busiest and most exposed part of the campground, but it has no neighbors on the right and no spaces in front of it. Vegetation hides the view of #2 on the left, and the spaces are far apart. Plus, it has no rear neighbors either, just a nice view of the mountains lining Sonora Canyon. It's a good spot for a trailer or RV.

**#5 Privacy Rating: B+**
**Reservable?** No. First-come, first-served.

We marked down the privacy rating on this one because you can see the camp host's trailer kitty corner from here. But pines block the view of any neighbors to the left and there are no spaces on the immediate right, so it has a good privacy cushion. Directly across the street, there is nothing but conifers and what look like tall bitterbrush. Another good spot for a trailer or RV, thanks to its pull through.

**#11 Privacy Rating: A+**
**Reservable?** No. First-come, first-served.

This beauty of a spot sits on an overlook, giving you a partial view of the mountains lining Sonora Canyon and the mountains to the east of Highway 395. Peer over the edge of the site, and far below you'll see the silver blue ribbon of the Walker River cutting its way through a meadow. Pines tower over the space and provide some shade. #11 is cushioned on all sides by privacy with no one to the right, behind, or across the street and just a hint of a view of #13 to the left. As a bonus, it's near the bathrooms. There might be faint road noise, but you're so far above Highway 108, it shouldn't pose much of a problem.

## #13 Privacy Rating: A+
**Reservable?** No. First-come, first-served.

Another exceptional campsite, #13 hugs the edge of a hill overlooking the Walker River. You can't see the river from the picnic table, but if you walk to the edge and look down, the river cuts through a meadow far below. What you *can* see from the campsite is a filtered view of a mountain rising up behind the Walker River that Mother Nature painted with alternating shades of rust and tan. #11 is barely visible to the right and to the left a small hill intervenes between you and the closest site on that side. Because the space is pushed far back from the campground road, the neighbor across the street seems far away. A tall Jeffrey pine provides some shade.

## #15 Privacy Rating: A+
**Reservable?** No. First-come, first-served.

A mountain intermingled with tan and rust hues looms up behind this site, an impressive backdrop to the picnic table. Many of the sites in this campground have a glimpse looking back down Sonora Canyon, but that vista mostly disappears here, replaced in the other direction by a view of the mountains by Sonora Pass. A short path behind the campsite leads to an overlook of the Walker River and Highway 108 far below. No neighbors on the left, right, behind, or directly across the street mean this site is in a world of its own. What looks like a Huckleberry Oak guards the entrance to the campsite, and a couple of pines partially protect campers from the warm blast of Sierra sun. There's just a hint of road noise from Highway 108 far below.

**#16 Privacy Rating: A+**
**Reservable?** No. First-come, first-served.

At first glance, #16 seems like it's too exposed to #17 on the left, which is a long stone's throw away from the driveway. But the fact that #16 is pushed far back from the road and faces the opposite direction from its only visible neighbor gives this site an isolated feel. Adding to the secluded ambiance is a short path to the right of the picnic table where a circle of tall bushes embrace the tent area. This area is almost completely invisible from the campground road or your neighbors. What looks like a slightly bigger version of Charlie Brown's Christmas tree pokes up in the middle of the tent area, so if you have a giant tent it might not fit, but you can squeeze in one two- or four-person tent here. And once you park your vehicle, it will hide most of your neighbor from view.

Of all the sites overlooking the Walker River, this one has the best view of the stream, which is visible from the picnic table. You also have a glimpse of the mountains by Sonora Pass. This site is nicely shaded thanks to a large juniper and other tall vegetation next to the picnic table and big pines surrounding the campsite. You'll hear just a hint of Highway 108 road noise here, too, but nothing that's bothersome.

**#17 Privacy Rating: A+**
**Reservable?** No. First-come, first-served.

A steep hill rises to the left of the last site on this loop, providing total privacy on that side. #17's only neighbor (#16 on the right) is pushed back far enough from the road and faces a different direction, making its existence a non-issue (see description for #16). Plus, your vehicle will obscure the view of #16 when you're sitting at the picnic table or campfire.

A little path departs from the picnic table and fire pit to a sheltered spot to pitch your tent away from the campground road. This site is big enough to fit at least one other two- or four-person tent, although in a more visible location. Behind #17, the trees open up to distant views of the granite peaks near Sonora Pass and some interesting rocky outcroppings poking out of a mountain across the canyon. A few big pines provide some shade.

## #22 Privacy Rating: B
**Reservable?** No. First-come, first-served.

A long and narrow site ideally suited to a trailer or RV thanks to a pull through driveway, #22 backs up to a hill. It has no neighbors immediately across the street. The space to the left is invisible from here, and vegetation partially blocks the view of the right-hand neighbor. Not as private as some of the other sites we've described due to its proximity to the campground road, but still a nice spot.

## #23 Privacy Rating: B+
**Reservable?** No. First-come, first-served.

Set off by itself and anchoring this end of the campground, #23 has no immediate neighbors on any side. Like #22, the hill rising up immediately behind #23 forces the space into a long and narrow area. The tent area here is a bit close to the campground road, which is the only reason I marked this space down to a B+ from what would normally be an A site. But you shouldn't have a ton of people driving past, since there are only five other sites on this loop. This is a good spot for a small trailer, pickup truck with a camper shell, or a van.

## Leavitt Meadows Campground

**Directions:** From Bridgeport, travel 17 miles north on Highway 395. Turn left on Highway 108 at Sonora Junction and drive approximately six miles to campground on the left.

### What's It Like?

Set in a beautiful grove of aspens alongside the Walker River, this campground features many spaces next to the river — but these spaces aren't the most private in the campground. In view of many of the riverside spaces, a picturesque pedestrian bridge crosses over a deep emerald green pool and leads to hiking trails, swimming holes, and fishing spots.

Because of all the aspens surrounding many of the campsites, I thought the privacy factor here would be better. But many of the spaces, especially along the river, are in clear view of each other and pressed close together. However, we did find three spaces we really liked.

Some of the campsites across from the river might be acceptable to you from a privacy perspective, but we ruled those out because the tent area of the sites was too close to the campground road and the spaces seemed too near their neighbors across the street. Likewise, for a few of the spaces next to the river, aspens provide a partial privacy screen, but we didn't include those spaces because the proximity of the neighbors felt intrusive and the picnic tables and fire pits sit too close to the campground road. Other spaces are too close to Highway 108.

Still, if you have your heart set on camping near the river, you might bite the bullet and choose one of the riverside spaces where the aspens at least shelter some of your campsite from view of the neighbors. There aren't many spaces like that, though, so it will be slim pickings. If you like privacy, we think you'll like the three spaces below better than the riverside sites.

**Words of Warning:** A marine military base is located a few miles down the highway, so expect to hear helicopters and planes buzzing overhead in the daytime. Also know that the closest restaurant is in Walker, a curvy 20-mile drive away. So bring plenty of food.

**What's It Near?**

• Fishing for trout in the West Walker River.

• The Leavitt Meadows trailhead, with hikes to Roosevelt and Lane Lakes (5 miles round trip) and a loop hike leading to Poore Lake and Secret Lake (6 miles round trip). Roosevelt Lake is a serene little gem with cattails and grass growing on floating logs. Leavitt Meadows is spectacular in the fall, with the aspen on the surrounding mountainsides ablaze in yellow, orange, and red, and willows adding splashes of yellow along the banks of the Walker River.

• Technical climbing and scrambling to reach Tower Peak.

• Horseback riding at Leavitt Meadows Pack Station.

• A scenic drive up to Sonora Pass.

• Hiking on the Pacific Crest Trail. The trailhead is at Sonora Pass.

**Elevation:** 7,800 feet

**Toilets:** Vault

**Verizon Cell Service?** Yes, surprisingly, two bars.

**Takes Reservations?** No. First-come, first-served.

**Number of Campsites:** 16

**Bear Boxes?** Yes

## Campsites with the Most Privacy

**#3 Privacy Rating: A-**
**Reservable?** No. First-come, first-served.

This site is located across the campground road from the Walker River, but it's upstream from all the other riverside spaces and off by itself, giving it more privacy. The campground road curls around this spot, so you will have a road on two sides. The table and grill are a bit closer to the campground road than we like, but some low-growing aspens and other vegetation partially filter the view of both the road and the only neighboring site, which is across the street and in front of this campsite.

A semi circle of aspens embrace the tent area on three sides, creating a sort of Mother-Nature-made bedroom. You can see the Walker River from the campsite when you're standing. #3 is above the river, so you might have to walk downstream a little ways to reach the water, or scramble down a steep hill.

**#13 Privacy Rating: A-**
**Reservable?** No. First-come, first-served.

A spacious spot, we gave this a high privacy rating due to its lack of neighbors on three sides and the fact you can't see the neighbor on the left. A rather open spot in the sagebrush and sprinkled with a handful of conifers, it's clearly visible from the campground road. A large pine shades the picnic table.

Its two biggest disadvantages are that it's not the most aesthetically pleasing campsite due to an eyesore of a fence surrounding some unknown object (a transformer maybe?). The fence, though, serves a purpose: it eliminates the left-side neighbor from sight and if you position your chair facing the other direction you'll never know that space is there. The other disadvantage to this spot? Highway 108 is up a small hill behind the campsite and in the daytime especially you'll hear a little road noise. The good news: because the highway is up a hill from the campsite, it's not as visible as it is in a few of the other campsites. Aspens flutter in the breeze across the street from #13. A pull through also makes this a nice spot for an RV or trailer.

**#15 Privacy Rating: A**
**Reservable?** No. First-come, first-served.

Aspens grow to the right and behind the site. To the left is sagebrush, but no other campsites. Aspens partially screen the space across the street and it's pushed back enough to remain unobtrusive. This is a pleasant spot among the aspens, and has the most privacy of any of the sites in the campground.

# TWIN LAKES

## Buckeye Campground

**Directions:** From Bridgeport, at the intersection of Highway 395 and Twin Lakes Road, turn south on Twin Lakes Road and follow it approximately 7 miles to Doc and Al's Resort. There, turn right on Buckeye Road and drive for 3 miles. Turn left at the fork and drive 0.7 miles to the campground. The road is dirt, but passenger cars can easily make it to the campground, where it becomes paved again.

### What's It Like?

The campground is nestled among Jeffrey and lodgepole pines, with some sites along the stream in the aspens, others set back in the forest, and some sites more open in the sagebrush with a smattering of Jeffrey pines. The first loop that you encounter on the left of the road has the most activity, is closest to Buckeye Creek, and is the least private although there are several good spaces there, including my favorite one in the campground. On the second loop on the right, the campsites are well-spaced, and it's surprisingly private given that most of the understory is low-growing sagebrush and bitterbrush. The farthest loop away from the entrance has spaces that are closer together. Plus, on this loop, there isn't much vegetation growing under the pines, so that even though there are tall trees between the campsites, without aspens or bushes to screen out neighbor views you'll have less of a pick of spaces with privacy.

**Words of Warning:** There is no potable water in this campground. Bring your own. The campground also is lacking bear boxes. Make sure your food and any fragrant toiletries are locked in your trunk or, if your car has no trunk, toss a blanket or tarp over anything that even looks or smells like food.

---

## What's It Near?

• Soak in the Buckeye Hot Springs, a half mile east of the campground.

• Hikes on the Buckeye Canyon Trail to Big Meadow (8.2 miles round trip), sprinkled with wild iris in late May, or to The Forks (18.8 miles round trip to where the North and South Forks of Buckeye Creek join together). Walk as far as you like in this canyon, but if you can make it to at least Big Meadow it will reward you with stunning vistas. Well-conditioned hikers also can tackle the strenuous trek up to Eagle Peak.

• Fishing in Buckeye Creek for primarily brook and rainbow trout and some brown trout.

**Elevation:** 7,000 feet

**Toilets:** Vault

**Verizon Cell Service?**

Check our website at **www.ilovetheeasternsierra.com** for updates on this. Patrick, who has an iPhone, wasn't at the campground with me. My cell phone is an older model and not as reliable.

**Takes Reservations?** No. First-come, first-served.

**Number of Campsites:** 68

**Bear Boxes?** No.

# Campsites with the Most Privacy

**#3 Privacy Rating: C+**
**Reservable?** No. First-come, first-served.

Sometimes, my husband and I sacrifice complete privacy if a campsite has a great view. #3 in Buckeye Creek is worth considering for this reason. I give it a low privacy rating because it's out in the open, well-visible from the campground road, and you can see site #4 really well from #3. However, it's set on the edge of a green-velvet meadow with a great view of the snow-capped peaks of Buckeye Canyon. At least, snow-capped earlier in the season. There's nobody camped behind you, and that's also an advantage. Plus, none of your neighbors are pressed up right next to you.

**#9 Privacy Rating: B+**
**Reservable?** No. First-come, first-served.

I can't say this space has tons of personality in regards to views of anything interesting but it's peaceful and private. Its nearest neighbor, site #8, is far enough away on the right—a few steps more than a stone's throw away and barely visible—and there are no spaces to the left, behind, or across the street. Pines provide shade and the bathroom is a short walk away. There are other sites on this loop that are acceptable—in other words not jammed in together—but this space is the most private on the loop.

**#23, #24, #26 Privacy Rating: B+**
**Reservable?** No. First-come, first-served.

Your nearest neighbors to the left and right are far enough away, you won't have any neighbors behind you, and the picnic tables and fire pits are tucked back far from the campground road. Pines spread their boughs over the picnic table, offering up some welcome shade. All three sites are good for small trailers and RVs. These sites are located on the second (middle loop), which curves around through sagebrush and pines. This loop seemed the most quiet and peaceful because most of its spaces are far apart from each other.

**#34 Privacy Rating: A+**
**Reservable?** No. First-come, first-served.

There's no other space across the street nor will you have any neighbors in sight on either side. Through the pines, looking towards The Roughs, there's a filtered view of the snow-capped peaks of Buckeye Canyon. Despite a lot of sagebrush and bitterbrush—which was blooming yellow during my visit on Memorial Day—some tall Jeffrey pines provide shade.

**#35 Privacy Rating: A**
**Reservable?** No. First-come, first-served.

From here, to the east, you have a glimpse of Bridgeport valley and the mountains beyond. To the west, through the trees, catch a filtered glimpse of the mountains in Buckeye Canyon. Tall Jeffrey pines gather around the picnic table, offering some protection against the afternoon sun. This site boasts good privacy, with no neighbors too close on any side. This one might get blasted by sun in the morning (I visited in the afternoon) thanks to the open view to the East.

**#38 Privacy Rating: A+**
**Reservable?** No. First-come, first-served.

This is the most private site on the loop. Sitting under a tall Jeffrey pine and surrounded by a carpet of sagebrush and bitterbrush, #38 has no neighbors on either side, across the street, or behind. The big pine shades much of the campsite, but the picnic table isn't completely under the tree's limbs and is bathed by the afternoon sun.

## #41 Privacy Rating: A-
**Reservable?** No. First-come, first-served.

Another beauty of a campsite with plenty of elbow room. There are no neighboring campsites on either side and behind the site a carpet of sagebrush is dotted with tall Jeffrey pines. The only neighbor is a space across the campground road, but it's a good distance away. You'll also have a view of a pine-covered mountain. And, as an added bonus, it's near the bathroom. Pines provide shade, but some dappled afternoon sunlight sneaks through the branches.

## #52 Privacy Rating: B
**Reservable?** No. First-come, first-served.

In the busiest section of the campground (the first loop on the left), #52 punctuates the far right end of that loop. Tall pines and their shorter offspring gather behind the campsite, ensuring forested privacy in that direction, and no other sites sit to the left or right, either. Your nearest neighbor is across the street. It's also a short walk to Buckeye Creek.

## #64 Privacy Rating: A+
**Reservable?** No. First-come, first-served.

This was one of my favorite campsites in this campground. Although it's located in the busiest section, it's on a more peaceful spur loop. There's nothing more serene than camping next to a stream—as long as the campsites aren't jammed up next to each other. Buckeye Creek flows immediately behind this campsite. And even though this space is near to the right of site #65, aspens curtain off the view of the neighbor. Plus, the two spaces are stacked—#65 is close to the road whereas #64 is pushed farther back near the creek. It's a shady spot, thanks to aspens and a cluster of pines towering over the picnic table. You could cast your fishing line from your campsite.

**#66 Privacy Rating: B+**
**Reservable?** No. First-come, first-served.

Not as nice as #64, because it's not right next to the stream and isn't surrounded by aspens. But it's far enough away from its closest neighbor—#65—to give it a fair amount of privacy. And it's a close walk to the creek from here. Four tall Jeffrey pines stand guard over the picnic table, bestowing some shade upon this sagebrush-surrounded campsite. One disadvantage: Buckeye Creek Road is behind #66, but there's not much traffic on the road to begin with, and as the evening wears on the traffic will die down.

## Lower Honeymoon Flat Campground

**Directions:** From Bridgeport, at the intersection of Highway 395 and Twin Lakes Road, turn south on Twin Lakes Road (toward the Sierra) and follow it approximately 8 miles to the campground on the right.

## What's It Like?

While Upper Honeymoon Flat is known for its nice views of Sawtooth Ridge, Lower Honeymoon Flat boasts many creekside campsites in the conifers and willows. This is one of the nicest campgrounds in the Twin Lakes area and was a pleasant surprise after viewing other campgrounds in the canyon that were what Patrick calls "condo camping," where all the spaces are pressed right up next to each other.

## What's It Near?

• Fishing for rainbow, brown, and brook trout at Twin Lakes, a couple of miles away from the campground, and in Robinson Creek.

• Boating, kayaking, and canoeing at Twin Lakes.

• Hikes to Barney Lake (7.5 miles round trip), Peeler Lake (15.5 miles round trip), Tamarack Lake (9 miles round trip), Hunewill Lake (11 miles round trip), and Crown Lake (15 miles round trip).

• Delicious meals at the Café at Annette's Mono Village, which will cook your fresh caught fish for you along with tasty side dishes. Be sure to give the chef enough notice.

**Elevation:** 7,000 feet

**Toilets:** Vault

**Verizon Cell Service?** Visit the campground updates section at www.ilovetheeasternsierra.com for information on cell phone service availability.

**Takes Reservations?** Yes. Visit www.recreation.gov for reservations. Only one of the campsites (#3) is first-come, first-served.

**Number of Campsites:** 13

**Bear Boxes?** Yes

# Campsites with the Most Privacy

**#3 Privacy Rating: A+**
**Reservable?** No. First-come, first-served.

It doesn't get any better than this. Set off by itself with no close neighbors on any side, this well-shaded site sits next to Robinson Creek, which flows behind #3. This is a dream spot for an angler or anyone who loves to hear the symphonic sound of a stream flowing past. You can see the creek from here, too. Wild irises will add a splash of color in early summer. If there are any disadvantages it would be the pond to the left of the site, which looks tranquil but may give birth to a lot of mosquitoes earlier in the summer. The bathroom is also a little farther away compared to other spots, but this is such a nice site, the walk is worth it.

**#5 and #7 Privacy Rating: B+**
**Reservable?** Yes. Visit www.recreation.gov for reservations. These are double sites so they cost more.

These double sites are ideal for families or groups of friends. #5 is more exposed and sunny and fringed by aspens and willows. #7 has more shade, thanks to its location in the pines, and sits far back from the campground road. Both #5 and #7 are near Robinson Creek. You might be able to see Robinson Creek from #7, but the day we were at the campground, someone was camped here and we couldn't access the site to be certain.

**#9 Privacy Rating: A-**
**Reservable?** Yes. Visit www.recreation.gov for reservations.

The willows embrace this cozy, creekside spot. No neighbors are visible on any side. The only reason we didn't give this an

A+ rating is because the tent pad is too close to the campground road. However, this might not be much of an issue since #9 is located on a loop with only five sites, so there won't be a ton of cars driving past.

**#10 Privacy Rating: A+**
**Reservable?** Yes. Visit www.recreation.gov for reservations.

Some campsites—the really magical ones—I think about for days after I visit them. This was one of those campsites.

Willows enclose it on three sides, blocking the view of its two adjoining neighbors, and Robinson Creek flows close behind it. The willows conceal most of the view of the creek, except for one little peek of the water. Mother Nature makes up for robbing you of your view of the creek by providing a view of the mountains beyond instead. No other campsites are across the street. As an added bonus, wild roses border the site, adding a touch of pink color in June or early July.

**#11 Privacy Rating: A+**
**Reservable?** Yes. Visit www.recreation.gov for reservations.

Tucked back in the willows and trees, this double site—meant for larger groups—is sheltered from the campground road and has no neighbors visible on any side. Twin Lakes Road is up a little hill next to the site. But at night traffic should die down. Plus, the willows cushion most of the site from the road.

## Upper Honeymoon Flat Campground

**Directions:** From Bridgeport, at the intersection of Highway 395 and Twin Lakes Road, turn south on Twin Lakes Road (toward the Sierra) and follow it approximately 8 miles to the campground on the left.

**What's It Like?**

Upper Honeymoon Flat is located on the opposite side of Twin Lakes Road from the lower campground. Campsites are either more in the open, etched out of the sage and rabbitbrush, with a smattering of low-growing aspens, or more sheltered in taller aspens and pines. Lower Honeymoon Flat is a little more appealing, just because it's next to Robinson Creek, but you can find some nice spots at Upper Honeymoon with spectacular views of Sawtooth Ridge. Compared to some of the campgrounds on the Twin Lakes Road, which jam the spaces in right next to each other, this campground has some good spacing in between many—but not all—of the sites.

**What's It Near?**

• Fishing for rainbow, brown, and brook trout at Twin Lakes, a couple of miles away from the campground, and in Robinson Creek.

• Boating, kayaking, and canoeing at Twin Lakes.

• Hikes to Barney Lake (7.5 miles round trip), Peeler Lake (15.5 miles round trip), Tamarack Lake (9 miles round trip), Hunewill Lake (11 miles round trip), and Crown Lake (15 miles round trip).

• Delicious meals at the Café at Annette's Mono Village, which will cook your fresh caught fish for you along with tasty side dishes. Be sure to give the chef enough notice.

**Elevation:** 7,000 feet

**Toilets:** Vault

**Verizon Cell Service?** Visit the campground updates section at www.ilovetheeasternsierra.com for information on cell phone service availability.

**Takes Reservations?** No. Upper Honeymoon is first-come, first-served. Lower Honeymoon does take reservations at www.recreation.gov.

**Number of Campsites:** 15

**Bear Boxes?** Yes

### Campsites with the Most Privacy

**#18 Privacy Rating: A-**
**Reservable?** No. First-come, first-served.

Pines, aspen, and greenery line either side of this cozy space. Willows and other greenery, topped by a mountain view, serve as a backdrop. To the right, past aspens and a small meadow, sits neighboring site #17, but it's not close enough to feel intrusive. To the left, there's a hint of a view of the neighbor's tent. Overall, one of the most private spaces in the Twin Lakes area. This site, and the other spaces on this spur loop (sites #15 - #21), are tent only.

**#23 Privacy Rating: A-**
**Reservable?** No. First-come, first-served.

Located on the left hand spur loop as you drive into the campground, this site is out in the open, surrounded by sagebrush and rabbitbrush. Pines and aspens in the distance politely open up for a nice view of Sawtooth Ridge from the left side of the camp space. Thanks to a well-placed tent pad, once you pitch your tent, it might partially conceal the view of the bathroom to the right and another campsite that's beyond the restrooms across the campground road. There are no spaces behind #23 — nothing but sagebrush, rabbitbrush, and conifers, although Twin Lakes Road interrupts the view about 35 feet away. A tall pine provides some shade. Aspens and a conifer team up to partially block the view of the campsite that's directly across the campground road. The view of the Sawtooth Ridge and the lack of nearby neighbors makes this a very nice site.

**#25 Privacy Rating: B**
**Reservable?** No. First-come, first-served.

A double site, #25 is a nice home away from home for a family or group of friends, especially if you enjoy high desert camping. Low-growing aspens sprinkled around the site add a bit of pizazz to the sagebrush scenery while the pull through adds convenience for people pulling trailers or driving RVs. The tent pads are nicely situated with a line of aspens on either side. There's a filtered view of Sawtooth Ridge from here (although not as nice as in #23). There are no neighbors to the left or behind, but space #24 is closer on the right than we like to see. Still, this isn't a bad spot.

## Robinson Creek North and South Campgrounds

**Directions:** From Bridgeport, travel south on Twin Lakes Road for about 9.2 miles. The campground is on the left.

**What's It Like?**

Sitting under a canopy of Jeffrey and lodgepole pines next to Robinson Creek, this campground falls short of privacy nirvana due to the fact you're going to rub elbows with your neighbors in most of the campsites. The only campsites with any privacy in this campground are the walk-in sites in the south section of the campground (see description below). The rest of the campground, however, feels like a mini-city in the woods. Still, its creekside location is heaven for anglers.

**What's It Near?**

• Fishing at Twin Lakes (Lower Twin Lake is .9 miles from the campground) and in Robinson Creek for rainbow, brook, and brown trout.

• Boating, canoeing, and kayaking at Twin Lakes.

• Hikes to Barney Lake (7.5 miles round trip), Peeler Lake (15.5 miles round trip), Tamarack Lake (9 miles round trip), Hunewill Lake (11 miles round trip), and Crown Lake (15 miles round trip).

• Delicious meals at the Café at Annette's Mono Village, which will cook your fresh caught fish for you along with tasty side dishes. Be sure to give the chef enough notice.

**Elevation:** 7,000 feet

**Toilets:** Flush and Vault

**Verizon Cell Service?** Visit the campground updates section at www.ilovetheeasternsierra.com for information on cell phone service availability.

**Takes Reservations?** Yes. Visit **www.recreation.gov** for reservations. A small number of sites are first-come, first-served.

**Number of Campsites:** 52

**Bear Boxes?** Yes

### Campsites with the Most Privacy

**#10 - #12, #16 Privacy Rating: See Description Below**
**Reservable?** Yes. Visit www.recreation.gov for reservations.

We made it a point to personally visit the majority of campsites mentioned in this book. Unfortunately, when we were driving through this campground, we were unable to visit these four campsites. We believe, however, that they have the most privacy in the campground. #10, #11, #12, and #16 are close to the creek and #16 likely has the most privacy. Visit the campground updates section at **www.ilovetheeasternsierra.com** where we'll give you a full description of these sites as soon as we return to the Twin Lakes area.

### PAHA Campground

**Directions:** From Bridgeport, travel south on Twin Lakes Road for about 9.5 miles. The campground is on the left.

## What's It Like?

One redeeming quality of this campground is that Robinson Creek curls around behind it and many sites overlook the water. Unfortunately, this is a very busy campground with spaces rubbing up next to each other. However, if you need to camp here or if the rest of the campgrounds near Twin Lakes are full, we did find three sites that are acceptable. (See campsite description below).

## What's It Near?

• Fishing at Twin Lakes (Lower Twin Lake is a half mile from the campground) and in Robinson Creek for rainbow, brook, and brown trout.

• Boating, kayaking, and canoeing at Twin Lakes.

• Hikes to Barney Lake (7.5 miles round trip), Peeler Lake (15.5 miles round trip), Tamarack Lake (9 miles round trip), Hunewill Lake (11 miles round trip), and Crown Lake (15 miles round trip).

• Delicious meals at the Café at Annette's Mono Village, which will cook your fresh caught fish for you along with tasty side dishes. Be sure to give the chef enough notice.

**Elevation:** 7,000 feet

**Toilets:** Flush

**Verizon Cell Service?** Visit the campground updates section of **www.ilovetheeasternsierra.com** for information on cell phone service availability.

**Takes Reservations?** Yes. Visit **www.recreation.gov** for reservations. A small number of sites are first-come, first-served.

**Number of Campsites:** 21

**Bear Boxes?** Yes

## Campsites with the Most Privacy

**#2 Privacy Rating: B+**
**Reservable?** Yes. This is a double site so it costs more. Visit **www.recreation.gov** for reservations.

This double site has a nice view of the green and rusty-hued mountain that dominates the skyline on the north side of the canyon. Sawtooth Ridge also rubs shoulders with the sky, clearly visible in the distance. #2 is a very sunny spot, with the only shade provided by some pines on the outskirts of the site. But despite its openness and proximity to the campground road it has the most privacy in the campground, well-spaced from its neighbors on the left and right, and no other sites behind it. #1 is visible across the street, but it's far enough away that #2 retains its private feel.

**#6 Privacy Rating: B-**
**Reservable?** Yes. Visit **www.recreation.gov** for reservations.

From a privacy perspective, this space stood out due to its lack of neighbors behind it and the distance between it and the spaces to the left and right. It does have shade, provided by tall Jeffrey pines, which is a bonus in this sunny transition zone between sage and pine. You'll have a neighbor across the street, but the fire pit and picnic table for #6 are back far enough that it doesn't feel like those neighbors are breathing down your neck. Compared to many of the sites in PAHA, which are joined at the hip with their neighbors, this one has plenty of breathing room.

**#9 Privacy Rating: B**
**Reservable?** Yes. Visit **www.recreation.gov** for reservations.

Robinson Creek ambles along behind this ideal spot for anglers. No other campsites exist to the immediate right. There is a neighbor to the left, but there's a goodly amount of space between the two sites and your vehicle may at least partially hide the view of that site. There's no one across the street either. Set your camp chair facing the stream and you won't even know you're in a campground, although you might have an angler or two wandering past you from time to time. Shade provides relief from the heat of the day.

## Crags Campground

**Directions:** From Bridgeport, follow Twin Lakes Road south for about 10 miles. Turn left on South Twin Road and travel about 0.2 miles to the campground on the left.

**What's It Like?**

In a canyon where most of the campgrounds have sites squished together like sardines in a can, this campground was a pleasant surprise. Sage, rabbitbrush, and scattered Jeffrey pines make this a very open campground, but because many of the sites are spaced far apart, there's a lot of privacy here. The two loops of the campground are named for the mountains visible from most sites: the Matterhorn and Sawtooth Ridge. Unlike the other campgrounds in the Twin Lakes area, Crags is not located next to Robinson Creek, but it's a pleasant campground nonetheless, and seems to have less commotion than many of the other more crowded campgrounds in the canyon.

The only National Forest Service campground closer to Twin Lakes than Crags is Lower Twin Lakes campground. But Crags boasts more privacy between spaces. Although it's not streamside, Crags is an easy drive away from Robinson Creek or Twin Lakes for anglers yearning to reel in a catch.

**Words of Warning:** Spaces in both the Sawtooth and Matterhorn loops have the same numbers, so when reading our descriptions below, make certain you take note on which loop the campsite is located.

**What's It Near?**

• Fishing at Twin Lakes and in Robinson Creek, a short drive away from the campground, for rainbow, brown, and brook trout.

• Boating, kayaking, and canoeing at Twin Lakes.

• Hikes to Barney Lake (7.5 miles round trip), Peeler Lake (15.5 miles round trip), Tamarack Lake (9 miles round trip), Hunewill Lake (11 miles round trip), and Crown Lake (15 miles round trip).

• Delicious meals at the Café at Annette's Mono Village, which will cook your fresh caught fish for you along with tasty side dishes. Be sure to give the chef enough notice.

**Elevation:** 7,000 feet

**Toilets:** Vault and flush

**Verizon Cell Service?** Visit the campground updates section of www.ilovetheeasternsierra.com for information on cell phone service availability.

**Takes Reservations?** Yes. Visit **www.recreation.gov** for reservations. Some sites in the campground are first-come, first-served.

**Number of Campsites:** 52

**Bear Boxes?** Yes

## Campsites with the Most Privacy
### Sawtooth Loop

**#4 Privacy Rating: C+**
**Reservable?** No. First-come, first-served.

Despite a neighbor that's clearly visible on the right, the lack of any spaces to the immediate left and the fact there's nothing but a sage- and pine-covered hill behind it, make #4 worthy to include in this book. A big boulder partially eliminates the view of people across the street when you're sitting down. We gave this a C+ rating due to the closeness of the neighbor on the right, but on that side the partial views of the Sawtooth Ridge and the Matterhorn through gaps in the tall pines will steal your attention away anyway. This is a very sunny site, so bringing a canopy to put over the picnic table is a good idea. Not the best site in the campground, but we wouldn't hesitate to camp here if the other good spaces were filled.

**#5 Privacy Rating: B**
**Reservable?** Yes. Visit **www.recreation.gov** for reservations.

This one is a bit close to its neighbor on the left and right. The space on the left is about 18 feet away from #5's driveway, but the sites are staggered so that #5 is farther back from the campground road while the other site is farther up. Same with the campsite on the right. Plus, your parked car, trailer, or camper van will mostly conceal the view of your neighbor to the left. Tall sagebrush and rabbitbrush also add some privacy. One large pine shades the driveway but the picnic table and bear box sit in the sun. This is another space where you'll want to bring a canopy to put over the picnic table.

**#6 Privacy Rating: A**
**Reservable?** Yes. Visit **www.recreation.gov** for reservations.

This is a sweet spot thanks to the lack of any nearby neighbors on any side and the tall pine shading the picnic table and bear box. A large hill anchors the rear of the site and there's a filtered view of the Matterhorn and Sawtooth Ridge. Plenty of room means there's space for three tents.

**Words of Warning:** During July and August thunderstorms you'll want to think twice about staying in this spot because

the camp host warned us that the tent pad floods.

**#9 Privacy Rating: A+**
**Reservable?** Yes. Visit **www.recreation.gov** for reservations.

One of the nicest campsites in the Sawtooth loop, #9 has no nearby neighbors on either side. A large hill with sagebrush and pines rises up behind the site. Like many spaces in this campground, #9 is exposed to the sun with only one large pine by the driveway to provide some shade. The picnic table and bear box are surrounded by a sea of sagebrush, rabbitbrush, and bitterbrush. A filtered view of the Matterhorn and Sawtooth Ridge will draw your gaze.

**#15 Privacy Rating: A+**
**Reservable?** Yes. Visit **www.recreation.gov** for reservations. This is a double site, so it will cost more.

A gem of a site for groups of friends or families, #15 is backed by tall Jeffrey pines and is surrounded by a field of sage. A Jeffrey pine also provides welcome shade over the picnic table. There are no spaces anywhere near to the right and to the left. Of all the sites on this loop, #15 has one of the nicest views of Sawtooth Ridge and the Matterhorn. Plus, it's near the bathrooms.

**#16 Privacy Rating: A+**
**Reservable?** Yes. Visit **www.recreation.gov** for reservations.

Although from #16 you can see the double campsite on the right, there's still some nice spacing between. To the left, the closest space is far away. And behind the site, sage and pine trees give way to a view of a mountain painted with rust and green hues. There's not much shade by the picnic table in the early afternoon, but by mid-afternoon the large pine next to it will likely cast some cooling shadows. You can see the Matterhorn and Sawtooth Ridge from some areas in the site.

**#18 Privacy Rating: A+**
**Reservable?** Yes. Visit **www.recreation.gov** for reservations.

This was one of our favorite campsites in Crags Campground. A paved 18-foot long pathway leads from the driveway to the picnic table and bear box, set back from the campground road. Another path—lined with pine cones to give it a whimsical touch—leads to the shady tent pad.

A hill to the left hides the view of your neighbor on that side and the space to the right is far away. The neighbor across the street also is far away.

Behind you is nothing but sagebrush, rabbitbrush, bitterbrush,

Jeffrey pines, and a nice view of a green and rusty hued mountain.

## Campsites with the Most Privacy
## Matterhorn Loop

### #4 Privacy Rating: A+
No. First-come, first-served.

This tent-only, walk-in site features a panoramic view of the Matterhorn and Sawtooth Ridge, interrupted by only a smattering of pine trees. In the opposite direction, there's also a distant view of the mountains east of Bridgeport. Its location up on a hill means it overlooks the Matterhorn Loop, yet the tent and fire pit are hidden from view of the campground road. Even though it's a walk-in site, you won't have to trek very far to reach it — about 18 feet up a little hill.

You'll look down at the neighboring space to the right, but that space is far enough away, you're far above them, and thanks to the bitterbrush, you won't see your neighbors from where you pitch your tent. To the left there are no other spots, behind is a large scrubby hill, and there are no neighbors across the street. The Sierra sun will blast this site in the afternoon, but there are some pines on the outskirts of the space where you can set a chair and read. This site is nirvana for anyone who likes to view the stars.

## Lower Twin Lakes Campground

**Directions:** From Bridgeport, follow Twin Lakes Road south for about 10 miles. At the campground sign, turn left on South Twin Road. Drive about a half mile to Lower Twin Lakes Campground sign and turn right into the campground.

**What's It Like?**

Lower Twin Lakes Campground brushes up against the

shores of Robinson Creek, but the beautiful, shady location is wasted in that all the campsites are a little too close together. Despite the name, the campground is not located on the shore of the lakes, although lower Twin Lake is within walking distance. Anglers may enjoy this campground since you can fish from most of the campsites.

**What's It Near?**

• Fishing for rainbow, brook, and brown trout at Twin Lakes and in Robinson Creek.

• Boating, kayaking, and canoeing at Twin Lakes.

• Hikes to Barney Lake (7.5 miles round trip), Peeler Lake (15.5 miles round trip), Tamarack Lake (9 miles round trip), Hunewill Lake (11 miles round trip), and Crown Lake (15 miles round trip).

• Delicious meals at the Café at Annette's Mono Village, which will cook your fresh caught fish for you along with tasty side dishes. Be sure to give the chef enough notice.

**Elevation:** 7,000 feet

**Toilets:** Flush

**Verizon Cell Service?** Visit the campground updates section of www.ilovetheeasternsierra.com for information on cell phone service availability.

**Takes Reservations?** Yes. Visit **www.recreation.gov** for reservations. Only a few sites in the campground are first-come, first-served.

**Number of Campsites:** 15

**Bear Boxes?** Yes

## Campsites with the Most Privacy

None.

# GREEN CREEK–VIRGINIA LAKES

## Green Creek Campground

**Directions:** From Bridgeport, travel on Highway 395 south for 3.8 miles to the Green Creek Road sign. Turn right on Green Creek Rd. (Forest Service Road 142) and drive 3.5 miles to a "T" intersection. Turn right, continuing on Road 142, and drive 5.4 miles to the campground. The road is dirt, but easily manageable by passenger cars.

**What's It Like?**

The drive up to this campground is a treat in itself, offering sublimely beautiful vistas. A spectacular view of the Bridgeport Valley and Bridgeport Reservoir greets you as you drive up the first part of the road. Not long after you leave that view behind and just before the campground, an aspen-ringed meadow opens up to a spectacular view of the jagged mountain peaks towering above Hoover Wilderness. This is a spectacular sight any time of year, but never more so than in the fall, when the aspens blaze yellow, orange, and red.

Green Creek meanders past this single loop campground. There are some creekside sites while other spaces are either a short distance from the creek and nestled in the lodgepole pines or surrounded by the quaking leaves of aspens. It has some of the best privacy of any campground in the Eastern Sierra, with all but one site boasting plenty of personal space. In this quieter canyon, you won't find the hustle and bustle of places like Mammoth Lakes. What you will find is plenty of opportunity to etch out your own slice of serenity.

**Words of Warning:** In fall of 2014 there was a boil water order in effect.

**What's It Near?**

• Hikes to Green Lake (4.8 miles round trip), West Lake (7.6

miles round trip), East Lake (7.6 miles round trip), Gilman Lake (9.6 miles round trip), Hoover Lakes (11.2 miles round trip).

• Fishing for rainbow trout in Green Creek or the other lakes mentioned above.

• Wonderful Italian food at Virginia Creek Settlement, two miles south of Green Creek Road on Highway 395. Some dishes are even available with gluten free pasta. You can also try their giant pizzas. A great place to stop on the way to the campground, but it's a long enough drive from the campground to the restaurant to make it an impractical choice for a dinner out after you've already set up camp.

• The turn off to the road that leads to the ghost town of Bodie is located only a few miles south from Green Creek Road on Highway 395.

**Elevation:** 7,500 feet

**Toilets:** Vault

**Verizon Cell Service?** Weak to non-existent.

**Takes Reservations?** No. All campsites are first-come, first served.

**Number of Campsites:** 11

**Bear Boxes?** Yes.

# Campsites with the Most Privacy

### #1 Privacy Rating: A
**Reservable?** No. First-come, first-served.

The creek runs behind this partly shady campsite and you can watch the water flow peacefully past. A lodgepole pine forest grows to the left of #1 so your only neighbors on that side are trees. Aspens and conifers filter the view of the space on the right. Aspens grow across the street, where the closest neighbor is just a bit down the campground road.

### #2 Privacy Rating: B+
**Reservable?** No. First-come, first-served.

This site is close to its neighbor on the right (#3), but low-growing aspens, willows, and some tall grass partially screen the view. Conifers and aspens mostly conceal the neighbor to the left (#1) from view. Green Creek is your only neighbor behind the site, and the water is in clear view, just a few feet from the fire pit. No neighbors are visible across the street—just a grove of aspens. This space has more shade than #1.

### #3 Privacy Rating: A-
**Reservable?** No. First-come, first-served.

Pines tower over this mostly shady spot with a grass understory. The creek flows behind #3, but it's farther away compared to sites #1 and #2 and thanks to a grove of willows growing along the stream banks, you can barely see it from the campsite. Site #2 sits on the left of this camp space, but aspens, willows, and tall grass shoulder their way in between the two sites for added privacy. To the right, there are no other campsites within view, just pines, aspens, and tall vegetation. No neighbors across the street, either.

**#5 Privacy Rating: A+**
**Reservable?** No. First-come, first-served.

With no neighbors on the left, right, across the street, or behind, #5 is loaded with privacy. This site is perched above the creek flowing behind it and you get a glimpse of the water from certain spots within the campsite. Plenty of pines shade #5, which is lacking the aspens that grow around many of the other sites in this campground. Through the trees, there's a partial view of the mountains rising above Green Creek Canyon. Another plus: the bathrooms are nearby.

**#6 Privacy Rating: B+**
**Reservable?** No. First-come, first-served.

This site is across from the camp host, but aspens and pines block the view of the host's picnic table and fire pit area even though you might be able to see the host's trailer from here. Still, the two sites are spaced far apart. A conifer-covered hill rises up behind #6, and to the left your only neighbors are lots of low-growing aspens. You'll have a partial glimpse of the neighbor to the right, but willows and lodgepole pines cancel out much of the view. In front of the campsite, low-growing aspens partially obscure the view of the campground road. #6 has a pull-through driveway, making it an easy in/out for small trailers.

**#8 Privacy Rating: A+**
**Reservable?** No. First-come, first-served.

Nestled in the pine forest, #8 is a beauty of a campsite with no nearby neighbors. The nearest neighbor to the left is a long

way away. There are no neighbors to the right, across the street, or behind. The rocky hill behind the campsite begs to be explored to see if it has a view from the top. The trees in that direction part to allow for a mountain vista in the distance. This site is close to the campground road, but it's located on a peaceful loop in such a small campground that its nearness to the road won't matter. A forest of pines, willows, and aspens grows across the street.

**#9 Privacy Rating: A+**
**Reservable?** No. First-come, first-served

Statuesque aspens lining the long driveway on either side welcome you to this camp spot. #9 is across from the camp host, but it's tucked so far back from the road and mostly hidden behind the aspens that it doesn't feel like you have a neighbor across the street.

The tent pad here is especially nice. Surrounded on three sides by aspens and two large pines towering over a big boulder, it almost feels like you're sleeping in a bedroom.

A pine-covered hill serves as the backdrop for the campsite and an aspen forest grows on the left.

## #10 Privacy Rating: A
**Reservable?** No. First-come, first-served.

This one's close to the campground road, but small aspens and pines partially hide the view of anyone passing by. Plus, the tent pad is far back from the road, near a miniature meadow between some low-growing aspens. A cluster of aspens in front of the tent pad acts as a privacy screen. No other spaces are visible to the left, right, or behind and no other campsites are across the street. You can hear the stream, even though this spot is not a streamside site. As an added convenience, #10 is near the bathroom.

## #11 Privacy Rating: A+
**Reservable?** No. First-come, first-served.

Across from the pay station, #11 is wrapped in aspens and willows with no neighbors on any side. It's also tucked back from the campground road. The tent pad is surrounded by aspens, which mostly block it from view of the campground road. There's room for another tent to the rear, in an area that's also embraced by trees, although that bonus tent spot isn't completely level.

# Trumbull Lake Campground

**Directions:** From Bridgeport, CA, drive south on Highway 395 for 12.3 miles to Conway Summit. Turn right just past the Virginia Lakes sign and drive approximately 6 miles to the campground on the right.

## What's It Like?

In a lodgepole pine forest near the shores of Trumbull Lake, this campground is nirvana for both anglers and hikers who enjoy spending time admiring glimmering alpine lakes set against a backdrop of massive mountain peaks. Aspens line Virginia Lakes Road and shimmer in the breeze along the shores of nearby Little and Big Virginia Lakes, making this an especially lovely destination in the fall. Throughout the area, ten lakes rest in glacier-carved cirques or sit serenely in alpine meadows. Some of the lakes are an easy walk from the campground or hiker's parking area, others take more of an effort to reach them.

Many campsites in this campground interfere with each other's space, but there's still a good selection of spaces with privacy (see campsite descriptions below). Even though the campground is next to Trumbull Lake, only a handful of campsites overlook the lake and only one of those lakeview sites has any privacy. In the woods and in a sagebrush meadow, you'll have a better choice.

**Words of Warning:** Trumbull Lake Campground and the surrounding area is just under 10,000 feet in elevation. If you're arriving to the area from sea level, it's a good idea to camp at 7,000 to 8.000 feet for a couple of days to acclimate yourself before camping at Trumbull Lake.

**What's It Near?**

• Fishing in Little Virginia, Big Virginia, and Trumbull Lakes for rainbow, brown, and brook trout. Rainbow and cutthroat trout are found at Cooney and Frog Lakes.

• Boating, canoeing, or kayaking on Trumbull Lake. Power boats are limited to electric motors.

• Hikes to Blue Lake (less than a mile round trip), Cooney Lake (2 miles round trip), Frog Lakes (3.6 miles round trip), Summit Lake (12 miles round trip), Hoover Lakes (12 miles round trip).

• Horseback riding through Virginia Lakes Pack Station.

• On the way to or from Virginia Lakes, be certain to stop at Virginia Creek Settlement for an Italian dinner or giant pizza. They even have gluten-free pasta. We've never had a bad dinner there, and it's a highlight of our Eastern Sierra excursions to treat ourselves to one of their meals. Ice cream comes with dinner, but take our advice and have the tapioca pudding instead (it's also included in the price of the dinner.) They also serve breakfast and lunch. Virginia Creek Settlement is located to the North of Conway Summit on Highway 395, between Virginia Lakes Road and Green Creek Road.

• The turn off to the road that leads to the ghost town of Bodie is located only a few miles north from Virginia Lakes Road on Highway 395.

• Breakfast, lunch, or an early dinner at Virginia Lakes Resort. Notice all the signatures on one of the lodge doors. Many of these are from movie stars who visited the resort in the 1920s and 30s as well as the 1938 USC football championship team.

• Showers are available for a fee at Virginia Lakes Resort.

**Elevation:** 9,500 feet

**Toilets:** Vault

**Verizon Cell Service?** Limited

**Takes Reservations?** Yes. Visit **www.recreation.gov** for reservations. Some sights are first-come, first-served.

**Number of Campsites:** 44

**Bear Boxes?** Yes.

## Campsites with the Most Privacy

**#5 Privacy Rating: B+**
**Reservable?** Yes. Visit **www.recreation.gov** for reservations.

This spot would deserve an A+ rating if it wasn't for one thing marring its complete privacy—there's a campsite a stone's throw to the left and widely spaced lodgepole pines only partially conceal it from view. But this site has no other visible neighbors and it's nestled back in the woods a fair distance from the campground road. The pines and willows shelter it from view of anyone driving past. To the right are willows and evergreens where we spotted a couple of deer the day we visited. A nice tent pad sits under the pines with room for a medium-sized tent.

**#10 Privacy Rating: C+**
**Reservable?** Yes. Visit **www.recreation.gov** for reservations.

This is one of the few C+ sites we've included in the book—but for good reason. It's the only lakeview site in this campground that even comes close to meeting our privacy criteria. If you have your heart set on camping within view of Trumbull Lake, we wanted to give you one choice.

#10 is an elongated site, stretched out alongside the campground road. Plenty of pines grow on the spot, but they're widely spaced and with no understory #10 is in clear view of anyone driving or walking past. Because it's a long narrow site, the tent pad, picnic table, and fire pit are all closer to the campground road than we'd like to see. There's a neighbor on the left, but they're about 48 feet away. On the right no other sites are visible.

The closest threat to your privacy is a campsite that's behind and a little to the right, although because the space to the rear is on top of a small hill that partially blocks it from view, it doesn't feel as if it's in your face. And, you'll probably be looking the other direction anyway, staring at the peaceful meadow across the street and beyond that a view of Trumbull Lake through gaps in the pines. The pull-through makes this a good site for a small trailer—the maximum vehicle length for this site is 26 feet.

**#28 Privacy Rating: B**
**Reservable?** No. First-come, first-served.

Although not the best spot in the campground, #28 is well-spaced from its neighbors and a good choice for a large family. It's a spacious, shady spot—in fact, we wondered if it might be a double space, but the campground host wasn't there to ask. To the right is a grove of trees and beyond that the bathroom, so no nearby neighbors exist on that side. The pines partially conceal a neighboring site to the left. Lodgepole pines filter the view of a neighbor across the street. You won't have any company behind you, either.

**#35 Privacy Rating: A-**
**Reservable?** No. First-come, first-served.

Conveniently located next to the bathrooms on the right, #35 has a good amount of privacy. Another campsite sits to the left about 20 feet away, but because you're tucked back from the road more than that space and thanks to low-growing aspens and conifers in between the two sites, you're not overly exposed to your neighbor. To the rear, there are no other campsites, only a cluster of low-growing aspens and a view of the mountains bordering Virginia Creek Canyon. A shield of low-growing aspens mostly hide the site across the street from view. This is a sunny spot, but a big conifer offers some shade.

Two small disadvantages: If the wind is blowing the right way, you might smell the bathrooms. Also, the tent pad is near the campground road, but you might be able to find another place to pitch your tent farther back.

**#36 Privacy Rating: A+**
**Reservable?** No. First-come, first-served.

Set back from the campground road in a forested setting, #36 is the camping equivalent of a hotel suite. It's a spacious spot surrounded by pines, although it is bathed in afternoon sunlight. Its only visible neighbor is #35 to the right, but because the campground road curves here, #35 isn't immediately to the right, but rather more to the front. Low-growing aspens and pines also provide some privacy between the two sites. A pine forest grows to the left and behind and a path wanders off through the trees, probably leading to Trumbull Lake. There are no neighbors immediately across the campground road, and #36 is set so far back it wouldn't matter anyway.

**#38 Privacy Rating: A+**
**Reservable?** Yes. Visit **www.recreation.gov** for reservations.

A sunny, roomy site with lots of privacy on the outskirts of the campground, #38 has no neighbors to the right—only a sagebrush meadow and scattered pines. There are no neighbors behind or to the left and the bathrooms are across the street. Although there's a lot of sun here, scattered conifers offer some shade over the picnic table and bear box. Trumbull Lake is a short walk away. You'll also have a good view of the mountain soaring up behind Trumbull Lake. In the night sky, the stars will shine above like glitter sprinkled on black velvet.

# LUNDY CANYON

## Lundy Campground

**Directions:** From Lee Vining, travel north for about 7 miles on Highway 395 to Lundy Lake Road. Turn left and travel approximately 5 miles to the campground on the left.

**What's It Like?**

Operated by Mono County (not the U.S. Forest Service), Lundy Campground settles in among the aspens alongside Mill Creek. Aspens surround most of the campsites, although a few are in pines or sagebrush. This campground is in a beautiful setting, filled with the music of aspen leaves shivering in the afternoon Zephyr breezes. Even though it is a developed campground, it has the feel of dispersed camping. I would rank the nearby hike into Lundy Canyon as one of the top 10 most beautiful hikes in the Eastern Sierra. Wildflowers and waterfalls in summer and a spectacular foliage show in fall make this canyon a must-visit spot during all of the camping season.

**Words of Warning:** No potable water is available.

**What's It Near?**

• Fishing for rainbow and brown trout in Lundy Lake and Mill Creek.

• Boating, canoeing, and kayaking in Lundy Lake.

• Hikes to Oneida Lake (7 miles round trip), Lower Lundy Falls (1.2 miles round trip), base of Upper Lundy Falls (5 miles round trip), Lake Helen (6 miles round trip).

• A short drive to Mono Lake with its interesting tufa formations and volcanic craters.

• The Whoa Nellie Deli (a.k.a. "The Gourmet Gas Station") is about fifteen minutes drive away from the campground, south on Highway 395 and then right on Highway 120 toward Tioga Pass. Colorful and delicious fish tacos, wild buffalo meatloaf, and a variety of other entrees served on glass plates with a beautiful presentation, all from a Mobile gas station store. Food is served together with a view of Mono Lake or Mount Dana, if you eat outside. Pizza and BBQ items are also on the menu. Stopping here at least once every summer is a tradition.

• Other good options for dining in Lee Vining: Nicely's (a casual coffee shop atmosphere), Bodie Mike's Barbeque, and the historic Mono Inn for fine dining. Mono Inn, built in 1922, has a beautiful outdoor dining area. I once sat there eating while watching a lightning storm on the other side of Mono Lake. Mono Inn also has an excellent wine list.

**Elevation:** 7,700 feet

**Toilets:** Vault and Port-A-Potties

**Verizon Cell Service?** Limited. One bar.

**Takes Reservations?** No. First-come, first-served.

**Number of Campsites:** 37

**Bear Boxes?** Available in some but not all campsites.

# Campsites with the Most Privacy

**#1 Privacy Rating: A+**
**Reservable?** No. First-come, first-served.

Surrounded by aspens with no neighbors visible to the left, right, or behind, this spot gets our privacy seal of approval. It is right by the entrance, but still sheltered with a good amount of late afternoon shade. It's supposed to be a tent spot, but the day we visited a small trailer was parked there with plenty of room.

**#2 Privacy Rating: A+**
**Reservable?** No. First-come, first-served.

Aspens gather around on the left and right while tall pines stand like sentinels protecting the forest to the rear of the site. There's some shade. Plenty of privacy in this site, too.

**Words of Warning:** This site does not have a bear box.

**#3 Privacy Rating: B+**
**Reservable?** No. First-come, first-served.

Another nice campsite among the aspens, #3 has no neighbors visible to the left. The aspen forest doesn't grow as thickly here so the space to the right is visible although partially hidden behind a screen of trees. You can see the campsite behind this one, mostly due to a path leading between the two spaces, but lots of aspens interfere with the view of the neighbor to the rear. There are no spaces immediately across the street, although there is a neighbor just down the road.

**Words of Warning:** This site does not have a bear box.

**#4 Privacy Rating: A**
**Reservable?** No. First-come, first-served.

This site is more open than its aspen-surrounded neighbors, but it's set back from the campground road so you don't feel like you're on display. Because it's more open, it makes for great star-gazing. Low-growing aspens gather in back of the site and it has a view of the hill that runs alongside the canyon. To the left, you have a glimpse of neighboring #3, although it doesn't feel too intrusive thanks to the aspen forest between the two sites. No neighbors are visible to the right. Across the campground road, sagebrush mingles with aspen. One flaw? It doesn't have a lot of afternoon shade. Also, the picnic table was in bad shape when we were there but it looks like they might be replacing some of the tables in the campground so maybe this one's next.

**Words of Warning:** This site does not have a bear box.

**#5 Privacy Rating: A+**
**Reservable?** No. First-come, first-served.

In a grassy clearing, #5 leaves plenty of room to roam. Willows grow to the rear of the site, aspens reach up to the sky on the left and right. No neighbors are visible on any side. Despite its location in a meadow area, the aspens give the site some shade.

**#11 Privacy Rating: A**
**Reservable?** No. First-come, first-served.

A spacious spot among the aspens, #11 also boasts a big pine, which graces the site with shade. You have a peek of the neighbor to the right through a forest of aspens, which is why we marked this down to an A rating, but so many trees grow between here and there that the argument could be made that this should be an A+ camp space. No other neighbors are visible on any side.

**#16 Privacy Rating: A**
**Reservable?** No. First-come, first-served.

Another aspen-shielded site, #16 has no neighbors in sight to the left, right, or behind. A neighboring campsite is across the campground road, but #16 is tucked back far enough that the presence of that neighbor doesn't matter.

**Words of Warning:** This site does not have a bear box.

**#24 Privacy Rating: A**
**Reservable?** No. First-come, first-served.

Sprawled out in a meadow with aspens to the left and willows across the meadow to the right, this tent-only spot is more open than some of the campsites in this campground. But with no neighbors visible on any side, it's a very private spot. The only reason we didn't give it an A+ rating is because it's within clear view of the campground road. Some conifers growing behind it mixed in with the aspens and willows offer some shade even though the spot is out in the open. A nice campsite for stargazing

**Words of Warning:** This site does not have a bear box.

**#25 Privacy Rating: A+**
**Reservable?** No. First-come, first-served.

The creek pokes along behind this tent-only campsite, which has a good cushion of privacy with no visible neighbors on any side. Willows and aspen surround the spot.

**Words of Warning:** This site does not have a bear box.

**#26 Privacy Rating: A+**
**Reservable?** No. First-come, first-served.

Another tranquil tent-only site in the aspens with a grassy understory, #26 is swaddled in privacy. The only neighbor within sight is on the left, but you can barely see them through the forest of aspens. From the entrance to the campsite, you'll have a view of a mountain peak. The picnic table here isn't in the greatest shape, but it looked like they were replacing some of the old ones and maybe this one is on the list.

**Words of Warning:** This site does not have a bear box.

## #31 Privacy Rating: A+
**Reservable?** No. First-come, first-served.

A large creekside site with room for several tents, #31 is enclosed on three sides by aspens. The trees and other vegetation block the view of the stream behind, but there's a path leading to it. Across the campground road is a sagebrush-studded meadow and beyond that a view of a rust- and tan-colored mountain.

**Words of Warning:** This site does not have a bear box.

## #32 Privacy Rating: A+
**Reservable?** No. First-come, first-served.

With the creek flowing behind it, #32 is a spot to envy. You can see the creek through the aspens when you're sitting at the picnic table or by the fire pit and you can hear it, too. A path leads from the campsite to the creek. It's more open than some of the sites, because on the right is a sagebrush meadow, but it's back from the campground road. Aspens grow to the left. A couple of big pines shade the campsite. No other camp spaces are in view to the left, right, or behind. Across the street there's only a sagebrush meadow and beyond that a rust- and cream-colored mountain rubs shoulders with the sky.

**Words of Warning:** No tents allowed in this spot, although we can't figure out why. Also, it has no bear box.

**#36 Privacy Rating: A**
**Reservable?** No. First-come, first-served.

The creek flows to the left of #36, and although you can't see it from the picnic table or where you pitch your tent, you can hear it. Behind #36 is an aspen forest and no spaces exist across the road, where you have a mountain view. A neighboring site to the right is well-spaced from this one and the view of it is partially filtered by some aspens. Our favorite part about this campsite is the short path that leads through the vegetation to the fire pit, located streamside in clear view of the water. The only reason we didn't give this site an A+ is because of the slight view of the space to the right, but the argument can be made that this deserves an A+, especially due to the location of the fire pit, which is completely hidden from view of the campground road.

**Words of Warning:** This site does not have a bear box.

# LEE VINING CANYON/TUOLUMNE MEADOWS

## Lower Lee Vining Campground

**Directions:** From Highway 395 in Lee Vining, turn right on Highway 120 (as if you were going up to Tioga Pass and Yosemite.) The campground is located on the left, about 2 miles west of Highway 395.

**What's It Like?**

In the aspens and conifers near Lee Vining Creek, this campground is in a peaceful setting, but many of the campsites are stacked on top of each other. There's one section of the campground that feels like camping in a dirt parking lot. If you're looking for privacy, overall this isn't the best campground in Lee Vining Canyon. But as we point out in our campsite descriptions below, there are a couple of spots that are more secluded than the rest.

**What's It Near?**

• Tuolumne Meadows and the high country of Yosemite National Park are about 10 miles away up a steep grade with spectacular views looking up towards Tioga Pass and down the dizzying expanse of Lee Vining Canyon.

• Saddlebag Lake, just outside the border of Yosemite, is worth a visit. Take the boat taxi across the lake and let the Sierra breeze whisper sweet nothings in your ear while you admire the snow-speckled walls of massive mountain peaks. The taxi shortens the trip to Twenty Lakes Basin, stretched out below the imposing face of Mount Conness, where you can take an easy loop hike past some of the most beautiful lakes in the Sierra. To reach such spectacular scenery you usually have to hike long and hard in the Eastern Sierra, but the hardest thing about this hike is that it's at 10,000 feet above sea level.

- Yosemite Hikes:
    - Glen Aulin High Sierra Camp (11 miles round trip, spectacular waterfalls along the way),
    - Elizabeth Lake (4.8 miles round trip, at the base of Unicorn Peak),
    - Mono Pass (7 miles round trip),
    - Lower Gaylor Lake (4.5 miles—beware of the mosquitoes, they're vicious here),
    - Tuolumne River Bridges of Lyell Canyon (2 miles round trip and only 150 feet elevation gain),
    - Lyell Canyon (12 to 16 miles round trip). The Tuolumne River slows down through Lyell Canyon, in some spots so clear it looks like the fish are swimming through glass. In other places along the river, it looks like a jeweler melted some of his finest emerald gems and poured them into the water, turning the stream to a beautiful shade of green.
    - Lembert Dome (4 miles round trip).

- Lundy Canyon is about nine miles away from here, north on Highway 395 and is worth a visit in the summer for the wildflowers and waterfalls and in the fall for the colorful foliage. Hikes: Lower Lundy Falls (1.2 miles round trip), base of Upper Lundy Falls (5 miles round trip).

- Mono Lake is several miles away from the campground. Kayak its salty waters, walk along the shore and admire the tufa formations, or hike to the top of Mono Craters (2 miles round trip).

- Whoa Nellie Deli, known affectionately as the gourmet gas station and one of the best restaurants in the Eastern Sierra, is a couple miles away from the campground. Inside the Mobile Gas Mart, the restaurant serves fish tacos, wild buffalo meatloaf, barbecue dishes, pizza, giant breakfast burritos, and a lot more. Sit outside and enjoy the view of Mono Lake or Mount Dana or bring your food back to your campsite.

• If you crave a good cup of Joe or like homemade baked goods (including gluten free treats), Latte Da Coffee Café is the place to go in Lee Vining for breakfast or lunch. Great breakfast sandwiches, too.

• Fishing for rainbow, brown, brook, and golden trout in Saddlebag Lake. The Saddlebag Lake boat taxi will get you to another batch of lakes within easy walking distance from where the boat leaves you on shore. You can also cast a line for trout at Lundy Lake, Lee Vining Creek, Tioga Lake, and Ellery Lake.

• Other good options for dining in Lee Vining: Nicely's (a casual coffee shop atmosphere), Bodie Mike's Barbeque, and the historic Mono Inn for fine dining. Mono Inn, built in 1922, has a beautiful outdoor dining area. I once sat there eating while watching a lightning storm on the other side of Mono Lake. Mono Inn also has an excellent wine list.

• Showers are available to the public about three miles away at Mono Vista RV Park (North on Highway 395 in Lee Vining).

**Elevation:** 7,300 feet

**Toilets:** Vault

**Verizon Cell Service?** Yes

**Takes Reservations?** No. First-come, first-served.

**Number of Campsites:** 60

**Bear Boxes?** Yes

# Campsites with the Most Privacy

**#1 Privacy Rating: A**
**Reservable?** No. First-come, first-served.

Off by itself, #1 has no neighbors on any side. It's a long, narrow spot that is a bit close to the campground road, but a row of aspens grow between the site and the road. Aspens and conifers grow to the right of the space and behind it. Campers who own trailers or motorhomes will enjoy the pull-through. This is a nice spot that outshines most of the other sites in the campground.

**#18 Privacy Rating: A-**
**Reservable?** No. First-come, first-served.

Immersed in aspens and greenery, this creekside site is a gem compared to the other offerings in this campground. It has no neighbors on the right and conifers and greenery hide the view of the neighbor to the left. Lee Vining Creek putters along behind it. Any neighbors across the street are insignificant, due to #18's location amid the trees.

## Moraine Campground

**Directions:** From Lee Vining, head west on Highway 120 (as if you were going up to Tioga Pass and Yosemite) for about 2 ½ miles. Turn left at the sign for Poole Power Plant Road and then take an immediate left again onto Poole Power Plant Road, which parallels Highway 120 and dead ends a short distance away at the campground.

## What's It Like?

Boasting spectacular views of Mount Dana, Moraine Campground nudges the shores of Lee Vining Creek. Some of the less-private sites sit out in the sagebrush and rabbitbrush, while other more secluded spaces are in willows, aspens, and conifers. This is supposed to be a spillover campground used during busy times, but it has been open during every one of my visits to the area in July and August.

**Words of Warning:** There is no water available here so you'll have to bring your own drinking and wash water. But if you need water to put out your fire, you can fill some jugs in Lee Vining Creek.

## What's It Near?

• Tuolumne Meadows and the high country of Yosemite National Park are about 10 miles away up a steep grade with spectacular views looking up towards Tioga Pass and down the dizzying expanse of Lee Vining Canyon.

• Saddlebag Lake, just outside the border of Yosemite, is worth a visit. Take the boat taxi across the lake and let the Sierra breeze whisper sweet nothings in your ear while you admire the snow-speckled walls of massive mountain peaks.

The taxi shortens the trip to Twenty Lakes Basin, stretched out below the imposing face of Mount Conness, where you can take an easy loop hike past some of the most beautiful lakes in the Sierra. To reach such spectacular scenery you usually have to hike long and hard in the Eastern Sierra, but the hardest thing about this hike is that it's at 10,000 feet above sea level.

- Yosemite Hikes:
  - Glen Aulin High Sierra Camp (11 miles round trip, spectacular waterfalls along the way),
  - Elizabeth Lake (4.8 miles round trip, at the base of Unicorn Peak),
  - Mono Pass (7 miles round trip),
  - Lower Gaylor Lake (4.5 miles—beware of the mosquitoes, they're vicious here),
  - Tuolumne River Bridges of Lyell Canyon (2 miles round trip and only 150 feet elevation gain),
  - Lyell Canyon (12 to 16 miles round trip). The Tuolumne River slows down through Lyell Canyon, in some spots so clear it looks like the fish are swimming through glass. In other places along the river, it looks like a jeweler melted some of his finest emerald gems and poured them into the water, turning the stream to a beautiful shade of green.
  - Lembert Dome (4 miles round trip).

- Lundy Canyon is about nine miles away from here, north on Highway 395 and is worth a visit in the summer for the wildflowers and waterfalls and in the fall for the colorful foliage. Hikes: Lower Lundy Falls (1.2 miles round trip), base of Upper Lundy Falls (5 miles round trip).

- Mono Lake is several miles away from the campground. Kayak its salty waters, walk along the shore and admire the tufa formations, or hike to the top of Mono Craters (2 miles round trip).

• Fishing for rainbow, brown, brook, and golden trout in Saddlebag Lake. The Saddlebag Lake boat taxi will get you to another batch of lakes within easy walking distance from where the boat leaves you on shore. You can also cast a line for trout at Lundy Lake, Lee Vining Creek, Tioga Lake, and Ellery Lake.

• Whoa Nellie Deli, known affectionately as the gourmet gas station and one of the best restaurants in the Eastern Sierra, is a couple miles away from the campground. Inside the Mobile Gas Mart, the restaurant serves fish tacos, wild buffalo meatloaf, barbecue dishes, pizza, giant breakfast burritos, and a lot more. Sit outside and enjoy the view of Mono Lake or Mount Dana or bring your food back to your campsite.

• If you crave a good cup of Joe or like homemade baked goods (including gluten free treats), Latte Da Coffee Café is the place to go in Lee Vining for breakfast or lunch. Great breakfast sandwiches, too.

• Other good options for dining in Lee Vining: Nicely's (a casual coffee shop atmosphere), Bodie Mike's Barbeque, and the historic Mono Inn for fine dining. Mono Inn, built in 1922, has a beautiful outdoor dining area. I once sat there eating while watching a lightning storm on the other side of Mono Lake. Mono Inn also has an excellent wine list.

• Showers are available to the public about 4 1/2 miles away at Mono Vista RV Park (North on Highway 395 in Lee Vining).

**Elevation:** 7,350 feet

**Toilets:** Porta Potties

**Verizon Cell Service?** Yes

**Takes Reservations?** No. First-come, first-served.

**Number of Campsites:** 27

**Bear Boxes?** Yes

## Campsites with the Most Privacy

**#3 Privacy Rating: A**
**Reservable?** No. First-come, first-served.

#3 is surrounded by willows, which hide it from view of its closest neighbor (#4). As a bonus, it's located next to Lee Vining Creek.

**#4 Privacy Rating: A**
**Reservable?** No. First-come, first-served.

The near twin to #3, this site also is set back in the willows next to the stream. It's nicely blocked from view of the neighbors thanks to a willow privacy screen.

**#10 Privacy Rating: A+**
**Reservable?** No. First-come, first-served.

Lots of aspens and other greenery give this site not only privacy, but also an element of serenity. Tall conifers provide additional shade. This site has no neighbors visible on any side. The campground road is in front and on the left of #10, but pines and greenery obscure it. It's across the campground road from the creek. If you like forested campsites, this one is a beauty.

**#15 Privacy Rating: A**
**Reservable?** No. First-come, first-served.

Lee Vining Creek flows peacefully by this angler-friendly site. You can't camp any closer to a stream without actually pitching your tent on the water. Your only neighbor is on the left (#16), but it's far away. This site is visible from the road (unless you have a trailer, which will hide most of the campsite from view). It's a peaceful spot where you'll be serenaded by the stream all night long. This is a very popular campsite, so you may have to fight for it by getting to the campground as early in the day as possible and hoping the previous occupant vacated.

**#16 Privacy Rating: B+**
**Reservable?** No. First-come, first-served.

Out in the open among the sage and rabbitbrush with a solitary pine standing guard over the picnic table, #16 is well-spaced from its neighbors. I've camped here several times and loved being able to gaze up at the view of Mount Dana in front of the site. Because it's not in the trees, there's also a spectacular view of the stars at night. You can just barely hear the stream from here, too, adding an extra element of pleasantness. Its only close neighbor is #15 to its right, but there's plenty of space between the two sites. There's also room for two tents here. The fact there are no other campsites across the street seals the deal.

## Aspen Grove Campground

**Directions:** From Lee Vining, head west on Highway 120 (as if you were going up to Tioga Pass and Yosemite) for about 3 ½ miles. Turn left at the sign for Poole Power Plant Road and then take an immediate right onto Poole Power Plant Road, which parallels Highway 120. Drive for about 1 1/2 miles to the campground on the left.

**What's It Like?**

As its name implies, many sites are nestled in the aspens. Other camp spaces are located in the conifers along Lee Vining Creek, some in view of a waterfall. A third group of campsites are located in the sagebrush and rabbitbrush with aspens and some conifers. Electrical towers mar the view from some of the sites farthest from the creek, but even with this blemish, put your chair facing the other direction and you'll barely notice they're there. Overall, even though many of the sites near the stream are jammed together, there's still a nice selection of campsites with privacy here. See below for our privacy picks.

**What's It Near?**

• Tuolumne Meadows and the high country of Yosemite National Park are about 10 miles away up a steep grade with spectacular views looking up towards Tioga Pass and down the dizzying expanse of Lee Vining Canyon.

• Saddlebag Lake, just outside the border of Yosemite, is worth a visit. Take the boat taxi across the lake and let the Sierra breeze whisper sweet nothings in your ear while you admire the snow-speckled walls of massive mountain peaks.

The taxi shortens the trip to Twenty Lakes Basin, stretched out below the imposing face of Mount Conness, where you can take an easy loop hike past some of the most beautiful lakes in the Sierra. To reach such spectacular scenery you usually have to hike long and hard in the Eastern Sierra, but the hardest thing about this hike is that it's at 10,000 feet above sea level.

• Yosemite Hikes:
  o Glen Aulin High Sierra Camp (11 miles round trip, spectacular waterfalls along the way),
  o Elizabeth Lake (4.8 miles round trip, at the base of Unicorn Peak),
  o Mono Pass (7 miles round trip),
  o Lower Gaylor Lake (4.5 miles—beware of the mosquitoes, they're vicious here),
  o Tuolumne River Bridges of Lyell Canyon (2 miles round trip and only 150 feet elevation gain),
  o Lyell Canyon (12 to 16 miles round trip). The Tuolumne River slows down through Lyell Canyon, in some spots so clear it looks like the fish are swimming through glass. In other places along the river, it looks like a jeweler melted some of his finest emerald gems and poured them into the water, turning the stream to a beautiful shade of green.
  o Lembert Dome (4 miles round trip).

• Lundy Canyon is about nine miles away from here, north on Highway 395 and is worth a visit in the summer for the wildflowers and waterfalls and in the fall for the colorful foliage. Hikes: Lower Lundy Falls (1.2 miles round trip), base of Upper Lundy Falls (5 miles round trip).

• Mono Lake is several miles away from the campground. Kayak its salty waters, walk along the shore and admire the tufa formations, or hike to the top of Mono Craters (2 miles round trip).

• Fishing for rainbow, brown, brook, and golden trout in Saddlebag Lake. The Saddlebag Lake boat taxi will get you to another batch of lakes within easy walking distance from where the boat leaves you on shore. You can also cast a line for trout at Lundy Lake, Lee Vining Creek, Tioga Lake, and Ellery Lake.

• Whoa Nellie Deli, known affectionately as the gourmet gas station and one of the best restaurants in the Eastern Sierra, is a couple miles away from the campground. Inside the Mobile Gas Mart, the restaurant serves fish tacos, wild buffalo meatloaf, barbecue dishes, pizza, giant breakfast burritos, and a lot more. Sit outside and enjoy the view of Mono Lake or Mount Dana or bring your food back to your campsite.

• If you crave a good cup of Joe or like homemade baked goods (including gluten free treats), Latte Da Coffee Café is the place to go in Lee Vining for breakfast or lunch. Great breakfast sandwiches, too.

• Other good options for dining in Lee Vining: Nicely's (a casual coffee shop atmosphere), Bodie Mike's Barbeque, and the historic Mono Inn for fine dining. Mono Inn, built in 1922, has a beautiful outdoor dining area. I once sat there eating while watching a lightning storm on the other side of Mono Lake. Mono Inn also has an excellent wine list.

• Showers are available to the public about 6 miles away at Mono Vista RV Park (North on Highway 395 in Lee Vining).

**Elevation:** 7,490 feet

**Toilets:** Vault and Porta Potties

**Verizon Cell Service?** No

**Takes Reservations?** No. First-come, first-served.

**Number of Campsites:** 56

**Bear Boxes?** Yes

## Campsites with the Most Privacy

### #5 Privacy Rating:  A-
**Reservable?** No. First-come, first-served.

An aspen-lined avenue leads to #5, far back from the campground road with no rear neighbors. There is a glimpse of the campsites on the left and right, but an aspen forest screens the view. #5 is staggered back from #6, so it doesn't seem as if you have a neighbor to the left.

### #6 Privacy Rating: B
**Reservable?** No. First-come, first-served.

Your only neighbor to the rear is a peaceful grove of aspens. #5 is to the right, but aspens partially shield the view. Some well-placed aspens intervene between the site and a section of the campground road to the left.

### #11 Privacy Rating: A+
**Reservable?** No. First-come, first-served.

A spacious spot in the woods, #11 has no neighbors to the left, right, or behind. This shady site is surrounded on three sides by aspens and tall conifers.

There is a campsite across the campground road — although not directly across — and the view of it is filtered by trees.

#11 is an ideal site for privacy-loving campers.

**#12 Privacy Rating: B+**
**Reservable?** No. First-come, first-served.

Boxed in by aspens and conifers, this site has only one minor flaw, which caused us to bump down its privacy rating from an A to a B+. The edge of the driveway for the space behind brushes up against #12, so that you'll have a clear view of any vehicle parked there. Still, I camped here once with my brother and sister-in-law and it was a surprisingly pleasant spot. Aspens obscure the neighboring space to the left of the driveway, and no one is visible on the right either. #11 is across the street, but it's down the road a little bit and tucked back in the woods.

**#13 Privacy Rating: A+**
**Reservable?** No. First-come, first-served.

This site is in the sagebrush, but a few pines provide shade. Its claim to fame is that it has no neighbors to the left, right, behind, or across the campground road. To the right of the site, aspens dance in the breeze. Its one flaw? Some trees partially conceal the wooden power tower behind the space. At the same time, power lines cut apart the view of the mountains to the north of Highway 120. Due to the privacy of this campsite, I'd be willing to overlook that one disadvantage.

**#14 Privacy Rating: A-**
**Reservable?** No. First-come, first-served.

With no neighbors to the left, right, or behind, #14 is cushioned in privacy. From certain places in the campsite, you can see the mountains north of Highway 120 rising up behind it. Pines gathered around the picnic table and tent pad provide shade. It has no dramatic features, but it's a pleasant enough spot. Some power lines stretch out above and behind the site, but the pines hide most of them from view, and at least you can't see the big wooden power towers that are visible from a few other campsites.

**#17 Privacy Rating: B**
**Reservable?** No. First-come, first-served.

Sitting out in the sagebrush and bushes, this spot is sunny but reasonably private. It's nicely spaced from its neighbors on the left and right. The bushes are tall enough that when you sit down, they partially conceal the neighboring sites. A Jeffrey pine grows on the fringes of the campsite and it might provide some shade to the picnic table at certain parts of the day. It's a close walk from here to the cascade. The biggest disadvantage to this spot is the fact one of the big wooden power towers is to the rear, in clear view, and power lines stretch out over the campsite.

**#19 Privacy Rating: B+**
**Reservable?** No. First-come, first-served.

At first glance, it would not seem like this campsite fits our definition of privacy, because there's a neighboring campsite about 15 feet away on the left. However, this campsite is the closest one to the waterfall. Not only is the cascade in full view of the campsite, but the sound of the water drowns out the voices from the neighbors on the left. Plus, that campsite on the left is #19's only nearby neighbor. Behind #19 Lee Vining Creek rushes over the rocks. To the right is a granite outcropping. In front of the site, across the campground road, #17 is far away. From the picnic table, to give the privacy an added boost, a tall conifer partially blocks the view of the neighbor to the left. We camped in this spot on a trip to celebrate our first wedding anniversary, and even though we had next door neighbors we barely noticed them.

**#24 Privacy Rating: B-**
**Reservable?** No. First-come, first-served.

If you have your heart set on a creekside spot, here's another option. It doesn't have the privacy of some of the other sites in the campground, but it is separated a little from its neighbors. You'll see the space to the right through a screen of willows. Trees screen out the neighbors on the left. You can see the cascade from here and can fish from the campsite.

**#25 Privacy Rating: B-**
**Reservable?** No. First-come, first-served.

Another campsite with Lee Vining Creek flowing behind it, #25 is a good choice for anglers or anyone who likes to fall asleep to the sound of water. Trees partially hide from view the campsite to the right. The neighbor to the left is a long stone's throw away, and lots of trees intervene between the two campsites. The nearest neighbor across the street is a good distance away.

## #27 Privacy Rating: A
**Reservable?** No. First-come, first-served.

With no neighbors on the left, right, or behind, #27 has good privacy. Aspens provide a peaceful backdrop for the campsite. The bathrooms are across the street.

## #44 Privacy Rating: A
**Reservable?** No. First-come, first-served.

After its burst of energy to get over the cascade, Lee Vining Creek recovers in this section of the campground, moving lazily along behind site #44. In the forest and very shady, #44 has neighbors on the right, but pines and deciduous trees help shelter them from view. Trees and vegetation completely obscure from view the neighbor on the left (#45). Another great campsite for an angler.

## #45 Privacy Rating: A+
**Reservable?** No. First-come, first-served.

Enclosed in vegetation and mostly hidden from the road, #45 is a beauty of a spot that boasts a lot of privacy. Willows sprout up on the left, eliminating the view of any campsites on that side. On the right, conifers and reedy plants block #45 from view. The stream flows behind the campsite. This peaceful spot is a tent-only campsite, but we have seen very small trailers camped here, too.

**#46 Privacy Rating: B**
**Reservable?** No. First-come, first-served.

While this isn't the most private site next to the stream, it isn't bad. On the right, there are no neighbors, just green deciduous trees. The neighbor to the left is close but not so close that you'll feel as if they're breathing down your neck. Plus, there's a light screen of pines and greenery in between the two sites. Lee Vining Creek ambles along behind #46, so anglers and anyone who likes to camp next to a stream will feel content here.

## Big Bend Campground

**Directions:** From Lee Vining, head west on Highway 120 (as if you were going up to Tioga Pass and Yosemite) for about 3 ½ miles. Turn left at the sign for Poole Power Plant Road and then take an immediate right onto Poole Power Plant Road, which parallels Highway 120. Drive for about 2 1/2 miles to the campground on the left. For the last .6 of a mile, the road is gravel.

**What's It Like?**

Under a conifer forest alongside Lee Vining Creek, this campground located deepest in Lee Vining Canyon certainly has a peaceful location. However, remember the "which one of

these things doesn't belong with the other game?" This campground is sort of like that. With spaces jammed in next to each other and little underbrush, nearly every space in the campground is a disappointment from a privacy perspective—with one notable exception (see campsite description below).

# What's It Near?

• Tuolumne Meadows and the high country of Yosemite National Park are about 10 miles away up a steep grade with spectacular views looking up towards Tioga Pass and down the dizzying expanse of Lee Vining Canyon.

• Saddlebag Lake, just outside the border of Yosemite, is worth a visit. Take the boat taxi across the lake and let the Sierra breeze whisper sweet nothings in your ear while you admire the snow-speckled walls of massive mountain peaks. The taxi shortens the trip to Twenty Lakes Basin, stretched out below the imposing face of Mount Conness, where you can take an easy loop hike past some of the most beautiful lakes in the Sierra. To reach such spectacular scenery you usually have to hike long and hard in the Eastern Sierra, but the hardest thing about this hike is that it's at 10,000 feet above sea level.

• Yosemite Hikes:
   o Glen Aulin High Sierra Camp (11 miles round trip, spectacular waterfalls along the way),
   o Elizabeth Lake (4.8 miles round trip, at the base of Unicorn Peak),
   o Mono Pass (7 miles round trip),
   o Lower Gaylor Lake (4.5 miles—beware of the mosquitoes, they're vicious here),
   o Tuolumne River Bridges of Lyell Canyon (2 miles round trip and only 150 feet elevation gain),
   o Lyell Canyon (12 to 16 miles round trip). The Tuolumne River slows down through Lyell Canyon, in some spots so clear it looks like the fish are swimming through glass. In other places along the river, it looks like a jeweler melted some of his finest emerald gems and poured them into the water, turning the stream to a beautiful shade of green.
   o Lembert Dome (4 miles round trip).

• Lundy Canyon is about nine miles away from here, north on Highway 395 and is worth a visit in the summer for the wildflowers and waterfalls and in the fall for the colorful foliage. Hikes: Lower Lundy Falls (1.2 miles round trip), base of Upper Lundy Falls (5 miles round trip).

• Mono Lake is several miles away from the campground. Kayak its salty waters, walk along the shore and admire the tufa formations, or hike to the top of Mono Craters (2 miles round trip).

• Fishing for rainbow, brown, brook, and golden trout in Saddlebag Lake. The Saddlebag Lake boat taxi will get you to another batch of lakes within easy walking distance from where the boat leaves you on shore. You can also cast a line for trout at Lundy Lake, Lee Vining Creek, Tioga Lake, and Ellery Lake.

• Whoa Nellie Deli, known affectionately as the gourmet gas station and one of the best restaurants in the Eastern Sierra, is a couple miles away from the campground. Inside the Mobile Gas Mart, the restaurant serves fish tacos, wild buffalo meatloaf, barbecue dishes, pizza, giant breakfast burritos, and a lot more. Sit outside and enjoy the view of Mono Lake or Mount Dana or bring your food back to your campsite.

• If you crave a good cup of Joe or like homemade baked goods (including gluten free treats), Latte Da Coffee Café is the place to go in Lee Vining for breakfast or lunch. Great breakfast sandwiches, too.

• Other good options for dining in Lee Vining: Nicely's (a casual coffee shop atmosphere), Bodie Mike's Barbeque, and the historic Mono Inn for fine dining. Mono Inn, built in 1922, has a beautiful outdoor dining area. I once sat there eating while watching a lightning storm on the other side of Mono Lake. Mono Inn also has an excellent wine list.

• Showers are available to the public about 7 miles away at Mono Vista RV Park (North on Highway 395 in Lee Vining).

**Elevation:** 7,800 feet

**Toilets:** Vault

**Verizon Cell Service?** No.

**Takes Reservations?** No.

**Number of Campsites:** 17

**Bear Boxes?** Yes

### Campsite with the Most Privacy

**#17 Privacy Rating: A+**
**Reservable?** No. First-come, first-served.

Your own slice of serenity in an otherwise busy campground. After looking at all the other jammed-together spaces in this campground, #17 was a pleasant surprise. Encircled by deciduous vegetation and aspens, #17 is one of the most private campsites in the Eastern Sierra. No other campsites are visible from #17, although you do have a filtered view of Poole Power Plant Road through pines, aspens, and greenery on the left. There are no neighbors directly across the street, either.

### Ellery Lake Campground

**Directions:** From Lee Vining turn west on Highway 120, towards Yosemite National Park. Ellery Lake Campground is approximately 9.8 miles from the intersection of Highways 395 and 120 on the left side of the road.

## What's It Like?

At the top of Tioga Pass, just outside Yosemite National Park's entrance station, Ellery Lake campsites are etched out of the willows or set among the conifers and boulders. The lake isn't visible from any of the sites, but the campground offers some impressive views of the mountains rising up behind the lake and you can get to the lake via a short stroll up and over a hill behind campsite #14. Privacy is scarce here, but we encountered two campsites that received our Campsites with Privacy official seal of approval (see campsite descriptions below).

## What's It Near?

• Tioga Pass Resort's cozy restaurant, which serves breakfast, lunch, and dinner as well as homemade pies, cakes, and desserts baked by the resort's own pastry chef. Try an omelet or homemade granola for breakfast, hearty sandwiches and burgers for lunch, or their tender pot roast or lemon garlic chicken for dinner, among other specialties.

• An approximately 20-minute drive away from Saddlebag Lake. Take the boat taxi across the lake and let the Sierra breeze whisper sweet nothings in your ear while you admire the snow-speckled walls of massive mountain peaks. The taxi shortens the trip to Twenty Lakes Basin, stretched out below the imposing face of Mount Conness, where you can take an easy loop hike past some of the most beautiful lakes in the Sierra. To reach such spectacular scenery you usually have to

hike long and hard in the Eastern Sierra, but the hardest thing about this hike is that it's at 10,000 feet above sea level, so acclimating well is a good idea.

• Wonderful chili and homemade pies and cakes at Saddlebag Lake Resort.

- Yosemite Hikes:
    - Glen Aulin High Sierra Camp (11 miles round trip, spectacular waterfalls along the way),
    - Elizabeth Lake (4.8 miles round trip, at the base of Unicorn Peak),
    - Mono Pass (7 miles round trip),
    - Lower Gaylor Lake (4.5 miles—beware of the mosquitoes, they're vicious here),
    - Tuolumne River Bridges of Lyell Canyon (2 miles round trip and only 150 feet elevation gain),
    - Lyell Canyon (12 to 16 miles round trip). The Tuolumne River slows down through Lyell Canyon, in some spots so clear it looks like the fish are swimming through glass. In other places along the river, it looks like a jeweler melted some of his finest emerald gems and poured them into the water, turning the stream to a beautiful shade of green.
    - Lembert Dome (4 miles round trip).

- Other nearby hikes: Gardinsky Lake (2.4 miles round trip, trailhead on Saddlebag Lake Road about 1 ¼ miles from Highway 120). Glacier Canyon and Dana Lakes (5 miles round trip, trailhead is at the Tioga Lake Overlook parking area). The Bennettville mine, a 0.7 mile walk from Junction Campground.

- Fishing for rainbow, brown, brook, and golden trout in Saddlebag Lake. The Saddlebag Lake boat taxi will get you to another batch of lakes within easy walking distance from where the boat leaves you on shore. You can also cast a line for trout at Lundy Lake, Lee Vining Creek, Tioga Lake, and Ellery Lake.

**Elevation:** 9,500 feet

**Toilets:** Vault

**Verizon Cell Service?** No

**Takes Reservations?** No. First-come, first-served.

**Number of Campsites:** 12

**Bear Boxes?** Yes.

## Campsites with the Most Privacy

**#7 Privacy Rating: A-**
**Reservable?** No. First-come, first-served.

A pathway shared with #8 leads to this site, which is barely visible from the campground road. In August, bright pink fireweed flowers serve as the hostesses greeting you as you set foot on the path. Set back in the pines, this campsite has only one neighbor, #8 to its left, which isn't visible thanks to a wall of willows. It's a cozy spot, much smaller than #8, but definitely one of the best sites in the campground.

**#8 Privacy Rating: A+**
**Reservable?** No. First-come, first-served.

Compared to the other spaces in the campground, #8 is a luxury suite. It shares a path with #7, but once you pass by that other site — your only neighbor — you're in a world of your own. Mother nature built a wall of willows between this space and #7 for added privacy. A spacious spot surrounded by conifers and set against a backdrop of rust- and tan-colored cliffs, it has the feel of being wrapped in Mother Nature's arms.

## Junction Campground

**Directions:** From Lee Vining turn west on Highway 120 towards Yosemite National Park. Drive approximately 10 miles from the intersection of Highways 395 and 120 to Saddlebag Road. Take a right on Saddlebag Road and then an immediate left into the campground.

**What's It Like?**

Junction is a small campground located at the intersection of Highway 120 and Saddlebag Road. The Dana Plateau and Tioga Peak watch over the campground from a distance. Campsites are either in the lodgepole pines or out in the open

by a meadow that's bordered by Lee Vining Creek on one side and Mine Creek on the other. Some sites are located streamside. To find the most private sites, you'll need to travel to the far end of the campground to a loop where long trailers or RVs are prohibited.

**What's It Near?**

• Tioga Pass Resort's cozy restaurant, which serves breakfast, lunch, and dinner as well as homemade pies, cakes, and desserts baked by the resort's own pastry chef. Try an omelet or homemade granola for breakfast, hearty sandwiches and burgers for lunch, or their tender pot roast or lemon garlic chicken for dinner, among other specialties.

• An approximately 20-minute drive away from Saddlebag Lake. Take the boat taxi across the lake and let the Sierra breeze whisper sweet nothings in your ear while you admire the snow-speckled walls of massive mountain peaks. The taxi shortens the trip to Twenty Lakes Basin, stretched out below the imposing face of Mount Conness, where you can take an easy loop hike past some of the most beautiful lakes in the Sierra. To reach such spectacular scenery you usually have to hike long and hard in the Eastern Sierra, but the hardest thing about this hike is that it's at 10,000 feet above sea level, so acclimating well is a good idea.

• Wonderful chili and homemade pies and cakes at Saddlebag Lake Resort.

• Yosemite Hikes:
  o Glen Aulin High Sierra Camp (11 miles round trip, spectacular waterfalls along the way),
  o Elizabeth Lake (4.8 miles round trip, at the base of Unicorn Peak),
  o Mono Pass (7 miles round trip),
  o Lower Gaylor Lake (4.5 miles—beware of the mosquitoes, they're vicious here),
  o Tuolumne River Bridges of Lyell Canyon (2 miles round trip and only 150 feet elevation gain),
  o Lyell Canyon (12 to 16 miles round trip). The Tuolumne River slows down through Lyell Canyon, in some spots so clear it looks like the fish are swimming through glass. In other places along the river, it looks like a jeweler melted some of his finest emerald gems and poured them into the water, turning the stream to a beautiful shade of green.
  o Lembert Dome (4 miles round trip).

• Other nearby hikes: Gardinsky Lake (2.4 miles round trip, trailhead on Saddlebag Lake Road about 1 ¼ miles from Highway 120). Glacier Canyon and Dana Lakes (5 miles round trip, trailhead is at the Tioga Lake Overlook parking area).

• The Bennettville mine, a 0.7 mile walk from Junction Campground.

• Fishing for rainbow, brown, brook, and golden trout in Saddlebag Lake. The Saddlebag Lake boat taxi will get you to another batch of lakes within easy walking distance from where the boat leaves you on shore. You can also cast a line for trout at Lundy Lake, Lee Vining Creek, Tioga Lake, and Ellery Lake.

**Elevation:** 9,600

**Toilets:** Vault

**Verizon Cell Service?** No.

**Takes Reservations?** No. First-come, first-served.

**Number of Campsites:** 13

**Bear Boxes?** Yes

## Campsites with the Most Privacy

**#6 Privacy Rating: A+**
**Reservable?** No. First-come, first-served.

You'll have to lug your stuff up a small hill, but your efforts are rewarded with a nice view of the creek, a tranquil meadow, and the mountains towering in the distance. The creek serenades you in your campsite and a short path leads down to it. You're wrapped up in nature here with no immediate neighbors on any side. There is a campsite across the street but they're far away. An interesting tree shaped like a giant Bonzai grows to the rear of the site.

#### #9 Privacy Rating: B+
**Reservable?** No. First-come, first-served.

Trek up a path leading past the campsite in front of #9 to the top of a little hill, where you'll have your own slice of nature under a canopy of conifers. The hill also partially hides from view the neighbor in front of you. From this well-shaded spot near the far end of the campground, you won't see any other campers to the left and a hill serves as the campsite's backdrop. Trees partially conceal the neighbors to the right, which are far away across a meadow. This is a walk-in site, but you won't have to travel far from where you park.

#### #13 Privacy Rating: B+
**Reservable?** No. First-come, first-served.

You'll feel lucky to camp in site #13, which anchors the end of the campground. Its only neighbor — #12 on the right — is far enough away so as not to feel as if they are breathing down your neck. A stream cuts through the willows behind it, and beyond that a granite outcropping serves as a backdrop. Conifers gather at the rear of the site, providing some shade to the picnic table and bear box. It's close to the bathrooms, too. This is another walk-in site that's near where you park.

## Saddlebag Lake Campground

**Directions:** From Lee Vining turn west on Highway 120, towards Yosemite National Park. Drive approximately 10 miles from the intersection of Highways 395 and 120 to Saddlebag Road. Take a right on Saddlebag Road and then drive 2.5 miles to the campground on the right. Saddlebag Road alternates between pavement and gravel and is easily accessible to passenger cars.

## What's It Like?

Some of the most spectacular scenery in the Sierra surrounds this campground, which is on a hill above Saddlebag Lake. Most—but not all—of the campsites have a view of the lake. The dark royal blue waters of the lake are punctuated by a medley of 12,000 foot mountain peaks including Mount Conness at 12,590 feet and the rusty-hued metamorphic rock of Excelsior Mountain at 12,446 feet. Lodgepole and whitebark pine grow in the campsites, and the shady areas under their branches offer campers a respite from the high altitude sun. If you have a large RV this campground is not for you, but smaller trailers will do fine here.

**Words of Warning:** This campground is located at 10,100 feet above sea level. If you're arriving from sea level, it's a good idea to camp at a lower elevation campground (7,000 to 8,000 feet) for a night or two before moving up here to make sure you're well acclimated.

## What's It Near?

• Take the boat taxi across Saddlebag Lake and let the Sierra breeze whisper sweet nothings in your ear while you admire the snow-speckled walls of massive mountain peaks. The taxi shortens the trip to Twenty Lakes Basin, stretched out below the imposing face of Mount Conness, where you can take an easy loop hike (8.3 miles total distance, 310 feet elevation gain) past some of the most beautiful lakes in the Sierra. To reach such spectacular scenery you usually have to hike long and hard in the Eastern Sierra, but the hardest thing about this hike is that it's at 10,000 feet above sea level, so acclimating well is a good idea.

• Wonderful chili and homemade pies and cakes at Saddlebag Lake Resort.

• Yosemite Hikes:
    o Glen Aulin High Sierra Camp (11 miles round trip, spectacular waterfalls along the way),
    o Elizabeth Lake (4.8 miles round trip, at the base of Unicorn Peak),
    o Mono Pass (7 miles round trip),
    o Lower Gaylor Lake (4.5 miles—beware of the mosquitoes, they're vicious here),
    o Tuolumne River Bridges of Lyell Canyon (2 miles round trip and only 150 feet elevation gain),
    o Lyell Canyon (12 to 16 miles round trip). The Tuolumne River slows down through Lyell Canyon, in some spots so clear it looks like the fish are swimming through glass. In other places along the river, it looks like a jeweler melted some of his finest emerald gems and poured them into the water, turning the stream to a beautiful shade of green.
    o Lembert Dome (4 miles round trip).

• Other nearby hikes: Gardinsky Lake (2.4 miles round trip, trailhead on Saddlebag Lake Road about 1 ¼ miles from Highway 120). Glacier Canyon and Dana Lakes (5 miles round trip, trailhead is at the Tioga Lake Overlook parking area). The Bennettville mine, a 0.7 mile walk from Junction Campground.

• Fishing for rainbow, brown, brook, and golden trout in Saddlebag Lake. The Saddlebag Lake boat taxi will get you to another batch of lakes within easy walking distance from where the boat leaves you on shore. You can also cast a line for trout at Lundy Lake, Lee Vining Creek, Tioga Lake, and Ellery Lake.

**Elevation:** 10,100 feet

**Toilets:** Vault

**Verizon Cell Service?** No.

**Takes Reservations?** No. First-come, first-served.

**Number of Campsites:** 19

**Bear Boxes?** Yes

### Campsites with the Most Privacy

**#11 Privacy Rating: A**
**Reservable?** No. First-come, first-served.

With only one nearby neighbor and a location that's farther back from the campground road, #11 is the most private spot in the campground–although it lacks the spectacular view of Saddlebag Lake and the mountains beyond that some of the other sites have. A big stump and some low-growing conifers mostly block from view the neighbor to the right about 24 feet away. A trail leads away from #11 on the left, where you'll likely have a view of the lake when the water isn't too low. Tall evergreens shade #11. The bathrooms are directly in front of the site, making this a convenient choice.

**#16 Privacy Rating: B+**
**Reservable?** No. First-come, first-served.

This campsite has a spectacular view of one of the prettiest sights in the Sierra: Royal blue Saddlebag Lake in the foreground with the 12,000 foot peaks reaching up toward the sky in the background. It's not as private as #11, since it's closer to its neighbors and the campground road, but some pines growing between #16 and the road add some privacy. Its nearest neighbors are closer than we would like but not so close that they're breathing down your neck. The picnic table and bear box are in the sun a good part of the day, but pines provide some shade to sections of the campsite.

**#18 Privacy Rating: A-**
**Reservable?** No. First-come, first-served.

A path from the driveway leads to the picnic table and fire pit perched on a natural platform above the lake. From here, there's a lovely view of Saddlebag Lake and rust-colored Excelsior Mountain looming up beyond it. A neighboring space is close on the left, but because #18 is pushed back from the road and its neighbor is closer to the road, it doesn't feel as if that spot is right next to you. Ditto with the campsite across the street. Another campsite sits to the right, but it's far enough away that you've got plenty of breathing room. If you like having a view from your campsite, this is an ideal choice.

## Sawmill Walk-In Campground

**Directions:** From Lee Vining turn west on Highway 120, towards Tioga Pass and Yosemite National Park. Drive approximately 10 miles from the intersection of Highways 395 and 120 to Saddlebag Road. Take a right on Saddlebag Road and then travel about 1.6 miles to the campground on the left.

**What's It Like?**

This walk-in campground is a privacy lover's dream. It has the feel of backpacking out in the wilderness. From some of the campsites, you can't see any neighbors, adding to this impression. But you're going to have to work for your privacy. It's about 300 paces (.15 miles) from the parking lot to the first campsite. And some of the best campsites are quite a hike from where you park your car. Still, load up your gear on to a hand cart and you'll be rewarded with campsites that are not only some of the most private in the Eastern Sierra—they also have views of some of the most spectacular scenery. The area has some history attached to it, since it's the site of the 1882 sawmill that supplied lumber for the mining town of Bennettville.

**Words of Warning:** There is no potable water available here. Bring your own or treat water that you get from the stream.

**What's It Near?**

• Take the boat taxi across Saddlebag Lake and let the Sierra breeze whisper sweet nothings in your ear while you admire the snow-speckled walls of massive mountain peaks. The taxi shortens the trip to Twenty Lakes Basin, stretched out below the imposing face of Mount Conness, where you can take an easy loop hike (8.3 miles total distance, 310 feet elevation gain) past some of the most beautiful lakes in the Sierra. To reach such spectacular scenery you usually have to hike long and hard in the Eastern Sierra, but the hardest thing about this hike is that it's at 10,000 feet above sea level, so acclimating well is a good idea.

• Wonderful chili and homemade pies and cakes at Saddlebag Lake Resort.

• Yosemite Hikes:
  o Glen Aulin High Sierra Camp (11 miles round trip, spectacular waterfalls along the way),
  o Elizabeth Lake (4.8 miles round trip, at the base of Unicorn Peak),
  o Mono Pass (7 miles round trip),
  o Lower Gaylor Lake (4.5 miles—beware of the mosquitoes, they're vicious here),
  o Tuolumne River Bridges of Lyell Canyon (2 miles round trip and only 150 feet elevation gain),
  o Lyell Canyon (12 to 16 miles round trip). The Tuolumne River slows down through Lyell Canyon, in some spots so clear it looks like the fish are swimming through glass. In other places along the river, it looks like a jeweler melted some of his finest emerald gems and poured them into the water, turning the stream to a beautiful shade of green.
  o Lembert Dome (4 miles round trip).

• Other nearby hikes: Gardinsky Lake (2.4 miles round trip, trailhead on Saddlebag Lake Road about 1 ¼ miles from Highway 120). Glacier Canyon and Dana Lakes (5 miles round trip, trailhead is at the Tioga Lake Overlook parking area).

• The Bennettville mine, a 0.7 mile walk from Junction Campground.

• Fishing for rainbow, brown, brook, and golden trout in Saddlebag Lake. The Saddlebag Lake boat taxi will get you to another batch of lakes within easy walking distance from where the boat leaves you on shore. You can also cast a line for trout at Lundy Lake, Lee Vining Creek, Tioga Lake, and Ellery Lake.

**Elevation:** 9,800 feet

**Toilets:** Vault

**Verizon Cell Service?** No

**Takes Reservations?** No. First-Come, First-Served

**Number of Campsites:** 12

**Bear Boxes?** Yes

## Campsites with the Most Privacy

**#1 Privacy Rating: A-**
**Reservable?** No. First-come, first-served.

You'll do the least amount of walking to reach this campsite since it's the first one on the path. Conifers grow behind the site and there are no immediate neighbors on the left or right. Across the path from #1 is the pay station. It's a little exposed, but it's far enough back from the path that it doesn't feel as if you're on display to anyone who walks past. To the front of the site, there's a filtered view of the majestic mountains towering over Sawmill Valley.

## #3 Privacy Rating: A+
**Reservable?** No. First-come, first-served.

Set back about 84 feet from the trail and with no neighbors anywhere in sight, this camp space is the ultimate in solitude. The walk to the campsite from the main path is stunning, with an unobstructed view of the Sawmill Valley meadow and a snow-speckled mountain beyond. It's perched above Lee Vining Creek, which you can't see from the campsite itself, but just a few steps past the tent pad is an overlook with views of the creek and the layered granite mountain across the meadow. It's a sunny site, but some medium-sized conifers provide a little shade.

## #4 Privacy Rating: A+
**Reservable?** No. First-come, first-served.

Out of all campsites with privacy in this campground, this one has an advantage of being closer to the parking lot—although still farther away than site #1. It's located far back from the trail on a bluff overlooking Sawmill Valley meadow with no neighbors in view on any side. It does receive a blast of high altitude sun, but one small conifer shades the tent pad and a few medium-sized evergreens shade the picnic table.

The scarcity of big trees within the campsite has one advantage—the site has a phenomenal view of the meadow and a mountain with a snow patch beyond. There's also a nice view of a brick-red mountain soaring up to the front of the campsite and a filtered view of a granite hunk of a mountain bursting up above the trees to the right. It's above the creek, which you can't see from the campsite. A nice spot for larger groups, thanks to the two tent pads. In front of the site is a phenomenon we've seen elsewhere: patches of grass growing in circles.

## #5 Privacy Rating: A+
**Reservable?** No. First-come, first-served.

A small hill partially curtains off the view of #5 from the trail and adds some geologic interest to the spot thanks to small rusty rock spires sticking out of the ground. The site also is a good distance from the campground trail. With no nearby neighbors on the left or across the trail and a hill to the right obscuring any view of the site on that side, this spot has a lot of privacy. It's above the creek, although you can't see the stream as well as from site #6. You do have a filtered view of Sawmill Valley meadow and the mountains beyond. A gap in the conifers affords a view of an impressive granite peak. As a bonus, there's ample shade here.

## #6 Privacy Rating: A
**Reservable?** No. First-come, first-served.

More private than its neighbor #7 to the right, #6 is set back from the campground trail. A hill with some rust-colored rocks stands between #6 and the space to the left. Behind this partially shady site is a spectacular view of Sawmill Valley meadow and beyond that a snow-speckled mountain. There is a glimpse of #7 to the right from the tent pad, but trees block the view from the picnic table and there's a fair distance between the two sites. You can set your tent on a bluff above the creek and through the tent windows see a view seldom acquired through car camping. There are no campsites across the trail from this campsite.

## #7 Privacy Rating: B+
**Reservable?** No. First-come, first-served.

We marked this one down to B+ due to its closeness to the campground trail and the fact it feels more exposed, but given the small number of sites in this campground and the campground's layout, you probably aren't going to have a parade of people walking past. This wouldn't be our first choice of a campsite, but it has some nice features. It looks out over the stream so you can hear nature serenading you with water music. It also has no nearby neighbors and plenty of shade. No other spaces are visible to the right or across the trail. You can see a campsite to the left, but it's far away.

## #8 Privacy Rating: A
**Reservable?** No. First-come, first-served.

The campground trail passes by to the right of this shady site, but it's not like there's going to be a parade of hikers walking past. It sits in a circle of conifers with some willows behind. To the left is a meadow. The bathroom is a stone's throw away. This doesn't have the dramatic view of some of the spaces in this campground, but it's a peaceful choice nonetheless.

## #9 Privacy Rating: A
**Reservable?** No. First-come, first-served.

An interesting old tree stump with striated patterns greets you as you step into this campsite. A hill rises up behind the site and it has no neighbors on the left and right. The bathroom is in front. It also has a view of a snow-speckled mountain. Plenty of conifers shade the site. The only reason we marked it down from an A+ to an A rating is because it's close to the trail. But this is a lightly used area and even if the campground is full there won't be hundreds of people trekking past.

## #10 Privacy Rating: A
**Reservable?** No. First-come, first-served.

Perched on a platform above the Sawmill Valley, #10 affords nice views of the creek flowing peacefully past in the meadow below. The creek also plays a continual concert of Mother Nature's music clearly audible from the campsite. Visible from the trail but off by itself, this partially shady campsite has a filtered view of the rocky spires on the mountain at the end of the valley as well as the peeling layers of granite on the mountain across the meadow. There are no neighboring campsites on any side.

## #11 Privacy Rating: A+
**Reservable?** No. First-come, first-served.

This site is far away from others in the campground, In fact, it's two-tenths of a mile walk from #11 to the bathrooms and it's quite a trek from the parking lot. If you like your solitude, the walk is worth it. No neighbors are in sight on any side. Behind the site a grassy meadow and some conifers cover a hillside. In front is a filtered view of the layered granite mountain that stretches alongside Sawmill Valley meadow. Tall pines provide ample shade.

**#12 Privacy Rating: A+**
**Reservable?** No. First-come, first-served.

This site is the ultimate in privacy, but you pay the price of camping far, far away from the bathrooms, which are about three-tenths of a mile away. The stream flows to the left of this campsite and you have a filtered glimpse of it through the vegetation. Good-sized conifers hide the view of site #11, which is a fair distance away up the trail. What isn't hidden is a view of an impressive mountain beyond the evergreens to the rear of the camp space. Since #12 doesn't overlook Sawmill Valley meadow and is closer to the stream, it has a different personality than a lot of the other campsites in this campground, but it's still a lovely spot. With more than a quarter mile trek from the parking lot to #12, it feels like you're backpacking.

### Tioga Lake Campground

**Directions:** From Lee Vining turn west on Highway 120, towards Yosemite National Park. Drive approximately 11 miles from the intersection of Highways 395 and 120 to the campground on the left.

## What's It Like?

God outdid himself when he created Tioga Lake. It's a High Sierra gem. The campground, however, is a privacy-seeker's nightmare. Most of the spaces are crammed together on a natural lawn overlooking the lake. Certainly, the spaces here have postcard-perfect views. But we couldn't find any that met our privacy criteria.

## What's It Near?

• Tioga Pass Resort's cozy restaurant, which serves breakfast, lunch, and dinner as well as homemade pies, cakes, and desserts baked by the resort's own pastry chef. Try an omelet or homemade granola for breakfast, hearty sandwiches and burgers for lunch, or their tender pot roast or lemon garlic chicken for dinner, among other specialties.

• An approximately 20-minute drive away from Saddlebag Lake. Take the boat taxi across the lake and let the Sierra breeze whisper sweet nothings in your ear while you admire the snow-speckled walls of massive mountain peaks. The taxi shortens the trip to Twenty Lakes Basin, stretched out below the imposing face of Mount Conness, where you can take an easy loop hike past some of the most beautiful lakes in the Sierra. To reach such spectacular scenery you usually have to hike long and hard in the Eastern Sierra, but the hardest thing about this hike is that it's at 10,000 feet above sea level, so acclimating well is a good idea.

• Wonderful chili and homemade pies and cakes at Saddlebag Lake Resort.

• Yosemite Hikes:
> o Glen Aulin High Sierra Camp (11 miles round trip, spectacular waterfalls along the way),

- Elizabeth Lake (4.8 miles round trip, at the base of Unicorn Peak),
- Mono Pass (7 miles round trip),
- Lower Gaylor Lake (4.5 miles—beware of the mosquitoes, they're vicious here),
- Tuolumne River Bridges of Lyell Canyon (2 miles round trip and only 150 feet elevation gain),
- Lyell Canyon (12 to 16 miles round trip). The Tuolumne River slows down through Lyell Canyon, in some spots so clear it looks like the fish are swimming through glass. In other places along the river, it looks like a jeweler melted some of his finest emerald gems and poured them into the water, turning the stream to a beautiful shade of green.
- Lembert Dome (4 miles round trip).

• Other nearby hikes: Gardinsky Lake (2.4 miles round trip, trailhead on Saddlebag Lake Road about 1 ¼ miles from Highway 120). Glacier Canyon and Dana Lakes (5 miles round trip, trailhead is at the Tioga Lake Overlook parking area). The Bennettville mine, a 0.7 mile walk from Junction Campground.

• Fishing for rainbow, brown, brook, and golden trout in Saddlebag Lake. The Saddlebag Lake boat taxi will get you to another batch of lakes within easy walking distance from where the boat leaves you on shore. You can also cast a line for trout at Lundy Lake, Lee Vining Creek, Tioga Lake, and Ellery Lake.

**Elevation:** 9,700 feet

**Toilets:** Vault

**Verizon Cell Service?** No.

**Takes Reservations?** No. First-come, first-served.

**Number of Campsites:** 13

**Bear Boxes?** Yes

## Campsites with the Most Privacy

None.

## Tuolumne Meadows Campground

**Directions:** From Lee Vining, travel about 16 miles west on Highway 120 into Yosemite National Park. The campground is on the left. The campground is located about 1 ½ hours away from Yosemite Valley.

**What's It Like?**

A large campground in the high country of Yosemite National Park, Tuolumne Meadows Campground rests in the forest under a canopy of primarily lodgepole pines. Some of the campsites in section A are located across the campground road from the Tuolumne River (although most of these campsites are not very private). Certain sections of this campground are filled with a lot of commotion, but there are campsites that are more peaceful and farther away from the crowds (see campsites with the most privacy descriptions below).

This campground also works a little differently. Rather than drive around the campground until you find a first-come, first-served site you like, you are assigned a first-come, first-served campsite when you check in. First, you pay for a site in the cabin at the campground entrance. Then, you drive up to the entrance booth, where they assign you a camp space. Your best bet is to request one of the sites below when you pay at the cabin at the campground entrance and then when you drive up to the entrance booth ask them again if one of the first-come, first-served sites below are available. If the sites are available, they should be willing to assign one of them to you at the entrance booth.

**What's It Near?**

• Tioga Pass Resort's cozy restaurant, which serves breakfast, lunch, and dinner as well as homemade pies, cakes, and desserts baked by the resort's own pastry chef. Try an omelet or homemade granola for breakfast, hearty sandwiches and burgers for lunch, or their tender pot roast or lemon garlic chicken for dinner, among other specialties. Tioga Pass Resort is just east of the Tioga Pass entrance station to Yosemite.

• An approximately 30-minute drive away from Saddlebag Lake. Take the boat taxi across the lake and let the Sierra breeze whisper sweet nothings in your ear while you admire the snow-speckled walls of massive mountain peaks. The taxi shortens the trip to Twenty Lakes Basin, stretched out below the imposing face of Mount Conness, where you can take an easy loop hike past some of the most beautiful lakes in the Sierra. To reach such spectacular scenery you usually have to hike long and hard in the Eastern Sierra, but the hardest thing about this hike is that it's at 10,000 feet above sea level, so acclimating well is a good idea.

• Wonderful chili and homemade pies and cakes at Saddlebag Lake Resort.

• Horseback riding through Tuolumne Meadows Stables.

• Yosemite Hikes:
  o Glen Aulin High Sierra Camp (11 miles round trip, spectacular waterfalls along the way),
  o Elizabeth Lake (4.8 miles round trip, at the base of Unicorn Peak),

- Mono Pass (7 miles round trip),
- Lower Gaylor Lake (4.5 miles—beware of the mosquitoes, they're vicious here),
- Tuolumne River Bridges of Lyell Canyon (2 miles round trip and only 150 feet elevation gain),
- Lyell Canyon (12 to 16 miles round trip). The Tuolumne River slows down through Lyell Canyon, in some spots so clear it looks like the fish are swimming through glass. In other places along the river, it looks like a jeweler melted some of his finest emerald gems and poured them into the water, turning the stream to a beautiful shade of green.
- Lembert Dome (4 miles round trip).

• Fishing for rainbow, brown, brook, and golden trout in Saddlebag Lake, just east of the Tioga Pass entrance station. The Saddlebag Lake boat taxi will get you to another batch of lakes within easy walking distance from where the boat leaves you on shore. You can also cast a line for trout at Lundy Lake, Lee Vining Creek, Tioga Lake, and Ellery Lake.

**Elevation:** 8,600 feet

**Toilets:** Flush

**Verizon Cell Service?** No

**Takes Reservations?** Yes, but since this campground is in a national park it's very difficult to find any open spots on recreation.gov unless you make reservations the second they become available six months in advance. You can usually find first-come, first-served sites if you arrive before 11 a.m. Sunday – Thursday.

**Number of Campsites:** 304

**Bear Boxes?** Yes

# Campsites with the Most Privacy

**#A49 Privacy Rating: C+**
**Reservable?** No. First-come, first-served.

Normally, we wouldn't include a campsite with a C+ privacy rating in this book. However, we believe this site has a place here for two reasons. First, it has a spectacular view of Lembert Dome across a tranquil, willow-dotted meadow on the other side of the campground road. The Tuolumne River flows lazily through the meadow. Second, many people want to stay in the A loop because it's next to the Tuolumne River. However, all the sites in the A loop, except for this one, are squished together.

#49 is a long and narrow site stretched out along the campground road. It's fully visible from the road but it has lots of trees. Through the trees and up a hill, you'll be able to see an RV parked in the spot above although it's far enough away not to feel as if it's in your face. Plus, your gaze will be drawn to the spectacular view across the street. Just be aware that if an RV is parked above you, then you might have to hear its generator running. There are no campsites visible to the right and the space to the left is far away. The grill and the picnic table are near the campground road. This would make a nice spot for a small trailer, pickup truck with a camper top, or camper van.

**Words of Warning:** In the long-range plan, the National Park Service is considering getting rid of the A loop in this campground. Visit the Campground Updates section of our website at **www.ilovetheeasternsierra.com** to stay abreast of this situation.

## #D3 Privacy Rating: B
**Reservable?** No. First-come, first-served.

On a quiet loop far back from the commotion of the main part of the campground, #D3 is in a forested setting with a fair amount of shade. A tiny seasonal stream cuts through the conifers to the right and beyond that sits a neighboring space that the trees partially filter from view. Another space sits to the left, but it's also partially screened by the pines. The forest is the only neighbor you'll have behind you and there's no neighbors across the street, either.

It's a short walk to Elizabeth Creek from here and it's not too far of a walk to reach Tuolumne Meadows for a nice stroll looking out toward Mount Dana. While this isn't the best site in the campground, it's a refreshing change of pace from the many Condo Camping spaces that are squished together in other places throughout the campground.

## #D11 Privacy Rating: A+
**Reservable?** No. First-come, first-served.

#D11 holds a soft spot in my heart. I camped here many times both with my brother and sister-in-law and alone before I met Patrick. The first time I requested this spot, the ranger assigning spaces in the booth said, "D11 is a sweet spot!"

What makes it a sweet spot? First, it has no neighbors on three sides. There's a campsite across the street, but because of the way the two sites are placed, that other site doesn't intrude on your solitude. Second, Elizabeth Creek is immediately behind the camp spot, in view from much of the site. Be forewarned, though, that in drought years the creek is barely a dribble by late August and may be completely dry by Labor Day. If you hit it at the right time, a patch of yellow wildflowers adds a splash of color to the campsite. It's also a short walk along the creek to Tuolumne Meadows.

If it has any disadvantages it's that the tent area is close to the campground road. But this is a quiet loop that doesn't see much traffic. If you have a smaller tent, you might be able to pitch it closer to the stream, which is what I did when sharing the site with my brother and sister-in-law. Another slight disadvantage is that a path runs between the campsite and the creek, so occasionally someone might pass by close to your campsite. But so few campers use the trail that it never bothered me when I camped there.

**#E13 Privacy Rating: A-**
**Reservable?** Yes. Visit www.recreation.gov for reservations.

With no one visible on three sides, #E13 offers up oodles of privacy, especially when you compare it to many of the right-on-top-of-your-neighbor campsites in this campground. Evergreens and its location set back a little from the campground road serves to shelter it from its only nearby neighbors across the street (#F2 and #F4). Trees conceal the view of one section of the campground road that sits to the left. There's lots of shade here, but the sun slips through.

**#F2 Privacy Rating: B**
**Reservable?** Yes. Visit www.recreation.gov for reservations.

A spacious, tent-only spot under the pines with some grass understory, #F2 is a peaceful home away from home. The space on the right (#F4) is about 30 feet away and mostly sheltered from view by a forest of pines. It has no neighbors on the left. The camp space across the street (#E13) isn't directly in front of #F2 and the trees in both campsites provide a cushion of privacy along with their locations slightly back from the campground road. This spot would rate a B+ except that the driveway for #F3—the space out of sight behind #F2—runs alongside this campsite to the left, so your neighbor to the rear will drive closely by your site. This space has a lot of shade but the sun manages to slip through the pines at parts of the day.

#### #F4 Privacy Rating: B+
**Reservable?** Yes. Visit www.recreation.gov for reservations.

This tent-only, mostly shady site sits at the intersection of two campground roads, but lots of tall conifers partially shelter it from view. There's a campsite to the left about 30 feet away, but the pines in between the two sites provide a fair amount of privacy. Another campsite is partially visible through the gaps in the evergreens behind the site, but it's a fair distance away. Trees do a good job of concealing the campground road, which runs along the right side of the site. Trees in #F4 screen out the campsite across the street, a little ways down the road.

#### #G3 Privacy Rating: B+
**Reservable?** No. First-come, first-served.

With no spaces visible to the left and none behind the site either, #G3 has some good privacy. It's well-spaced from #G5 on the right and big conifers filter the view. The site is set back from the campground road, giving it a fair amount of distance from the neighbor across the street. It's a forested spot with lots of boulders. It's also a tent-only campsite.

#### #G5 Privacy Rating: A
**Reservable?** No. First-come, first-served.

As far as privacy goes, #G5 gives #G16 and #D11 a run for their money. A small hill on the right blocks the view of the neighbor on that side (#G6). The space to the left is far enough away and partially filtered from view by conifers. Behind this tent-only campsite, there are no neighbors other than pines.

No neighbors immediately across the street, either. As a bonus, the tent area is far back from the road. A good amount of shade here, too.

**#G9 Privacy Rating: B**
**Reservable?** No. First-come, first-served.

Through the pines, you can see the neighbors to the left and right, but they're not too close. No neighbors are visible behind this partially shady, tent-only spot. This would not be our first choice in this campground, but it's not a bad spot if all the other good ones are taken.

**#G16 Privacy Rating: A+**
**Reservable?** No. First-come, first-served.

This is a huge spot, with plenty of room for at least three tents. I camped in this shady, tent-only site once when my favorite site—#D11—was taken. At first I went through #D11 withdrawal, but soon began to appreciate the solitude of #G16. To the right and behind the site, there's nothing but woods. Because #G16 is farther back from the road and the neighbor to the left is closer, you won't notice them there. Plus that site is far enough away on the other side of the pines. No other spaces sit immediately across the street, although you will catch a glimpse of one camp space slightly down the road.

**Words of Warning:** It's a bit of a hike to the bathrooms from #G16. But if you like privacy, the walk is well worth it.

# JUNE LAKE LOOP

## Grant Lake Campground

**Directions:** From Lee Vining, travel south on Highway 395 until you reach the northernmost section of the June Lake Loop (Highway 158). Turn right on Highway 158. The campground is the first one you will see on the June Lake Loop. It will be on the left.

## What's It Like?

Out of all the campgrounds on the June Lake Loop, if you like privacy this is the one to avoid. It's basically parking lot camping.

## What's It Near?

• Hikes to Parker Lake (4 miles round trip), Fern Creek Trailhead to Fern Lake (3.4 miles round trip), Yost Lake (4.8 miles round trip), and Walker Lake (2 miles round trip), Glass Creek Meadow (4 to 6 miles round trip).

• Obsidian Dome is a short drive away. From June Lakes, take Highway 395 about 3.7 miles south of the southernmost June Lake Junction. Turn right on Obsidian Dome Road (Forest Service Road 2S10) and drive 1.5 miles to Obsidian Dome where you can take an easy stroll up a gated road to the old pumice quarry at the top of the dome.

• Fishing in June Lake, Grant Lake, Gull Lake, and Silver Lake as well as in a number of creeks.

• Horseback riding through Frontier Pack Station.

• Swimming, waterskiing, wakeboarding, and boat rentals on Grant Lake after 10:00 am. Swimming, sailing, and windsailing on June Lake as well as docking for boats up to 24 feet. Boat rentals also available at Gull Lake and Silver Lake Marinas.

• Stop by the Silver Lake Resort for breakfast or lunch. Giant omelets and their Famous Silver Lake Burger are some of the popular items on the menu. And don't forget a slice of pie. Comfort food at its best.

**Elevation:** 7,135 feet

**Toilets:** Flush

**Verizon Cell Service?** Limited.

**Takes Reservations?** No. First-come, first-served.

**Number of Campsites:** 70

**Bear Boxes?** No.

### Campsites with the Most Privacy

None

### Silver Lake Campground

**Directions:** From Lee Vining, travel south on Highway 395 until you reach the northernmost section of the June Lake Loop (State Route 158). Turn right and travel about 7 miles to the campground on the left.

**What's It Like?**

Although this campground is far superior to Grant Lake, most of the sites lack privacy. They're either out in a meadow or within view of each other. The most private sites are on the right side of the campground in the willows and aspens. This campground does have spectacular views of the June Lake canyon and its majestic 11,000 and 12,000-foot mountain peaks. So staying here is very easy on the eyes. It's also in a peaceful location on the shores of Silver Lake and Rush Creek. The reason why we didn't include more campsites is because many of the campsites in the willows and aspens were in full view of their nearby neighbors. However, we did find a couple campsites here we really liked (see campsite descriptions below).

**Bonus:** The campground has paid showers.

**What's It Near?**

• Hikes to Parker Lake (4 miles round trip), Fern Creek Trailhead to Fern Lake (3.4 miles round trip), Yost Lake (4.8 miles round trip), and Walker Lake (2 miles round trip), Glass Creek Meadow (4 to 6 miles round trip).

• Obsidian Dome is a short drive away. From June Lakes, take Highway 395 about 3.7 miles south of the southernmost June Lake Junction. Turn right on Obsidian Dome Road (Forest Service Road 2S10) and drive 1.5 miles to Obsidian Dome where you can take an easy stroll up a gated road to the old pumice quarry at the top of the dome.

• Fishing for rainbow trout in June Lake, Grant Lake, Gull Lake, and Silver Lake as well as in a number of creeks.

• Horseback riding through Frontier Pack Station.

• Swimming, waterskiing, wakeboarding, and boat rentals on Grant Lake after 10:00 am. Swimming, sailing, and windsailing on June Lake as well as docking for boats up to 24 feet. Boat rentals also available at Gull Lake and Silver Lake Marinas.

• Stop by the Silver Lake Resort for breakfast or lunch. Giant omelets and their Famous Silver Lake Burger are some of the popular items on the menu. And don't forget a slice of pie. Comfort food at its best.

**Elevation:** 7,200 feet

**Toilets:** Flush

**Verizon Cell Service?** Limited cell reception.

**Takes Reservations?** Yes. Visit www.recreation.gov for reservations. Some campsites are first-come, first-served.

**Number of Campsites:** 62

**Bear Boxes?** Yes.

### Campsites with the Most Privacy

**#10 Privacy Rating: A**
**Reservable?** No. First-come, first-served.

This one is closer to the campground road than we like to see, but it's still a nice site. Willows surround it on three sides, hiding any neighbors to the left, right, or behind. Willows also grow to the front right of the campsite, conveniently obscuring the view of the neighbor across the road from your picnic table. A good view of the mountain peaks from here, too.

**#20 Privacy Rating: A+**
**Reservable?** Yes. Visit www.recreation.gov for reservations.

Willows enclose the site on the left and right. Behind the site, aspens tower above the willows, creating a thick wall of

vegetation. There are no spaces immediately across the street either. Above the willows to the rear, the craggy cliffs of the mountains lining June Lake Canyon are an imposing sight. It looks like a waterfall might wiggle its way down those cliffs in early spring and summer, and if so, would add a touch of pizazz to this campsite. #20 also is across from the lake, although willows interfere with the view.

## Gull Lake Campground

**Directions:** From Mammoth Lakes, travel north on Highway 395 to the southernmost June Lake Loop junction (Highway 158). Turn left on Highway 158 and travel 2.7 miles to the campground on the right (just past the town of June Lake).

**What's It Like?**

On the southern shore of Gull Lake, this campground sits on an aspen-lined road that parallels Highway 158. The campsites on the lake rest under a canopy of lodgepole pines with some aspen accents. The spaces across the campground road from the lake are tucked back in the aspens. A good campground for anglers due to its proximity to the water's edge, Gull Lake Campground is a scenic spot to camp in September and October when the foliage displays its fall finery. Its one flaw? You can hear road noise from Highway 158, but it should die down at night and you can always bring earplugs.

**What's It Near?**

• Hikes to Parker Lake (4 miles round trip), Fern Creek Trailhead to Fern Lake (3.4 miles round trip), Yost Lake (4.8 miles round trip), and Walker Lake (2 miles round trip), Glass Creek Meadow (4 to 6 miles round trip).

• Obsidian Dome is a short drive away. From June Lakes, take Highway 395 about 3.7 miles south of the southernmost June Lake Junction. Turn right on Obsidian Dome Road (Forest Service Road 2S10) and drive 1.5 miles to Obsidian Dome where you can take an easy stroll up a gated road to the old pumice quarry at the top of the dome.

• Fishing for rainbow trout in June Lake, Grant Lake, Gull Lake, and Silver Lake as well as in a number of creeks.

• Horseback riding through Frontier Pack Station.

• Swimming, waterskiing, wakeboarding, and boat rentals on Grant Lake after 10:00 am. Swimming, sailing, and windsailing on June Lake as well as docking for boats up to 24 feet. Boat rentals also available at Gull Lake and Silver Lake Marinas.

• Stop by the Silver Lake Resort for breakfast or lunch. Giant omelets and their Famous Silver Lake Burger are some of the popular items on the menu. And don't forget a slice of pie. Comfort food at its best.

**Elevation:** 7,600 feet

**Toilets:** Flush

**Verizon Cell Service?** Yes

**Takes Reservations?** No. First-come, first-served.

**Number of Campsites:** 11

**Bear Boxes?** Yes

## Campsites with the Most Privacy

**#6 Privacy Rating: A**
**Reservable?** No. First-come, first-served.

This is a nice site, with one exception: Highway 158 runs immediately behind it. Still, there are some aspens filtering the view of the highway, and the road noise here probably won't be any worse than anywhere else in the campground. To reach #6, climb up four stairs from the parking area. No neighbors are visible on the left, right, or across the street, thanks to the tall aspens. It's across the campground road from the lake.

**#9 Privacy Rating: A-**
**Reservable?** No. First-come, first-served.

An ideal site for an angler, #9 sits on the lakeshore under a canopy of pines. To the right is a forest of aspens with no neighbors. Pines and aspens partially obscure from view #11

on the left. There's some good distance between this campsite and the campsites across the street, and #9 is behind a screen of conifers. Like all the sites in this campground, you will hear some road noise.

**#11 Privacy Rating: A-**
**Reservable?** No. First-come, first-served.

The lake stretches out immediately behind this pine-shaded campsite. It's like camping on the edge of a sapphire jewel. Your parked vehicle will partially block from view another campsite sitting to the right of this one. Plus, aspens and evergreens filter some of the view. To the left, there are no other spaces, only a forest of aspens. A couple of willows on the banks of the water partially screen you from view of the houses across the lake. Like all the campsites in this campground, you'll hear some road noise.

## Reversed Creek Campground

**Directions:** From Mammoth Lakes, travel north on Highway 395 to the southernmost June Lake Loop junction (Highway 158). Turn left on Highway 158 and travel 2.7 miles to the campground on the left (just past the town of June Lake).

**What's It Like?**

Settled underneath a grove of aspens and pines, Reversed Creek Campground is sunken down from Highway 158, so it isn't plagued by road noise to any major extent. Across the main highway from Gull Lake, it's a convenient campground for anglers. It's also a nice hideaway for anyone who enjoys listening to the symphony of the aspens quaking in the breeze. Despite the campground's name, none of the campsites have a view of Reversed Creek.

**What's It Near?**

• Hikes to Parker Lake (4 miles round trip), Fern Creek Trailhead to Fern Lake (3.4 miles round trip), Yost Lake (4.8 miles round trip), and Walker Lake (2 miles round trip), Glass Creek Meadow (4 to 6 miles round trip).

• Obsidian Dome is a short drive away. From June Lakes, take Highway 395 about 3.7 miles south of the southernmost June Lake Junction. Turn right on Obsidian Dome Road (Forest Service Road 2S10) and drive 1.5 miles to Obsidian Dome where you can take an easy stroll up a gated road to the old pumice quarry at the top of the dome.

• Fishing for rainbow trout in June Lake, Grant Lake, Gull Lake, and Silver Lake as well as in a number of creeks.

• Horseback riding through Frontier Pack Station.

• Swimming, waterskiing, wakeboarding, and boat rentals on Grant Lake after 10:00 am. Swimming, sailing, and windsailing on June Lake as well as docking for boats up to 24 feet. Boat rentals also available at Gull Lake and Silver Lake Marinas.

• Stop by the Silver Lake Resort for breakfast or lunch. Giant omelets and their Famous Silver Lake Burger are some of the popular items on the menu. And don't forget a slice of pie. Comfort food at its best.

**Elevation:** 7,600 feet

**Toilets:** Flush

**Verizon Cell Service?** Yes

**Takes Reservations?** Yes. Visit **www.recreation.gov** for reservations. Some first-come, first-served sites are available.

**Number of Campsites:** 17

**Bear Boxes?** Yes

### Campsites with the Most Privacy

**#6 Privacy Rating: A+**
**Reservable?** Yes. Visit **www.recreation.gov** for reservations.

 A beautiful, forested, spacious spot, #6 has almost everything a privacy-loving camper is looking for including a location away from other campsites. A conifer-covered hill stands guard over the left side of the site. Willows and

aspens grow to the right. To the rear, a peaceful grassy area bordered by aspens and conifers adds more solitude. You'll have a neighbor across the campground road, but #6 is pushed back so far it won't feel like it. There's lots of shade here, too.

**Words of Warning:** I believe that on www.recreation.gov, the photograph they show for this campsite as of June 2015 is wrong. The photo shows it as being completely surrounded by aspens, when it is not.

### #8 Privacy Rating: B+
**Reservable?** Yes. Visit www.recreation.gov for reservations.

A nice site for an RV or trailer thanks to the pull-through driveway, #8 is surrounded on all sides by aspens with one small conifer serving as a centerpiece. Another large pine off to the right offers some extra shade. The space has no neighbors to the left or across the street. The campsite that's behind #8 is partially blocked from view by aspens and conifers. However, tent campers be warned: the most logical place for your tent is in full view of another campsite behind, although if you have a small tent you might be able to squeeze it in somewhere more private. Because of the tent pad placement, we gave this a B+, but if you have a trailer or RV you might consider this more of an A-.

### #12 Privacy Rating: A
**Reservable?** No. First-come, first-served.

Aspens enclose this spot on three sides. The aspens on the right give way to a path connecting #12 with its neighbor (#13), decreasing the privacy between the two sites just a little. But the trees still do a good job of filtering the view of the neighbors. Aspens shoulder their way into the area between #12 and the campground road, eliminating the view of the camp space across the street.

**#13 Privacy Rating: A**
**Reservable?** No. First-come, first-served.

As we mentioned in the description for #12, the path that runs between #13 and #12 slightly decreases the privacy between the two sites but not by an excessive amount. This is still a nicely private site, with no other neighbors in view. To the rear, conifers—including a giant pine tree—dwarf a sprinkling of aspens. The bathrooms are a stone's throw to the right of this partially shady spot.

**#14 Privacy Rating: B+**
**Reservable?** No. First-come, first-served.

With a pull-through driveway, #14 is an ideal spot for an RV or trailer up to 45 feet. You can see a couple of other campsites from here, including the one behind it, but the aspens, pines, and some bushes do a good job of filtering the view. To the left, there are no other campsites. The aspens that embrace this site on three sides are small and don't provide the privacy taller trees would, but they do a fair job of screening out the neighbors.

## June Lake Campground

**Directions:** From Mammoth Lakes, travel north on Highway 395 to the southern junction of June Lake Loop (State Route 158). Turn left and travel 2.3 miles to the campground on the right just past the fire station.

**What's It Like?**

June Lake Campground has a nice selection of campsites with privacy located under a canopy of aspens and pines. Wild roses provide bouquets of color to some of the campsites earlier in the summer and bright red rose hip berries in the fall. The campground is located on the shore of June Lake, where you can take a dip, go fishing, or simply say hello to the ducks waddling past. In addition, the campground is in walking distance to the town of June Lake. Even though it's considered to be in town, you would never know it, since it has a serene, secluded ambiance.

**What's It Near?**

• Hikes to Parker Lake (4 miles round trip), Fern Creek Trailhead to Fern Lake (3.4 miles round trip), Yost Lake (4.8 miles round trip), and Walker Lake (2 miles round trip), Glass Creek Meadow (4 to 6 miles round trip).

• Obsidian Dome is a short drive away. From June Lakes, take Highway 395 about 3.7 miles south of the southernmost June

Lake Junction. Turn right on Obsidian Dome Road (Forest Service Road 2S10) and drive 1.5 miles to Obsidian Dome where you can take an easy stroll up a gated road to the old pumice quarry at the top of the dome.

• Fishing for rainbow trout in June Lake, Grant Lake, Gull Lake, and Silver Lake as well as in a number of creeks.

• Horseback riding through Frontier Pack Station.

• Swimming, waterskiing, wakeboarding, and boat rentals on Grant Lake after 10:00 am. Swimming, sailing, and windsailing on June Lake as well as docking for boats up to 24 feet. Boat rentals also available at Gull Lake and Silver Lake Marinas.

• Stop by the Silver Lake Resort for breakfast or lunch. Giant omelets and their Famous Silver Lake Burger are some of the popular items on the menu. And don't forget a slice of pie. Comfort food at its best.

**Elevation:** 7,600 feet

**Toilets:** Flush

**Verizon Cell Service?** Yes

**Reservations:** Yes. Visit **www.recreation.gov** for reservations. Some sites are first-come, first-served.

**Number of Campsites:** 28

**Bear Boxes?** Yes

# Campsites with the Most Privacy

**#1 Privacy Rating: A+**
**Reservable?** Yes. Visit **www.recreation.gov** for reservations.

This site is a good choice for an RV, because there's tons of room to park for a vehicle up to 60 feet. Because State Route 158 is right next to #1, it's probably more suited to an RV or trailer due to possible road noise. However, aspens growing in front of the highway reduce the view of the road, and tent campers might still enjoy the spot, given that traffic on State Route 158 should die down at night. A pair of tall junipers add some shade. Where the campsite ends an aspen forest begins. No other campsites are visible from #1.

**#4 Privacy Rating: A+**
**Reservable?** Yes. Visit **www.recreation.gov** for reservations.

Surrounded by aspens with no neighbors in view on any side, #4 has plenty of privacy. Although it's not the closest campsite to the lake, it's an easy walk to the water from here.

**T-1 Privacy Rating: A**
**Reservable?** Yes. Visit **www.recreation.gov** for reservations.

Low-growing aspens on all sides conceal any neighbors. The day we were there, the people in the campsite behind T-1 had a really tall tent and you could see the top of it over the aspens. Otherwise, you wouldn't know there was a campsite there. No campsites exist across the street from this spot. It's a short walk to June Lake from this site. Plus, to the rear is a nice view of the 11,000 and 12,000-foot mountain peaks in the distance. The site does have some afternoon shade and because of a couple of medium-sized evergreens, the bear box is in the shadows.

## T-2 Privacy Rating: B
**Reservable?** Yes. Visit **www.recreation.gov** for reservations.

The reason we marked this spot down to a B is because you can see the site to the right clearly through a path connecting the two spots, although aspens filter the view of the main part of that site. The neighbor on the right also will park their vehicle only about 15 feet away from T-2. But on all other sides there are no neighbors visible. One bonus: This site has a filtered view of June Lake.

## #14 Privacy Rating: A+
**Reservable?** Yes. Visit **www.recreation.gov** for reservations.

#14 is a privacy lover's paradise, although it has one flaw—it's next to State Route 158, so vehicle noise does intrude a little. However, the view of the road is partially screened by trees and bushes. To reach this spot, you take a short path from the driveway. It's completely surrounded by aspens and bushes. A big pine to the right contributes to the shadiness of this campsite. The aspen trunks here are curved and wiggled, making it look like they're stuck in a frozen dance. A beautiful campsite, maybe beautiful enough to ignore its proximity to Highway 158. And if you have a trailer, pickup with a camper top, or camper van, if there's any road noise after you hit the sack, it won't bother you.

## #16 Privacy Rating: A
**Reservable?** Yes. Visit **www.recreation.gov** for reservations.

Several pieces of volcanic rock that look like giant sponges greet you as you step down the three stairs leading into this sunken campsite. The only neighbor visible from this spot is to the right, but that space is closer to the road whereas #16 is tucked back. From your picnic table you'll be able to see the RV or vehicle parked in the neighboring spot. Even so, the view of the neighbor is mostly through a curtain of aspens and wild rose bushes that were dotted with red rose hips in the fall.

Even with the view of the neighbor to the right, with no neighbors visible to the left and no neighbors behind, this is still a very private campsite with vegetation on three sides. You can pitch your tent in the middle of a circle of willows and aspens. And because the campsite is sunken and back from the campground road, you won't see any neighbors across the street.

**#19 Privacy Rating: A**
**Reservable?** Yes. Visit **www.recreation.gov** for reservations.

Back from the campground road, #19 sits in a forest of aspens and evergreens. To the right, you can barely see another space through the trees. To the left, there are no other spaces, just an aspen forest. The bathrooms are behind this site, but you will only catch a glimpse of them through the quaking green leaves. Aspens, conifers, and wild rose bushes growing in #19 mostly hide the spot across the street. The trees provide some shade in the afternoon.

## Oh! Ridge Campground

**Directions:** From Mammoth Lakes, take Highway 395 north to its southern junction with Highway 158. Turn left and travel 1 mile to the campground on the right.

**What's It Like?**

The good news? Oh! Ridge has a great view of the towering

mountain peaks in the distance, with some campsites overlooking June Lake far below. It also has easy access to a sandy lakeside beach. The bad news? Oh! Ridge does not have a huge selection of campsites with privacy. Most of the campsites are in the sagebrush and jammed up close together to each other. Some of the campsites have wooden privacy screens between them, which helps a little. We found a few campsites with privacy here, including one with an amazing view of the lake (see campsites with privacy descriptions below). This is the closest campground on the June Lake Loop to Highway 395, so if you're looking for a quick getaway this campground might be a good choice for you.

**What's It Near?**

• Hikes to Parker Lake (4 miles round trip), Fern Creek Trailhead to Fern Lake (3.4 miles round trip), Yost Lake (4.8 miles round trip), and Walker Lake (2 miles round trip), Glass Creek Meadow (4 to 6 miles round trip).

• Obsidian Dome is a short drive away. From June Lakes, take Highway 395 about 3.7 miles south of the southernmost June Lake Junction. Turn right on Obsidian Dome Road (Forest Service Road 2S10) and drive 1.5 miles to Obsidian Dome where you can take an easy stroll up a gated road to the old pumice quarry at the top of the dome.

• Fishing for rainbow trout in June Lake, Grant Lake, Gull Lake, and Silver Lake as well as in a number of creeks.

• Horseback riding through Frontier Pack Station.

• Swimming, waterskiing, wakeboarding, and boat rentals on Grant Lake after 10:00 am. Swimming, sailing, and windsailing on June Lake as well as docking for boats up to 24 feet. Boat rentals also available at Gull Lake and Silver Lake Marinas.

• Stop by the Silver Lake Resort for breakfast or lunch. Giant omelets and their Famous Silver Lake Burger are some of the popular items on the menu. And don't forget a slice of pie. Comfort food at its best.

**Elevation:** 7,600 feet

**Toilets:** Flush

**Verizon Cell Service?** Yes

**Takes Reservations?** Yes. Visit www.recreation.gov for reservations.

**Number of Campsites:** 143
**Bear Boxes?** Yes

## Campsites with the Most Privacy

**#6 Privacy Rating: B+**
**Reservable?** Yes. Visit www.recreation.gov for reservations.

The privacy on this site may be a B+ but the view from the campsite is an A+. It looks out over the Caribbean blue waters of June Lake and beyond to the 11,000 and 12,000 foot mountain peaks. The campsite on the left is about 30 feet away, but bitterbrush, pines, and shrubs provide a partial privacy screen. There are no other neighbors to the right, behind, or across the street. Stay at this campsite and it's like living in a postcard. It's located on the Bear loop.

### #92 Privacy Rating: B-
**Reservable?** Yes. Visit www.recreation.gov for reservations.

We would have given this a higher privacy rating if only the space to the left (#93) was even 15 feet farther away. As it stands now, though, the two sites are joined like Siamese twins. However, #92 is still one of the best sites in the campground because there are no other campsites to the right. The bathrooms are immediately across the street, so there are no spaces there, either. Behind #92, tall pines provide shade, and between the trees you can see the mountains in the distance—so there are no threats to your privacy in that direction.

A wooden screen sits between #92 and #93, adding a little bit of privacy, especially when you're sitting at the campfire. From the tent pad, you'll also be able to see your neighbors to the left, but this is a large enough space that you might be able to find a place to pitch your tent farther away from the neighbors. This isn't a perfect spot, but again, it's one of the best in the campground and does have a lot going for it—just know that if a big RV pulls up next to you it could spoil your privacy party. And since the maximum vehicle length for neighboring #93 is 40 feet, you could have a rather large neighbor. This site is located on the Owl loop.

### #159 Privacy Rating: C+
**Reservable?** Yes. Visit www.recreation.gov for reservations.

Squeezed between its neighbor on the left and right, this site isn't perfect, but it has two advantages. First, a pine and some bushes partially block the view of the space to the right. On the left, a wooden privacy screen, some pines, bitterbrush, and a juniper shelter this site from view of the neighbor. Its second advantage is that it has a filtered view of June Lake. This is a better site for a trailer or RV than a tent. It's located on the Gull loop.

---

**Are You Enjoying This Book? Write a Review on Amazon.com**

Your input is important to us. Write a review on Amazon and let us know if we've succeeded in helping you find a peaceful campsite.

---

# HARTLEY SPRINGS – GLASS CREEK AREA

## Hartley Springs Campground

**Directions:** From Mammoth Lakes, go north on Highway 395 for about 11.3 miles. Turn left at the Hartley Springs sign onto Obsidian Dome/Glass Flow Road. Drive on the gravel road about 0.9 miles then veer right onto Forest Service Road 2S48. Travel 0.7 miles to campground on the right.

**What's It Like?**

Under a canopy of ponderosa and Jeffrey pines and white fir, Hartley Springs rests in a forested setting on a carpet of pine needles. There's not a lot of understory, but many spaces sit far enough apart so that you're not butting heads with your neighbor. Unlike the campgrounds in June Lake, which are a hop, skip, and a jump from restaurants and stores, it's a bit of a drive from here to any restaurant, at least 25 minutes away to those on the June Lakes Loop or in Mammoth Lakes.

When we visited in October, we were greeted by an energetic welcoming committee: little nuthatches that flitted about hyperactively—we almost had to duck to avoid them. They also liked to land on the tires of our car and on the windshield, making us afraid we were going to squish one of them when we drove away. This campground is popular not only with the nuthatches—off highway vehicle (OHV) owners like it here, too, so it might get noisy.

**Note:** Staying at this campground is the right price—free!

**Words of Warning:** There is no piped water so bring your own. No dumpsters are available either, so expect to pack out your garbage.

**What's It Near?**

• The hike to Glass Creek Meadow (4 to 6 miles round trip). A hike away from the crowds with lots of wildflowers in June and early July.

• Two of the closest hikes in the Mammoth Lakes area to this campground are Sherwin Lakes (4.6 miles round trip) and Valentine Lake (9.6 miles round trip)—trailheads are near Sherwin Creek Campground. The ¼ mile one-way hike to Inyo Craters is also nearby on the Mammoth Scenic Loop.

• Obsidian Dome is a short drive away. From the campground, return to Obsidian Dome Road (Forest Service Road 2S10), turn right, and drive about 0.6 miles to Obsidian Dome where you can take an easy stroll up a gated road to the old pumice quarry at the top of the dome.

• Fishing in Glass Creek and Deadman Creek for rainbow and brook trout.

• OHV travel on many of the dirt roads in the area.

**Elevation:** 8,400 feet

**Toilets:** Vault

**Verizon Cell Service?** Yes

**Takes Reservations?** No. First-come, first-served.

**Number of Campsites:** 20

**Bear Boxes?** No

# Campsites with the Most Privacy

**#4 Privacy Rating: B+**
**Reservable?** No. First-come, first-served.

Off by itself, #4 is a lot more private compared to many of the sites in this understory-less campground. No other sites exist behind this one and there are no nearby sites to the left. There's a neighbor to the right, but that site is about 60 feet away. Across the street, the nearest neighbor is down the road. Like all the sites in this campground, #4 is visible from the campground road, but it's in a forest of widely spaced towering pines so it doesn't feel too exposed.

**#12 Privacy Rating: B+**
**Reservable?** No. First-come, first-served.

Three massive pines stand guard over the entrance to this forested campsite. You can see your neighbor to the right, but pines intervene between the two sites, which are spaced far enough apart not to feel intrusive. No other campsites are to the immediate left, although #12 is on a loop and there are a couple other campsites on the far side of the loop. Even so, #12 is pushed far enough back from the road that it keeps its distance from its across-the-way neighbors. Behind the site, the view is of the pines and nothing else.

**#13 Privacy Rating: A-**
**Reservable?** No. First-come, first-served.

Despite its location squeezed between two loops of the campground road, #13 is tucked back far enough that any cars driving by won't be too disruptive. This spacious site seems like it's in a world of its own despite the fact it does have a couple of neighbors. A campsite sits across the street but it's a good distance from #13. The space on the right is also far enough away with plenty of pines in between. A massive pine towers over the picnic table.

## Glass Creek Campground

**Directions:** From Mammoth Lakes, take Highway 395 north and go 8.4 miles. Turn left on Glass Creek Road and travel 0.3 miles to a road on the right. Turn right and drive 0.2 miles to campground.

**What's It Like?**

It's in a pleasant location, nudged up against Glass Creek. Some of the campsites are at water's edge while others are under the pines or in a sagebrush meadow. However, nearly all the campsites are jammed together. We did find one beauty of a campsite here, though (see campsites with privacy description below). This is another campground that's popular with OHV drivers, so be aware it might get noisy.

**Note:** This campground is free, although donations are welcome.

**Words of Warning**: There is no drinking water. Bring plenty of water. And there's no dumpster here so expect to pack out your trash. Plus, there are no bear boxes here.

**What's It Near?**

• The hike to Glass Creek Meadow (4 to 6 miles round trip). A hike away from the crowds with lots of wildflowers in June and early July.

• Two of the closest hikes in the Mammoth Lakes area to this campground are Sherwin Lakes (4.6 miles round trip) and Valentine Lake (9.6 miles round trip) — trailheads are near Sherwin Creek Campground. The ¼ mile one-way hike to Inyo Craters is also nearby on the Mammoth Scenic Loop.

• Obsidian Dome is a short drive away. Return to Highway 395, turn left (North), and then turn left again on Obsidian Dome Road (Forest Service Road 2S10). Drive 1.5 miles to Obsidian Dome where you can take an easy stroll up a gated road to the old pumice quarry at the top of the dome.

• Fishing in Glass Creek and Deadman Creek for rainbow and brook trout.

• OHV travel on many of the dirt roads in the area.

**Elevation:** 7,600 feet

**Toilets:** Vault

**Verizon Cell Service?** 1 bar.

**Number of Campsites:** 50

**Takes Reservations?** No. First-come, first-served.

**Bear Boxes?** No.

### Campsite with the Most Privacy

**#43 Privacy Rating: A+**
**Reservable?** No. First-come, first-served.

This site was a pleasant surprise compared to the other ones

in the campground. Unlike all the other campsites, which are squished together, #43 is spacious and located far away from other campers. No nearby neighbors are visible on any side. Lots of pines provide plenty of shade and pine needles carpet the ground. Behind the campsite is a sagebrush meadow. Its only flaw: the bathroom is close to an 1/8 mile hike away.

## Lower Deadman Campground

**Directions:** From Mammoth Lakes, travel north on Highway 395 for about 8 miles and turn left (west) on the dirt Deadman Creek Road. At an intersection 1.2 miles in, veer left on Deadman Creek Road. The campground is about 0.4 mile farther on the left.

**What's It Like?**

In a shady, forested setting under lodgepole and Jeffrey pines, Lower Deadman Campground sits near Deadman Creek—although not many spaces are near the water's edge. There's also not a lot of privacy here. But we did find one campsite that had a lot going for it. (See campsites with the most privacy description below.) This campground is another one that attracts OHV enthusiasts, so don't be surprised if you hear the rumble of an off road vehicle engine or two while you're staying here.

**Note:** This campground is free.

**Words of Warning**: There is no drinking water in this campground. Bring plenty of water. And expect to lug out your trash, since there are no dumpsters. Plus, there are no bear boxes here.

### What's It Near?

• The hike to Glass Creek Meadow (4 to 6 miles round trip). A hike away from the crowds with lots of wildflowers in June and early July.

• Two of the closest hikes in the Mammoth Lakes area to this campground are Sherwin Lakes (4.6 miles round trip) and Valentine Lake (9.6 miles round trip)—trailheads are near Sherwin Creek Campground. The ¼ mile one-way hike to Inyo Craters is also nearby on the Mammoth Scenic Loop.

• Obsidian Dome is a short drive away. Return to Highway 395, turn left (North), and then turn left again on Obsidian Dome Road (Forest Service Road 2S10). Drive 1.5 miles to Obsidian Dome where you can take an easy stroll up a gated road to the old pumice quarry at the top of the dome.

• Fishing in Glass Creek and Deadman Creek for rainbow and brook trout.

• OHV travel on many of the dirt roads in the area.

**Elevation:** 7,800 feet

**Toilets:** Vault

**Verizon Cell Service?** 1 bar

**Takes Reservations?** No. First-come, first-served.

**Number of Campsites:** 11

**Bear Boxes?** No.

## Campsite with the Most Privacy

**#9 Privacy Rating: B-**
**Reservable?** No. First-come, first-served.

This campsite does have some flaws, but it's by far the best site in the campground and has some advantages, too. It's an elongated site stretched out along the left end of a cul de sac. Its biggest flaw is that it's really close to the campground road and despite all the pines towering over the campsite, it's fairly well exposed due to the lack of understory. But if you have a trailer, your parked vehicle will block your campsite from view of the road and from the gaze of any across-the-street neighbor. Plus, since #9 is on the cul de sac, the only people who have a reason to drive past your site are the people camped on the other side of the cul de sac and anyone searching for a camp space, so you probably won't get a lot of people driving past your spot. There's a campsite to the left, but it's at least 24 feet away and the trunks of some tall conifers stand in between.

On the plus side, the stream meanders past the right of this campsite, with grassy banks and willows adding a touch of tranquility. A small pine-covered hill serves as the backdrop to #9, so you'll have no neighbors there, either. This forested spot also has lots of shade.

## Upper Deadman Campground

**Directions:** From Mammoth Lakes, travel north on Highway 395 for about 8 miles and turn left (west) on the dirt Deadman Creek Road. At an intersection 1.2 miles in, veer left on Deadman Creek Road. The campground is about 0.6 mile farther on the left.

**What's It Like?**

Even though it's in a forested setting, Upper Deadman Campground feels slightly more open than its neighbor down the road, with a bit more sunlight spilling through the trees. The spaces here are close together, but we did find two campsites worthy of inclusion in this book. OHV enthusiasts use Upper Deadman as a base camp, so this is another campground where you might have to put up with the rumble of engines.

**Words of Warning:** There is no drinking water in this campground. Bring plenty of water. And expect to have to lug out your trash. Plus, there are no bear boxes here.

**Note:** This campground is free, although donations are welcome.

**What's It Near?**

• The hike to Glass Creek Meadow (4 to 6 miles round trip). A hike away from the crowds with lots of wildflowers in June and early July.

• Two of the closest hikes in the Mammoth Lakes area to this campground are Sherwin Lakes (4.6 miles round trip) and Valentine Lake (9.6 miles round trip) — trailheads are near Sherwin Creek Campground. The ¼ mile one-way hike to Inyo Craters is also nearby on the Mammoth Scenic Loop.

• Obsidian Dome is a short drive away. Turn left (north) on Highway 395, then take another left on Obsidian Dome Road (Forest Service Road 2S10), and drive 1.5 miles to Obsidian Dome where you can take an easy stroll up a gated road to the old pumice quarry at the top of the dome.

• Fishing in Glass Creek and Deadman Creek for rainbow and brook trout.

• OHV travel on many of the dirt roads in the area.

**Elevation:** 7,800 feet

**Toilets:** Vault

**Verizon Cell Service?** 1 bar

**Takes Reservations?** No. First-come, first-served.

**Number of Campsites:** 19

**Bear Boxes?** No

### Campsites with the Most Privacy

**#15 Privacy Rating: C+**
**Reservable?** No. First-come, first-served.

This was a hard spot to rate. For many reasons, it should be a

B- spot. On the right is a forest of pines and willows. Behind the site, widely spaced evergreens march off into the distance. Another site sits across the campground road, but the two sites are spaced far apart from each other and your parked car should hide part of the view of that space. The only reason we marked it down to a C+ is because there's a neighbor 20 feet away to the left and without much understory, they are really visible. But, some tall, thick-trunked pines between the two spots save the privacy day to a certain extent. If the space to the left was even 15 more feet away, #15 would have been a B campsite. Yet, #15 outshines most of the other spaces, which are jammed too close together.

**#18 Privacy Rating: B-**
**Reservable?** No. First-come, first-served.

This forested campsite is just slightly more private than #15, because #18 has no immediate neighbors across the campground road. Behind and to the left, there are no other campsites, either. The biggest threat to your privacy is the space to the right. Since #18 sits atop a little hill, it's looking down on its only neighbor. A smattering of pines filters out some of the view, but you're on display, especially without any understory. Still, this site is the best in the campground.

## Big Springs Campground

**Directions:** This campground is on the opposite side of Highway 395 from Glass Creek, Hartley Springs, and Upper and Lower Deadman Campgrounds—to the east of the highway instead of the west. From Mammoth Lakes, drive north on Highway 395 for 7.3 miles. Turn right on Owens River Road and travel 2.1 miles to campground on the left.

**What's It Like?**

Under a canopy of pines along the shore of Deadman Creek, Big Springs Campground is a collection of camp spaces that are mostly too close together for any privacy. About half of the spaces are farther away from the creek while the other half are closer to the water. We did find two campsites that were a pleasant change of pace from the rest. An OHV staging area is immediately next to the campground so this is a popular choice for off highway vehicle enthusiasts.

**Words of Warning**: There is no drinking water in this campground. Bring plenty of water. And expect to have to lug out your trash.

**Note:** This campground is free, although donations are welcome.

**What's It Near?**

• Follow Owens River Road past the campground where the road turns into dirt. Turn right at Forest Service Road 3S44, which will take you to the hot springs and geysers of Hot Creek Geological Site. After the hot springs, you'll pass the Hot Creek Fish Hatchery, which is open for tours, weather permitting, and you'll end up back on Highway 395.

• The hike to Glass Creek Meadow (4 to 6 miles round trip). A hike away from the crowds with lots of wildflowers in June and early July.

• Two of the closest hikes in the Mammoth Lakes area to this campground are Sherwin Lakes (4.6 miles round trip) and Valentine Lake (9.6 miles round trip)—trailheads are near Sherwin Creek Campground. The ¼ mile one-way hike to Inyo Craters is also nearby on the Mammoth Scenic Loop.

• Obsidian Dome is a short drive away. Turn left (north) on Highway 395, then take another left on Obsidian Dome Road (Forest Service Road 2S10), and drive 1.5 miles to Obsidian Dome where you can take an easy stroll up a gated road to the old pumice quarry at the top of the dome.

• Fishing in Glass Creek and Deadman Creek for rainbow and brook trout.

• OHV travel on many of the dirt roads in the area.

**Elevation:** 7,300 feet

**Toilets:** Vault

**Verizon Cell Service?** 1 bar

**Takes Reservations?** No. First-come, first-served.

**Number of Campsites:** 26 sites

**Bear Boxes?** Yes.

# Campsites with the Most Privacy

**#8 Privacy Rating: B-**
**Reservable?** No. First-come, first-served.

The good news? Unlike most of the other sites in the campground, #8 is far from its neighbors. The bad news? It's up on a hill, so some people might feel like they're on display. When you look behind you or to the right, all you see is a never-ending forest of pines, which makes up for the view of other campsites when you look down the hill to the left. Your nearest neighbor is actually across the campground road, but since #8 is tucked back quite a ways, unless they're noisy you probably won't notice they're there. The bathrooms sit at the entrance to #8 at the end of the site's long driveway.

**#19 Privacy Rating: B-**
**Reservable?** No. First-come, first-served.

The pine trees look like they're gathering around the picnic table for dinner at site #19. This spot backs up against a conifer-covered hill. If you sit at the picnic table facing the hill, you won't even know there are any other spaces nearby. However, if you turn to the left, you'll see another site about

18 feet away. Depending on the size of your parked vehicle, it might do a good job of sheltering you from that neighbor's view. To the right, there's also another site, but because #19 is farther back and its neighbor to the right is closer to the road, it doesn't feel like there's a neighbor in that direction at all. Deadman Creek is across the road and you can hear it singing a soft melody.

# MAMMOTH LAKES

## New Shady Rest Campground

**Directions:** Travel on Highway 395 to State Route 203. Drive west on 203 for 2.8 miles then turn right on Old Sawmill Road. Drive 0.1 mile to the campground on the right.

### What's It Like?

We couldn't warm up to New Shady Rest. It's in a forest of Jeffrey pines, but there is no understory and many of the camp spaces are close together, so on a busy weekend it might seem more like an RV city in the pines. A ranger also told us that because there's no separation between a housing development and this campground, a lot of the locals cut through here to walk their dogs. It does have the advantage (along with Old Shady Rest) of being the closest campground in the Mammoth Lakes area to the restaurants in the Town of Mammoth Lakes and The Village at Mammoth.

### What's It Near?

• The town of Mammoth Lakes and the Mammoth Lakes Visitor Center are within walking distance of the campground.

• The Village at Mammoth with shops and restaurants is a short drive away.

• A great place to dine at The Village is Campo Mammoth, owned by acclaimed chef Mark Estee and serving wood-fired Neapolitan pizzas, pastas, and handcrafted salumi. Estee uses only the best organic and seasonal ingredients, locally sourced when possible. While waiting for your food, compete with family and friends in a game of bocce ball on the restaurant's terrace.

• Another can't-go-wrong restaurant choice is Toomey's in The Village at Mammoth. It's owned by Matt Toomey, who for 16 years was the chef at Whoa Nellie Deli (the "gourmet" gas station) in Lee Vining. Try the Coconut Mascarpone Pancake or Smoked Trout Bagel for breakfast or the Seafood Jambalaya, Baby Back Ribs, or New Zealand Elk Ranch Chop for lunch or dinner. Top it off with Bananas Foster for dessert.

• Looney Beans is a good place to go for a cup of coffee or tea, smoothies, and pastries and to check your email. It's in the same shopping center as Rite-Aid.

• Hikes: Sherwin Lakes (4.6 miles round trip) and Valentine Lake (9.6 miles round trip) — trailheads are near Sherwin Creek Campground. Crystal Lake (5 miles round trip), Mammoth Crest Trail (6 miles round trip), Minaret Vista Trail (3 miles round trip), Panorama Dome (1 mile round trip), Duck Pass (12 miles round trip).

• Let the Mammoth Mountain Scenic Gondola carry you up to 11,053 feet with wonderful views of the Minarets along the way. There's an interpretative center at the summit. Fat tire fans can load their bikes on to the gondola and ride down from the top of the mountain.

• Conquer the mountain bike trails at the Mammoth Mountain Bike Park.

• Fishing for rainbow, brook, or brown trout in Lake Mary, Lake George, and Twin Lakes as well as nearby streams.

• Boating on Lake Mary, Lake George, and Twin Lakes.

• Golfing at Sierra Star.

• Horseback riding through Mammoth Lakes Pack Outfit.

**Elevation:** 7,800 feet

**Toilets:** Flush

**Verizon Cell Service?** Yes

**Takes Reservations?** Yes. Visit **www.recreation.gov** for reservations. Some campsites are first-come, first-served.

**Number of Campsites:** 93

**Bear Boxes?** Yes

### Campsites with the Most Privacy

None.

### Old Shady Rest Campground

**Directions:** In Mammoth Lakes, at the intersection of State Route 203 and Sawmill Cutoff, follow Sawmill Cutoff north 0.3 miles to the campground on the left.

**What's It Like?**

This wasn't our favorite campground, but it's better than New Shady Rest if you have your heart set on camping near civilization. The one exception is if you have a large RV: it's easier for larger vehicles to maneuver in New Shady Rest. The spaces at Old Shady Rest were farther apart, and we did find one space that fit our privacy qualifications (see below). The spaces sit in a peaceful Jeffrey pine forest, and like New Shady Rest, there's no understory. Be warned: on a busy weekend in this campground, it might seem like the city has followed you to the mountains. And even though there's a tall fence dividing the campground from the houses on one side of it, windows of homes peer down at some of the camp spaces.

## What's It Near?

• The town of Mammoth Lakes and the Mammoth Lakes Visitor Center is within walking distance of the campground.

• The Village at Mammoth with shops and restaurants is a short drive away.

• A great place to dine at The Village is Campo Mammoth, owned by acclaimed chef Mark Estee and serving wood-fired Neapolitan pizzas, pastas, and handcrafted salumi. Estee uses only the best organic and seasonal ingredients, locally sourced when possible. While waiting for your food, compete with family and friends in a game of bocce ball on the restaurant's terrace.

• Another can't-go-wrong restaurant choice is Toomey's in The Village at Mammoth. It's owned by Matt Toomey, who for 16 years was the chef at Whoa Nellie Deli (the "gourmet" gas station) in Lee Vining. Try the Coconut Mascarpone Pancake or Smoked Trout Bagel for breakfast or the Seafood Jambalaya, Baby Back Ribs, or New Zealand Elk Ranch Chop for lunch or dinner. Top it off with Bananas Foster for dessert.

• Looney Beans is a good place to go for a cup of coffee or tea, smoothies, and pastries and to check your email. It's in the same shopping center as Rite-Aid.

• Hikes: Sherwin Lakes (4.6 miles round trip) and Valentine Lake (9.6 miles round trip)—trailheads are near Sherwin Creek Campground. Crystal Lake (5 miles round trip), Mammoth Crest Trail (6 miles round trip), Minaret Vista Trail (3 miles round trip), Panorama Dome (1 mile round trip), Duck Pass (12 miles round trip).

• Let the Mammoth Mountain Scenic Gondola carry you up to 11,053 feet with wonderful views of the Minarets along the way. There's an interpretative center at the summit. Fat tire fans can load their bikes on to the gondola and ride down from the top of the mountain.

• Conquer the mountain bike trails at the Mammoth Mountain Bike Park.

• Fishing for rainbow, brook, or brown trout in Lake Mary, Lake George, and Twin Lakes as well as nearby streams.

• Golfing at Sierra Star.

• Horseback riding through Mammoth Lakes Pack Outfit.

**Elevation:** 7,800 feet

**Toilets:** Flush

**Verizon Cell Service?** Yes

**Takes Reservations?** Yes. Visit **www.recreation.gov** for reservations. Some first-come, first-served sites are available.

**Number of Campsites:** 47

**Bear Boxes?** Yes

### Campsite with the Most Privacy

**#20 Privacy Rating: B-**
**Reservable?** Yes. Visit **www.recreation.gov** for reservations.

This campsite isn't perfect. But compared to the rest of the sites in Old Shady Rest, it deserves a mention. Pines stretch off into the distance behind the site and pine needles blanket the ground everywhere. The neighbor on the right side is far away (about 40 feet) and pines filter the view, although without any understory you'll still see those neighbors. Same with the neighbor on the left. And because you're tucked back from the campground road, the neighbor across the street doesn't interfere with the privacy of this site. There's also a nice spot to pitch a tent.

## Sherwin Creek Campground

**Directions:** There are two ways to reach this campground:

1) From the intersection of Stare Route 203 and Highway 395, drive south 1.3 miles on Highway 395. Turn right on Sherwin Creek Road and drive 3.5 miles on the dirt road to the campground on the right.

2) From Highway 395, travel west on State Route 203 to Mammoth Lakes. Turn left on Old Mammoth Road at the first traffic light. Head south for 0.9 miles then turn left on Sherwin Creek Road and drive 1.5 miles to the campground.

**What's It Like?**

A large campground spread out under the Jeffrey pines and aspens with Sherwin Creek running alongside it, Sherwin Creek Campground is a combination of quiet camp spaces and sites that are in the middle of a hub of activity. A lot of the campsites here are really close together. In certain parts of the campground there is more understory intervening between campsites. In other parts, the understory is lacking. You can find a campsite with privacy here, but you have to really look for them. Read our description below to discover the best campsites.

**What's It Near?**

• The town of Mammoth Lakes and the Mammoth Lakes Visitor Center are a short drive from the campground.

• The Village at Mammoth with shops and restaurants is a short drive away.

• A great place to dine at The Village is Campo Mammoth, owned by acclaimed chef Mark Estee and serving wood-fired Neapolitan pizzas, pastas, and handcrafted salumi. Estee uses only the best organic and seasonal ingredients, locally sourced when possible. While waiting for your food, compete with family and friends in a game of bocce ball on the restaurant's terrace.

• Another can't-go-wrong restaurant choice is Toomey's in The Village at Mammoth. It's owned by Matt Toomey, who for 16 years was the chef at Whoa Nellie Deli (the "gourmet" gas station) in Lee Vining. Try the Coconut Mascarpone Pancake or Smoked Trout Bagel for breakfast or the Seafood Jambalaya, Baby Back Ribs, or New Zealand Elk Ranch Chop for lunch or dinner. Top it off with Bananas Foster for dessert.

• Looney Beans is a good place to go for a cup of coffee or tea, smoothies, and pastries and to check your email. It's in the same shopping center as Rite-Aid.

• Hikes: Sherwin Lakes (4.6 miles round trip) and Valentine Lake (9.6 miles round trip) — trailheads are near Sherwin Creek Campground. Crystal Lake (5 miles round trip), Mammoth Crest Trail (6 miles round trip), Minaret Vista Trail (3 miles round trip), Panorama Dome (1 mile round trip), Duck Pass (12 miles round trip).

• Let the Mammoth Mountain Scenic Gondola carry you up to 11,053 feet with wonderful views of the Minarets along the way. There's an interpretative center at the summit. Fat tire fans can load their bikes on to the gondola and ride down from the top of the mountain.

• Conquer the mountain bike trails at the Mammoth Mountain Bike Park.

• Fishing for rainbow, brook, or brown trout in Lake Mary, Lake George, and Twin Lakes as well as nearby streams.

• Boating on Lake Mary, Lake George, and Twin Lakes.

• Golfing at Sierra Star.

• Horseback riding through Mammoth Lakes Pack Outfit.

**Elevation:** 7,600 feet

**Toilets:** Vault

**Verizon Cell Service?** Yes

**Takes Reservations?** Yes. Visit **www.recreation.gov** for reservations. Some sites are first-come, first-served.

**Number of Campsites:** 85

**Bear Boxes?** Yes

### Campsites with the Most Privacy

**#10 Privacy Rating: A+**
**Reservable?** Yes. Visit **www.recreation.gov** for reservations.

To reach this walk-in site you cross two bridges over small streams. We estimated it's a 120-foot walk from the parking area and the bathrooms to the campsite. After taking this long trek, you're rewarded with a shady, peaceful spot surrounded by pines, aspens, and other greenery. There are no neighbors on three sides. One spot sits to the right, but it's more to the front whereas #10 is farther back in the woods so that it doesn't feel like there's someone right next to you. We visited in fall, when the vegetation between the two campsites had lost leaves, but it looks like your neighbor is either mostly or completely hidden behind greenery.

**#22 Privacy Rating: A+**
**Reservable?** Yes. Visit **www.recreation.gov** for reservations.

A spacious site on a forested cul de sac, #22 sits by itself with no neighbors visible on any side. The site is sandwiched between two hills. Behind, pine trees are visible as far as you can see. The spot also boasts plenty of shade. Definitely one of the best spots in the campground for privacy.

**#36 Privacy Rating: B-**
**Reservable?** Yes. Visit **www.recreation.gov** for reservations.

Patrick and I disagreed about whether to include this campsite. He didn't like it. His biggest complaint was that it's located at the intersection of two campground roads and seemed really exposed. However, if all the other sites we mention for this campground are reserved and if you really want to stay at Sherwin Creek, I believe this spot is a good alternative. Why? It has no neighbors visible to the left or behind it and it's back far enough from the spaces across the street that those neighbors don't feel intrusive. Pines provide some shade, although the sun sneaks through, too.

**#49 Privacy Rating: A**
**Reservable?** Yes. Visit **www.recreation.gov** for reservations.

With only one neighbor—a space across the campground road—#49 has a fair cushion of privacy. A hill on the left and right blocks the view of the campground in those directions, adding solitude. Recreation.gov says this is a streamside site, but to reach Sherwin Creek you must stroll down a path behind the campsite — the creek isn't right next to the site. Still, it's ideally located for an angler or anyone who likes to dip their toes in the water on a hot day. Plenty of pines grow in the site, but they open up in places to let sun through.

## #54 Privacy Rating: A
**Reservable?** Yes. Visit **www.recreation.gov** for reservations.

Thanks to the pull-through driveway and the private location of the spot, #54 is equally suited to RVs, trailers, and tent campers. A hill rises up in back of the site and curves around to the left and right, enclosing the site in privacy. #54 is set back from the road putting some good space between the site and the across-the-street neighbor. Your vehicle also will likely block out at least part of the view of the site across the road. It's a mostly shady spot, but gaps in the tall pines allow some sun to spill through. This is a spacious spot, with room for two tents.

## #75 Privacy Rating: B
**Reservable?** Yes. Visit **www.recreation.gov** for reservations.

Set against a backdrop of aspens, #75 rests in front of the creek — although you can't see the water from the campsite. Low-growing vegetation in #75 partially hides the neighboring spots on the left and right. It has no neighbors immediately across the campground road. The privacy of this spot is conditional upon who camps in the space on your right. If a 40-foot trailer pulls in there, #75 might feel less private. But if tent campers make their home in the neighboring spot, #75 will be quite tranquil.

## Upper and Lower Twin Lakes Campground

**Directions:** From the junction of Highway 395 and State Route 203, turn west on 203 toward the town of Mammoth Lakes. At the intersection of Main Street (State Route 203), Minaret Road, and Lake Mary Road stay straight on Lake Mary Road and travel 2.3 miles to the campground.

## What's It Like?

Not to be confused with the Twin Lakes area near Bridgeport, Twin Lakes Campground near Mammoth Lakes is divided into two sections. The upper section closest to the entrance is in a grove of lodgepole pines with no understory and lacks privacy, with spaces jammed together. To reach the really good spaces in the lower section, drive across a bridge that crosses a stream between the two peaceful, grassy lakes. Impressive cliffs tower over one of the lakes. The spaces in the lower section of the campground are under the lodgepole pines (less private) or in the willows (more private). Although there is a lot of commotion in some parts of the lower campground, you can carve out your slice of serenity here, in one of the more private spots.

## What's It Near?

• The town of Mammoth Lakes and the Mammoth Lakes Visitor Center are a short drive from the campground.

• The closest restaurant to the campground is Tamarack Lodge's The Lakefront Restaurant, on the shores of Twin Lakes. Fine dining featuring sustainable, locally sourced ingredients served in an intimate atmosphere (the restaurant has only ten tables). Listen to live piano on the weekends.

• The Village at Mammoth with shops and restaurants is a short drive away.

• A great place to dine at The Village is Campo Mammoth, owned by acclaimed chef Mark Estee and serving wood-fired

Neapolitan pizzas, pastas, and handcrafted salumi. Estee uses only the best organic and seasonal ingredients, locally sourced when possible. While waiting for your food, compete with family and friends in a game of bocce ball on the restaurant's terrace.

• Another can't-go-wrong restaurant choice is Toomey's in The Village at Mammoth. It's owned by Matt Toomey, who for 16 years was the chef at Whoa Nellie Deli (the "gourmet" gas station) in Lee Vining. Try the Coconut Mascarpone Pancake or Smoked Trout Bagel for breakfast or the Seafood Jambalaya, Baby Back Ribs, or New Zealand Elk Ranch Chop for lunch or dinner. Top it off with Bananas Foster for dessert.

• Looney Beans is a good place to go for a cup of coffee or tea, smoothies, and pastries and to check your email. It's in the same shopping center as Rite-Aid.

• Hikes: Sherwin Lakes (4.6 miles round trip) and Valentine Lake (9.6 miles round trip)—trailheads are near Sherwin Creek Campground. Crystal Lake (5 miles round trip), Mammoth Crest Trail (6 miles round trip), Minaret Vista Trail (3 miles round trip), Panorama Dome (1 mile round trip), Duck Pass (12 miles round trip).

• Let the Mammoth Mountain Scenic Gondola carry you up to 11,053 feet with wonderful views of the Minarets along the way. There's an interpretative center at the summit. Fat tire fans can load their bikes on to the gondola and ride down from the top of the mountain.

• Conquer the mountain bike trails at the Mammoth Mountain Bike Park.

• Fishing for rainbow, brook, or brown trout in Lake Mary, Lake George, and Twin Lakes as well as nearby streams.

- Boating on Lake Mary, Lake George, and Twin Lakes.

- Golfing at Sierra Star.

- Horseback riding through Mammoth Lakes Pack Outfit.

**Elevation:** 8,600 feet

**Toilets:** Flush

**Verizon Cell Service:** Limited

**Takes Reservations?** Yes. Visit **www.recreation.gov** for reservations. Some sites are first-come, first-served.

**Number of Campsites:** 95

**Bear Boxes?** Yes.

### Campsites with the Most Privacy

**#25 Privacy Rating: B+**
**Reservable?** Yes. Visit **www.recreation.gov** for reservations.

Willows embrace this tiny spot on three sides. It's a bit close to the campground road. But it still feels private since you can't see neighbors on any side. It's a lakeside spot, but the greenery interferes with your view of the water.

**#26 Privacy Rating: B+**
**Reservable?** Yes. Visit **www.recreation.gov** for reservations.

Similar to its neighbor #25, this site is surrounded on three sides by greenery and is close to the campground road. It, too, feels private thanks to the willows embracing it and the lack of neighbors directly across the campground road. Not a good spot for a trailer, but people who have a camper van, pickup with a camper shell, or a tent will all feel at home here.

### #28 Privacy Rating: B+
**Reservable?** Yes. Visit **www.recreation.gov** for reservations.

If this site were a person, I'd say it comes from the same gene pool as #25 and #26. But it has one advantage its nearby siblings don't have—through the greenery surrounding the campsite, there's a glimpse of a waterfall tumbling into Twin Lakes. There's also a view of a rusty hued mountain.

### #33 Privacy Rating: A+
**Reservable?** Yes. Visit **www.recreation.gov** for reservations.

Set back from the campground road and more spacious than sites #25, #26, and #28, site #33 has willows embracing it on three sides and pines towering above, providing welcome shade. There are no other spaces visible to the immediate left and there's no one visible to the immediate right or behind, either. The site is pushed back far enough from the road that the presence of the nearest neighbor across the street shouldn't bother you unless they were to get particularly rowdy. This is one of the best sites in the campground and more roomy than some of the other spaces with privacy.

### #64 Privacy Rating: A+
**Reservable?** Yes. Visit **www.recreation.gov** for reservations.

A beautiful spot, completely surrounded by willows, pines, and greenery. The only neighbor in sight is across the road, but thanks to the abundant vegetation surrounding #64 and the fact your neighbor across the street is far away, it feels like

you're in a world all your own here. As a bonus, you have view of a mountain ablaze with rust-colored rock.

**#68 Privacy Rating: B+**
**Reservable?** Yes. Visit **www.recreation.gov** for reservations.

Set in the willows, #68 is slightly less private than #64 because you can see the space to the right, although your car and the willows will eliminate some of the view of the neighbor. You can also see the campground road better from this campsite. But it's still a private spot, with no neighbors visible on the left or behind.

**#70 Privacy Rating: A+**
**Reservable?** Yes. Visit **www.recreation.gov** for reservations.

This site feels as if you've made camp in your own private mini-meadow, surrounded by willows and other greenery. It has no neighbors on the left, right, or across the street, and willows block the view of the space behind. Tall pines beyond the willows cast late afternoon shadows offering some welcome shade.

### Coldwater Campground

**Directions:** From the junction of Highway 395 and State Route 203, go west on State Route 203 toward Mammoth Lakes. At the intersection of Main St, (State Route 203), Minaret Road, and Lake Mary Road, go straight on Lake Mary Road 3.7 miles to campground sign.

## What's It Like?

Squeezed between Mammoth Creek and Coldwater Creek in a lodgepole pine forest, this campground has only a smattering of understory. Even so, some of the campsites are well-spaced from each other. The only reason we didn't include more campsites from this campground in this book is because many of the sites are too close to the campground road. Since the one-way road is narrow, being too close to the road often meant being too close to the neighbor across the street. However, we did find some sites we really liked (see descriptions below). One other characteristic of this campground: small, white boulders are flung around everywhere.

## What's It Near?

• The town of Mammoth Lakes, the Village at Mammoth with shops and restaurants, and the Mammoth Lakes Visitor Center are about a 15-minute drive from the campground.

• Tamarack Lodge's The Lakefront Restaurant, on the shores of nearby Twin Lakes, features fine dining with sustainable, locally sourced ingredients served in an intimate atmosphere (the restaurant has only ten tables). Listen to live piano on the weekends.

• A great place to dine at The Village is Campo Mammoth, owned by acclaimed chef Mark Estee and serving wood-fired Neapolitan pizzas, pastas, and handcrafted salumi. Estee uses only the best organic and seasonal ingredients, locally sourced when possible. While waiting for your food, compete with family and friends in a game of bocce ball on the restaurant's terrace.

• Another can't-go-wrong restaurant choice is Toomey's in The Village at Mammoth. It's owned by Matt Toomey, who for 16 years was the chef at Whoa Nellie Deli (the "gourmet" gas station) in Lee Vining. Try the Coconut Mascarpone Pancake or Smoked Trout Bagel for breakfast or the Seafood Jambalaya, Baby Back Ribs, or New Zealand Elk Ranch Chop for lunch or dinner. Top it off with Bananas Foster for dessert.

• Looney Beans is a good place to go for a cup of coffee or tea, smoothies, and pastries and to check your email. It's in the same shopping center as Rite-Aid.

• Hikes: Sherwin Lakes (4.6 miles round trip) and Valentine Lake (9.6 miles round trip)—trailheads are near Sherwin Creek Campground. Crystal Lake (5 miles round trip), Mammoth Crest Trail (6 miles round trip), Minaret Vista Trail (3 miles round trip), Panorama Dome (1 mile round trip), Duck Pass (12 miles round trip).

• Let the Mammoth Mountain Scenic Gondola carry you up to 11,053 feet with wonderful views of the Minarets along the way. There's an interpretative center at the summit. Fat tire fans can load their bikes on to the gondola and ride down from the top of the mountain.

• Conquer the mountain bike trails at the Mammoth Mountain Bike Park.

• Fishing for rainbow, brook, or brown trout in Lake Mary, Lake George, and Twin Lakes as well as nearby streams.

• Boating on Lake Mary, Lake George, and Twin Lakes.

• Golfing at Sierra Star.

• Horseback riding through Mammoth Lakes Pack Outfit.

**Elevation:** 8,900 feet

**Toilets:** Flush

**Verizon Cell Service?** No.

**Takes Reservations?** Yes. Visit **www.recreation.gov** for reservations. Some sites are first-come, first-served.

**Number of Campsites:** 77

**Bear Boxes?** Yes

### Campsites with the Most Privacy

**#3 Privacy Rating: B**
**Reservable?** Yes. Visit **www.recreation.gov** for reservations.

With no neighbors to the left or right and Coldwater Creek flowing behind it, we might have considered giving this a higher privacy rating but for one fact: it's a long, narrow site with everything from the tent area to the fire pit near the campground road. Its only neighbors are across the street, but because #3 is so close to the road, those neighbors don't seem all that far away. Still, its forested, streamside location make it a peaceful spot and the plentiful pines in the site mean its not right out in the open.

**#21 Privacy Rating: A+**
**Reservable?** Yes. Visit **www.recreation.gov** for reservations.

With no neighbors on any side and the bathrooms across the street, #21 sits quietly under the conifers. Mammoth Creek sings a soft tune behind the site. The tent pad is far away from the campground road, adding another element of privacy, but this is also a good choice for a small trailer. It's a well-shaded site, but the sun bathes the picnic table in late afternoon/evening light.

**#29 Privacy Rating: A+**
**Reservable?** Yes. Visit **www.recreation.gov** for reservations.

To reach this shady site under the conifers, you'll trek up a small hill, where the picnic table and fire pit are perched above the campground road. There are no neighbors to the immediate left or behind and the neighbor to the right is completely out of view behind a hill. #30 is right across the street, but both #29 and #30 are back from the road, so your across-the-street neighbor isn't breathing down your neck. You also have a filtered view of mountains through the trees.

**#30 Privacy Rating: A**
**Reservable?** No. First-come, first-served.

You'll carve out a slice of solitude in #30. It's a little farther back from the campground road compared to many other spots near the stream. You can pitch your tent among the pines, which filter the view of the tent from the campground road. Shaded by lots of evergreens, it has no neighbors on the left or right, and behind the site, your only neighbor is Coldwater Creek. #29 sits across the street, but #30 is back far enough from the campground road that it doesn't feel as if anyone else is camped nearby.

## Lake George Campground

**Directions:** From the junction of Highway 395 and State Route 203, go west on State Route 203 toward Mammoth Lakes. At the intersection of Main St, (State Route 203), Minaret Road, and Lake Mary Road, go straight on Lake Mary Road. When you reach Lake Mary, the road reaches an intersection where it splits and loops around the lake. To reach Lake George Campground you can go either to the left or right, but it will be shorter if you go to the right.

**What's It Like?**

This campground overlooks one of the most beautiful lakes in the Sierra, with Crystal Crag standing guard over water the color of thousands of liquefied sapphires and emeralds. That's the good news. The bad news is that if you want to camp overlooking the lake, you'll have to sacrifice privacy. The lakeview spaces are jammed together like alpine sardines. There was one site that met our privacy criteria, but it doesn't have a lake view (see campsite description below).

**What's It Near?**

• The town of Mammoth Lakes, the Village at Mammoth with shops and restaurants, and the Mammoth Lakes Visitor Center are about a 15-minute drive from the campground.

• Tamarack Lodge's The Lakefront Restaurant, on the shores of nearby Twin Lakes, features fine dining with sustainable, locally sourced ingredients served in an intimate atmosphere (the restaurant has only ten tables). Listen to live piano on the weekends.

• A great place to dine at The Village is Campo Mammoth, owned by acclaimed chef Mark Estee and serving wood-fired Neapolitan pizzas, pastas, and handcrafted salumi. Estee uses only the best organic and seasonal ingredients, locally sourced when possible. While waiting for your food, compete with family and friends in a game of bocce ball on the restaurant's terrace.

• Another can't-go-wrong restaurant choice is Toomey's in The Village at Mammoth. It's owned by Matt Toomey, who for 16 years was the chef at Whoa Nellie Deli (the "gourmet" gas station) in Lee Vining. Try the Coconut Mascarpone Pancake or Smoked Trout Bagel for breakfast or the Seafood Jambalaya, Baby Back Ribs, or New Zealand Elk Ranch Chop for lunch or dinner. Top it off with Bananas Foster for dessert.

• Looney Beans is a good place to go for a cup of coffee or tea, smoothies, and pastries and to check your email. It's in the same shopping center as Rite-Aid.

• Hikes: Sherwin Lakes (4.6 miles round trip) and Valentine Lake (9.6 miles round trip) — trailheads are near Sherwin Creek Campground. Crystal Lake (5 miles round trip), Mammoth Crest Trail (6 miles round trip), Minaret Vista Trail (3 miles round trip), Panorama Dome (1 mile round trip), Duck Pass (12 miles round trip).

• Let the Mammoth Mountain Scenic Gondola carry you up to 11,053 feet with wonderful views of the Minarets along the way. There's an interpretative center at the summit. Fat tire fans can load their bikes on to the gondola and ride down from the top of the mountain.

• Conquer the mountain bike trails at the Mammoth Mountain Bike Park.

• Fishing for rainbow, brook, or brown trout in Lake Mary, Lake George, and Twin Lakes as well as nearby streams.

• Boating on Lake Mary, Lake George, and Twin Lakes.

• Golfing at Sierra Star.

• Horseback riding through Mammoth Lakes Pack Outfit.

**Elevation:** 9,000 feet

**Toilets:** Flush

**Verizon Cell Service?** No.

**Takes Reservations?** No. First-come, first-served.

**Number of Campsites:** 16

**Bear Boxes?** Yes

### Campsite with the Most Privacy

**#16 Privacy Rating: A**
**Reservable?** No

This site is by no means the most aesthetically pleasing in the campground. It doesn't have the spectacular view of Lake George that many of the other sites have. But it's the only one with elbow room: no neighbors on the left or behind. You can see #15 to the right, but it's about 80 feet away. Your reward for giving up the view of Lake George is a filtered view of Lake Mary through the pines behind the site. It's a shady spot, with many thick-trunked pines towering above. To reach the space, you have to take a steep walk down a hill from the parking space.

## Lake Mary Campground

**Directions:** From the junction of Highway 395 and State Route 203, go west on State Route 203 toward Mammoth Lakes. At the intersection of Main St, (State Route 203), Minaret Road, and Lake Mary Road, go straight on Lake Mary Road. When you reach Lake Mary, the road reaches an intersection where it splits and loops around the lake. To reach Lake Mary Campground you can go either to the left or right, but it will be shorter if you go to the right.

**What's It Like?**

This campground is what Patrick calls condo camping, with spaces piled on top of each other. We could not find any spots with privacy here. A few walk-in campsites up a hill are at least set back from the parking area, but they're so close together with nothing in between that we couldn't include them in this book. Some of the campsites are perched above Lake Mary, with spectacular views, but they're also too close together.

**Words of Warning:** RVs over 32 feet not recommended.

**What's It Near?**

• The town of Mammoth Lakes, the Village at Mammoth with shops and restaurants, and the Mammoth Lakes Visitor Center are about a 15-minute drive from the campground.

• Tamarack Lodge's The Lakefront Restaurant, on the shores of nearby Twin Lakes, features fine dining with sustainable, locally sourced ingredients served in an intimate atmosphere (the restaurant has only ten tables). Listen to live piano on the weekends.

• A great place to dine at The Village is Campo Mammoth, owned by acclaimed chef Mark Estee and serving wood-fired Neapolitan pizzas, pastas, and handcrafted salumi. Estee uses only the best organic and seasonal ingredients, locally sourced when possible. While waiting for your food, compete with family and friends in a game of bocce ball on the restaurant's terrace.

• Another can't-go-wrong restaurant choice is Toomey's in The Village at Mammoth. It's owned by Matt Toomey, who for 16 years was the chef at Whoa Nellie Deli (the "gourmet" gas station) in Lee Vining. Try the Coconut Mascarpone Pancake or Smoked Trout Bagel for breakfast or the Seafood Jambalaya, Baby Back Ribs, or New Zealand Elk Ranch Chop for lunch or dinner. Top it off with Bananas Foster for dessert.

• Looney Beans is a good place to go for a cup of coffee or tea, smoothies, and pastries and to check your email. It's in the same shopping center as Rite-Aid.

• Hikes: Sherwin Lakes (4.6 miles round trip) and Valentine Lake (9.6 miles round trip) — trailheads are near Sherwin Creek Campground. Crystal Lake (5 miles round trip), Mammoth Crest Trail (6 miles round trip), Minaret Vista Trail (3 miles round trip), Panorama Dome (1 mile round trip), Duck Pass (12 miles round trip).

• Let the Mammoth Mountain Scenic Gondola carry you up to 11,053 feet with wonderful views of the Minarets along the way. There's an interpretative center at the summit. Fat tire fans can load their bikes on to the gondola and ride down from the top of the mountain.

• Conquer the mountain bike trails at the Mammoth Mountain Bike Park.

• Fishing for rainbow, brook, or brown trout in Lake Mary, Lake George, and Twin Lakes as well as nearby streams.

• Boating on Lake Mary, Lake George, and Twin Lakes.

• Golf at Sierra Star.

• Horseback riding through Mammoth Lakes Pack Outfit.

**Elevation:** 8,900 feet

**Toilets:** Flush

**Verizon Cell Service?** No.

**Takes Reservations?** Yes. Visit **www.recreation.gov** for reservations. Some sites are first-come, first-served.

**Number of Campsites:** 48

**Bear Boxes?** Yes

### Campsites with the Most Privacy

None

# RED'S MEADOW - DEVIL'S POSTPILE NATIONAL MONUMENT

**Directions:** At the intersection of Highway 395 and State Route 203, turn west on 203 and drive toward the town of Mammoth Lakes. Turn right on to Minaret Road (the second stoplight) and follow it up the mountain, past Mammoth Mountain's Main Lodge, to the Minaret Vista entrance station, where you will have to pay a fee. Continue driving past the entrance station towards Devil's Postpile National Monument. Look for the campground sign on the right.

**Words of Warning:** Past the entrance station, the road leading down into the valley is narrow and curvy and there are a lot of shuttle buses sharing the road with campers until the first Wednesday after Labor Day. Drive slowly and carefully.

**What's It Like?**

Upper Soda Springs sits on the banks of the Middle Fork of the San Joaquin River under a grove of lodgepole pines. The campsites near the stream are packed in together and with almost no understory not the best choice from a privacy perspective. The best sites for privacy are on a spur or pushed up against a granite wall on the edge of the campground (see our campsite descriptions below).

**What's It Near?**

• An easy 0.4 mile hike to Devil's Postpile National Monument. Trailhead is a short drive from the campground.

• Hikes to Rainbow Falls (easy 3 miles round trip from Red's Meadow, 5 miles round trip from the ranger station), Minaret Falls (2.8 miles round trip), Shadow Lake (7.8 miles round trip), Ediza Lake (13.4 miles round trip), the River Trail to Thousand Island Lake (14.6 miles round trip), which gets my vote as being one of the top ten most beautiful backcountry lakes in the Eastern Sierra, although I'm told that nearby Garnet Lake is just as stunning.

• Fishing in the San Joaquin River, a designated Wild Trout River, or in Sotcher or Starkweather Lakes.

• Horseback riding through Red's Meadow Pack Station.

• Grab breakfast, a burger, a sandwich, or daily dinner specials in the Mule House Café at Red's Meadow Resort. Top off your meal with a slice of homemade pie.

**Elevation:** 7,700 feet

**Toilets:** Vault

**Verizon Cell Service?** 1 bar

**Takes Reservations?** No. First-come, first-served.

**Number of Campsites:** 28

**Bear Boxes?** Yes

## Campsites with the Most Privacy

**#5 Privacy Rating: A+**
**Reservable?** No. First-come, first-served.

Located on a quiet spur road with only three spaces, site #5 rests under the pines. No nearby neighbors exist on any side, so you're surrounded by serenity. Behind the space, we

noticed a ditch that might be a seasonal miniature creek earlier in the year, but was bone dry when we looked at the site in September. If it is a creek, in early summer, this would be a sweet spot indeed.

## #6 Privacy Rating: A
**Reservable?** No. First-come, first-served.

This space is a little close to its only neighbor (#7), but it doesn't feel uncomfortable because of the way the two spots are positioned. #7 is to the left-front of #6, and #6 is pushed back a ways. A granite, glaciated hill rises up to the right of the space. Mother nature also conveniently placed a small hill behind #6, which conceals the rest of the campground stretched out below. To the immediate left, a big boulder adds some interest.

## #7 Privacy Rating: A
**Reservable?** No. First-come, first-served.

One of three campsites located on their own spur, #7 isn't as spacious as #6, but is just as tranquil. The tent area rests under a canopy of conifers. Your parked car or trailer will mostly hide from view your only neighbor (#6). The campground road runs behind and below the site, but thanks to a group of conifers and your location slightly above the road, you can barely see it.

## #24 Privacy Rating: B
**Reservable?** No. First-come, first-served.

This site is at the far end of the busiest part of the campground. But it's far back from the campground road, up against a peach-colored granite hill. A large log resting between this site and its neighbor to the right inserts a little bit more privacy between two spots that would normally be in full sight of each other. The neighboring site on the left is pushed forward more, closer to the campground road, so it feels as if there are no neighbors to the immediate left. Your parked car or trailer will block most of the view of the space across the street when you're sitting by the campfire or at the picnic table.

## #26 Privacy Rating: A-
**Reservable?** No. First-come, first-served.

This site is more sheltered from the commotion of the campground thanks to its location in a grove of lodgepole pines. A peach-colored granite hill to the right of the space ensures privacy on that side. Its only neighbor on the same side of the street is just barely visible to the left through a curtain of conifers. Another space is across the street, down the road just a little ways, but because #26 is pushed back from the road and it's located in the trees, you can barely see your across-the-street neighbor.

**Directions:** At the intersection of Highway 395 and State Route 203, turn west on 203 and drive toward the town of Mammoth Lakes. Turn right on to Minaret Road (the second stoplight) and follow it up the mountain, past Mammoth Mountain's Main Lodge, to the Minaret Vista entrance station, where you will have to pay a fee. Continue driving past the entrance station toward Devil's Postpile National Monument. Look for the campground sign on the right, past Upper Soda Springs Campground.

**Words of Warning:** Past the entrance station, the road leading down into the valley is narrow and curvy and there are a lot of shuttle buses sharing the road with campers until the first Wednesday after Labor Day. Drive slowly and carefully.

**What's It Like?**

With no understory and many spaces close together, we couldn't warm up to this campground because of its lack of privacy. The campground host had moved in to the only really private space (#17), which was off by itself away from all the other sites.

We'll check out this campground again sometime in the future to see if the campground ever plans to free up site #17, and if so, post it under the campground updates section on our website at www.ilovetheeasternsierra.com  But for now you're better off camping at one of the other campgrounds in the Devil's Postpile area.

**What's It Near?**

• An easy 0.4 mile hike to Devil's Postpile National Monument. Trailhead is a short drive from the campground.

• Hikes to Rainbow Falls (easy 3 miles round trip from Red's Meadow, 5 miles round trip from the ranger station), Minaret Falls (2.8 miles round trip), Shadow Lake (7.8 miles round trip), Ediza Lake (13.4 miles round trip), the River Trail to Thousand Island Lake (14.6 miles round trip), which gets my vote as being one of the top ten most beautiful backcountry lakes in the Eastern Sierra, although I'm told that nearby Garnet Lake is just as stunning.

• Fishing in the San Joaquin River, a designated Wild Trout River, or in Sotcher or Starkweather Lakes.

• Horseback riding through Red's Meadow Pack Station.

• Grab breakfast, a burger or a sandwich, or daily dinner specials in the Mule House Café at Red's Meadow Resort. Top off your meal with a slice of homemade pie.

**Elevation:** 7,700 feet

**Toilets:** Flush

**Verizon Cell Phone Service?** Limited.

**Takes Reservations?** No. First-come, first-served.

**Number of Campsites:** 17

**Bear Boxes?** Yes

### Campsites with the Most Privacy

None.

## Minaret Falls Campground

**Directions:** At the intersection of Highway 395 and State Route 203, turn west on 203 and drive toward the town of Mammoth Lakes. Turn right on to Minaret Road (the second stoplight) and follow it up the mountain, past Mammoth Mountain's Main Lodge, to the Minaret Vista entrance station, where you will have to pay a fee. Continue driving past the entrance station toward Devil's Postpile National Monument. Look for the campground sign on the right, past Pumice Flat Campground.

**Words of Warning:** Past the entrance station, the road leading down into the valley is narrow and curvy and there are a lot of shuttle buses sharing the road with campers until the first Wednesday after Labor Day. Drive slowly and carefully.

**What's It Like?**

Much of this campground is settled under lodgepole pines alongside a particularly pretty stretch of the San Joaquin River where it takes its time passing through a willow-dotted meadow. However, many of the spaces at Minaret Falls don't boast a lot of privacy. They're squeezed close together. But we did find three spaces we liked. I have read descriptions that you can see Minaret Falls from this campground, but we never saw a glimpse of it.

**What's It Near?**

• An easy 0.4 mile hike to Devil's Postpile National Monument. Trailhead is a short drive from the campground.

• Hikes to Rainbow Falls (easy 3 miles round trip from Red's Meadow, 5 miles round trip from the ranger station), Minaret

Falls (2.8 miles round trip), Shadow Lake (7.8 miles round trip), Ediza Lake (13.4 miles round trip), the River Trail to Thousand Island Lake (14.6 miles round trip), which gets my vote as being one of the top ten most beautiful backcountry lakes in the Eastern Sierra, although I'm told that nearby Garnet Lake is just as stunning.

• Fishing in the San Joaquin River, a designated Wild Trout River, or in Sotcher or Starkweather Lakes.

• Horseback riding through Red's Meadow Pack Station.

• Grab breakfast, a burger or a sandwich, or daily dinner specials in the Mule House Café at Red's Meadow Resort. Top off your meal with a slice of homemade pie.

**Elevation:** 7,600 feet

**Toilets:** Vault

**Verizon Cell Service?** Yes

**Takes Reservations?** No. First-come, first-served.

**Number of Campsites:** 23

**Bear Boxes?** Yes

### Campsites with the Most Privacy

**#11 Privacy Rating: B+**
**Reservable?** No. First-come, first-served.

Unlike a lot of the spaces in this campground, this one is spaced far enough from its neighbors to meet our requirements for inclusion in this book. The campsite to the right is about 60 feet away and the bathroom is to the left.

Across the campground road, the San Joaquin River tiptoes its way through a willow-studded meadow. Because the conifers shading the site are widely spaced and there's little understory, #11 does have an open feel to it, which is why we gave it a B+ rating, but your neighbors won't be breathing down your neck and the view of the river adds a splash of personality to what would otherwise be an ordinary site.

### #13 Privacy Rating: B-
**Reservable?** No. First-come, first-served.

This shady site is by no means perfect from a privacy perspective, but it's one of the best in the campground. Conifers partially filter the view of the space to the right and you'll have no neighbors on your left. A small hill rises up behind #13. A camp space sits across the campground road, but it's just far enough away to feel non-intrusive.

### #23 Privacy Rating: A+
**Reservable?** No. First-come, first-served.

Punctuating the cul de sac at the end of the campground road, this campsite is a refreshing change of pace from the other close together spaces in the campground. Through the conifers on the left, you'll have a view of the San Joaquin River brushing up next to the site and the willows beyond the water. If there's anything better than a campsite with privacy, it's a campsite with privacy that's also next to a stream. Anglers can cast their lines without having to leave their site. The forest grows behind the campsite and to the right is a small hill. The closest neighbor resides at the far end of the cul de sac.

## Devil's Postpile National Park Service Campground

**Directions:** At the intersection of Highway 395 and State Route 203, turn west on 203 and drive toward the town of Mammoth Lakes. Turn right on to Minaret Road (the second stoplight) and follow it up the mountain, past Mammoth Mountain's Main Lodge, to the Minaret Vista entrance station, where you will have to pay a fee. Continue driving past the entrance station toward Devil's Postpile National Monument. Drive into Devil's Postpile National Monument. The campground will be on your right.

**Words of Warning:** Past the entrance station, the road leading down into the valley is narrow and curvy and there are a lot of shuttle buses sharing the road with campers until the first Wednesday after Labor Day. Drive slowly and carefully.

**What's It Like?**

As a whole this campground isn't the best option for anyone who likes privacy. Most of the spaces are squeezed together with no understory separating them, including the campsites that are located on the banks of the San Joaquin River. However, we did find a beautiful spot here where you'll have all the privacy you want (see campsite description below). And this *is* the closest campground to the trailhead to Devil's Postpile and Rainbow Falls, both natural attractions worth adding to your bucket list.

**What's It Near?**

• An easy 0.4 mile hike to Devil's Postpile National Monument. Trailhead is a short walk from the campground.

• Hikes to Rainbow Falls (easy 3 miles round trip from Red's Meadow, 5 miles round trip from the ranger station), Minaret Falls (2.8 miles round trip), Shadow Lake (7.8 miles round trip), Ediza Lake (13.4 miles round trip), the River Trail to Thousand Island Lake (14.6 miles round trip), which gets my vote as being one of the top ten most beautiful backcountry lakes in the Eastern Sierra, although I'm told that nearby Garnet Lake is just as stunning.

• Fishing in the San Joaquin River, a designated Wild Trout River, or in Sotcher or Starkweather Lakes.

• Horseback riding through Red's Meadow Pack Station.

• Grab breakfast, a burger or a sandwich, or daily dinner specials in the Mule House Café at Red's Meadow Resort. Top off your meal with a slice of homemade pie.

**Elevation:** 7,500 feet

**Toilets:** Flush

**Verizon Cell Service?** Yes

**Takes Reservations?** No. First-come, first-served.

**Number of Campsites:** 21

**Bear Boxes?** Yes

## Campsite with the Most Privacy

**#B3 Privacy Rating: A+**
**Reservable?** No. First-come, first-served.

You'll feel like king of the hill in this walk-in campsite. Perched on top of a hill overlooking the San Joaquin River, you're in a world all your own with no other nearby spaces in sight. A clear view of the sky means you'll see millions of stars at night. Despite the openness of the site, some conifers shade parts of it. It's a stone's throw to the river, meaning easy access for anglers and a peaceful chorus provided by Mother Nature's orchestra.

It is about a 42-foot walk up a steep hill from your car to the campsite, so come prepared with either a pull cart or expect to lug your stuff a good distance. The bathroom is a long walk from the space, but that's the price you pay for privacy. Overall, this site is a pleasant surprise in an otherwise crowded campground. To reach #B3, go left over the bridge to the B Loop.

## Red's Meadow Campground

**Directions:** At the intersection of Highway 395 and State Route 203, turn west on 203 and drive toward the town of Mammoth Lakes. Turn right on to Minaret Road (the second stoplight) and follow it up the mountain, past Mammoth Mountain's Main Lodge, to the Minaret Vista entrance station, where you will have to pay a fee. Continue driving past the entrance station toward Devil's Postpile National Monument. Drive straight past the turnout for the National Monument. Red's Meadow campground is on the left.

**Words of Warning:** Past the entrance station, the road leading down into the valley is narrow and curvy and there are a lot of shuttle buses sharing the road with campers until the first Wednesday after Labor Day. Drive slowly and carefully.

## What's It Like?

Of all the campgrounds near Devil's Postpile, this one has the largest selection of spaces with a lot of privacy. Some of the sites are located near a peaceful little stream, others are in a forest with widely spaced trees. The forest, willows, water birch, and grassy meadows in this campground all combine to create a very peaceful setting.

**Words of Warning**: Nearby Mammoth Mountain is a dormant volcano. This particular campground is subject to frequent earth tremors so don't be surprised if things shake, rattle, and roll while you're there.

## What's It Near?

• An easy 0.4 mile hike to Devil's Postpile National Monument. Trailhead is a short drive from the campground.

• Hikes to Rainbow Falls (easy 3 miles round trip from Red's Meadow, 5 miles round trip from the ranger station), Minaret Falls (2.8 miles round trip), Shadow Lake (7.8 miles round trip), Ediza Lake (13.4 miles round trip), the River Trail to Thousand Island Lake (14.6 miles round trip), which gets my vote as being one of the top ten most beautiful backcountry lakes in the Eastern Sierra, although I'm told that nearby Garnet Lake is just as stunning.

• Fishing in the San Joaquin River, a designated Wild Trout River, or in Sotcher or Starkweather Lakes.

• Horseback riding through Red's Meadow Pack Station.

• Grab breakfast, a burger or a sandwich, or daily dinner specials in the Mule House Café at Red's Meadow Resort. Top off your meal with a slice of homemade pie.

**Elevation:** 7,600 feet

**Toilets**: Flush

**Verizon Cell Service?** Yes

**Takes Reservations?** No. First-come, first-served.

**Number of Campsites:** 52

**Bear Boxes?** Yes

### Campsites with the Most Privacy

**#7 Privacy Rating: A**
**Reservable?** No. First-come, first-served.

Located immediately after the condo camping zone—what Patrick calls spaces squeezed too closely together—this site has a lot of charm. A small stream flows to the right of the space. Walls of greenery enclose the rear of the site with tall conifers bursting up into view beyond. More vegetation lines the far bank of the stream, creating a lot of privacy from that side as well. A path leads back through a garden of tall flowers to a private tent cave encircled by trees and bushes. No neighbors across the street add to the desirability of the site.

The only flaw? The neighbors on the left are very close, but greenery and trees partially filter your view of them. And with your tent pitched far away and out of view of the next door neighbors, this is still a very private spot. As an added bonus, #7 is close to the bathrooms.

**#13 Privacy Rating: A-**
**Reservable?** No. First-come, first-served.

This is a peaceful meadow site with a few well-spaced evergreens that provide shade. There are no sites to the left and only willows across the street. Through the willows to the right of the space you catch glimpses of your neighbor. But that site is far enough away so as not to feel intrusive.

**#39 Privacy Rating: A**
**Reservable?** No. First-come, first-served.

Fringed on the left and right by willows, this site looks out on a grassy meadow behind it. Beyond that some pines stand guard over a granite hill. Across the street is nothing but a grassy meadow and large pines. The tent area is on the edge of the meadow, and from there you can see the site to the right, but even with that slight intrusion on privacy #39 still has a peaceful feel to it.

**#40 Privacy Rating: B**
**Reservable?** No. First-come, first-served.

Another meadow-side campsite, #40 is peaceful but doesn't have as much privacy as #13 and #39. If the people staying in site #39 are tent campers, you'll be able to see their tent. The space to the right is clearly visible, although partially curtained off by bushes. Still, it's not a bad spot. There are no spaces behind, only willows and greenery. Conifers provide plenty of shade. To create more privacy from the neighbor on the right, you can pitch your tent closer to the meadow.

**#47 Privacy Rating: A**
**Reservable?** No. First-come, first-served.

A very spacious spot, #47 gets high marks for privacy and personality. A granite hill rises up behind the site and no neighbors are visible to the left or right. You can also hear a little stream gurgling its way through the willows and bushes behind and to the right of #47. Bushes screen out the site across the street, and #47 is pushed back from the campground road, ensuring you'll have plenty of space and your privacy, too.

**#48 Privacy Rating: A+**
**Reservable?** No. First-come, first-served.

This space has the most privacy in the campground, set back from the road in a peaceful natural amphitheater. A granite hill watches over it from behind. Water birch and willows line either side of the little stream flowing next to the campsite, and there's lots of shade thanks to a conifer canopy. No neighbors anywhere in sight here.

# CONVICT CANYON

# Convict Lake Campground

**Directions:** From Highway 395, about 4.5 miles south of Mammoth Lakes, turn west on Convict Lake Road (near the Mammoth Yosemite Airport). Travel 2 miles to the campground on the left.

## What's It Like?

Sunken down below Convict Lake Road, Convict Lake Campground has a large selection of private spaces nudged in between the willows and aspens. Convict Creek meanders past some of the campsites. Other spaces sit out in the sagebrush. Although you can't see Convict Lake from the campground, many campsites have views of 11,812-foot Laurel Mountain, with its swirls of multicolored rock, and 12,268-foot Mount Morrison, with its ancient dolomite and marble slopes. From the road, looking down into the campground, I would never have guessed there would be so many spaces with privacy here.

**Words of Warning:** In 2015, there will be road construction on the Convict Lake Road. Delays of 30 minutes or more are possible and limited access to day use areas and the trail around the east side of the lake. And you might hear road construction noise in the campground, especially during the week.

## What's It Near?

• Fishing for rainbow or brown trout in Convict Lake and Convict Creek.

• Hikes: Walk around Convict Lake (2 mile loop hike), Convict Lake Trail (6 miles round trip to where a tributary joins Convict Creek at a very dangerous ford best done late in the summer or in fall), Mildred Lake (10 miles round trip), Lake Dorothy (12 miles round trip). If you don't feel safe crossing the ford, the trailheads for Sherwin Lakes (4.6 miles round trip) and Valentine Lake (9.6 miles round trip) are a 15-minute drive away, north on Highway 395 to Sherwin Creek Road.

• Dining at The Restaurant at Convict Lake, a four-star establishment. While feasting on rack of lamb, beef wellington, grass fed beef steaks, fresh seafood, and pastas you might have a glimpse of a deer grazing outside the window. Patrick proposed to me here so we have fond memories of the restaurant. They also serve lunch under the aspens and a Sunday brunch or you can have appetizers and a drink in the lounge. Dress is casual.

**Elevation:** 7,600 feet

**Toilets:** Flush

**Verizon Cell Service?** Minimal.

**Takes Reservations?** Yes. Visit **www.recreation.gov** for reservations. First-come, first-served sites also are available.

**Number of Sites:** 85

**Bear Boxes?** Most, but not all, campsites have bear boxes.

### Campsites with the Most Privacy

**#7 Privacy Rating: A**
**Reservable?** No. First-come, first-served.

Featuring a nice view of the ribbons of color weaving their way over the face of Laurel Mountain, #7 sits on the edge of a large meadow. A glimpse of the space to the right is visible through the willows. There are no neighbors visible on the left. A few aspens behind the site partially filter the view of the meadow. Some campsites far across the meadow are visible, but they don't feel intrusive. Due to the site's placement, the neighbors across the street seem far away.

**#8 Privacy Rating: A-**
**Reservable?** Yes. Visit **www.recreation.gov** for reservations.

Suitable only for tents, #8 is perched slightly above the road in the sagebrush and rabbitbrush. To reach it, you climb a few stairs from the pull-through driveway up to the picnic table, fire pit, and tent pad. The site on the left is far enough away that you're not rubbing shoulders with the people staying there. Tall sagebrush, bushes, and grass between you and the neighbor on the left add more privacy. You can see the space to the right, but it doesn't feel intrusive and some of that campsite is in the aspens. Behind #8, the land rises up toward a barren hill. Aspens growing between the campsite and the road contribute to the private feel.

The amphitheater is near this site, so during campfire programs you might have nearby company for an hour or so. This is a good choice for anyone who likes the openness of high desert camping, with a great view of the stars at night as well as the mountains towering over Convict Lake.

**Words of Warning:** This site doesn't have a bear box.

**#9 Privacy Rating: A-**
**Reservable?** No. First-come, first-served.

#9 sits on the same side of the road as #7 but has a more open feel, since the willows and aspens surrounding it are more widely spaced. But it still has a good amount of privacy. The willows on the left are thick enough to block your view of the space on that side. The aspens partially hide the space on the right, too, although they don't obliterate the view completely. Unlike #7, which has a handful of aspens partially filtering the view of the meadow, this site is more open on that side, and therefore the RVs parked across the meadow seemed more visible, although at least 50 feet separate #9 from those distant sites. Like #7, this space also has a good view of Laurel Mountain, which has some of the most interesting and colorful geology of any mountain in the Eastern Sierra. The placement of #9 and the fact the site across the street is back behind a screen of aspens means you won't feel like the across-the-street neighbors are in your face.

## #11 Privacy Rating: A-
**Reservable?** Yes. Visit **www.recreation.gov** for reservations.

This tent only, sunny site is perched above the campground road in tall rabbitbrush, sagebrush, and grass. It's out in the open, but aspens in front of it and lining the pull-through driveway shelter the space from the road. A few stairs lead up to this site from the parking area. Since #11 is perched on a hill, there's an especially good view of Laurel Mountain. Aspens partially filter the view of the space on the right. The space on the left is fully visible, but it's at least 50 feet away and good-sized sagebrush and rabbitbrush intervene between the two sites. Behind #11 is nothing but a barren hill. If you like looking at the stars at night, this is a good choice.

## #14 Privacy Rating: A
**Reservable?** No. First-come, first-served.

There's not a lot of room in this cozy campsite, which is squeezed into the space alongside the paved driveway, but what it lacks in room it makes up for in privacy. Willows, aspens, and tall grass block the view of the site on the left. A neighbor sits close to the right, but aspens cancel out about 70 to 80 percent of your view of it. Aspens and willows grow to the rear of #14 and far beyond that Laurel Mountain with its colorful striations serves as a stunning backdrop. A slight disadvantage is the tent pad is a bit closer to the campground road than we like to see, but even so a line of aspens and tall grass understory between the tent pad and the road means that you won't feel exposed even if you can hear an occasional car or RV passing by.

**#16 Privacy Rating: A-**
**Reservable?** No. First-come, first-served.

Aspens gather around the picnic table, tent pad, and fire pit, shading the site and making it feel as if you're sitting in an outdoor room. The space to the right is close to your driveway, but a thick forest of willows hides about 80 or 90 percent of the view. Plus, your parked vehicle will help obscure your neighbor from sight. You can also see site #14 to the left, but the aspen forest in between does a good job of cancelling out much of the view. Behind the site, aspens merge with the meadow. You can see the picnic table from the campground road here, but the table's location in the aspens means you won't feel overly exposed.

## #17 Privacy Rating: B+
**Reservable?** Yes. Visit **www.recreation.gov** for reservations.

The willows lining the driveway make way for two sets of stairs leading up to this two-tier campsite. The first tier houses the fire pit, picnic table, and bear box. The second tier is the tent pad. We marked it down to a B+ because on the other side of the bathroom, which is to the immediate left of #17, is another campsite with a picnic table that's in clear view. Except for that one nearby campsite, the rest of #17 is surrounded in privacy. On the right, a thick hedge of willows conceals the view of any spaces on that side. Behind #17, aspens here and there add splashes of color to the sagebrush and rabbitbrush landscape. Over the tops of willows and tall grass, we could just barely see the roof of the RV parked across the street.

## #18 Privacy Rating: A+
**Reservable?** No. First-come, first-served.

The driveway for this campsite passes through an alleyway of willows, which do a good job of blocking the view of the neighboring campsites on the left and right. The neighboring sites are also a good distance away, adding to the serenity of #18. Willows grow in back of the campsite, and Laurel Mountain towers above the vegetation.

## #19 Privacy Rating: B+
**Reservable?** No. First-come, first-served.

Nicely screened from the campground road by willows and other bushes, #19 is another spot carved out of the sagebrush and rabbitbrush with nice views of the mountains around Convict Lake. To reach the site, which is elevated from the campground road, climb up four stairs from the driveway. To the right, you can see a camp space on the other side of the bathrooms, but there's still plenty of elbow room between the two sites. A sage-covered hill dominates the view behind #19. To the left, there's plenty of space between you and your nearest neighbor. Another great star-gazing spot and a nice location to watch the full moon rise.

## #20 Privacy Rating: A-
**Reservable?** No. First-come, first-served.

Enclosed in a rectangle of willows, this site is peaceful and private. Its only flaw is that over the willows you can just barely see the top of an RV parked in the adjoining space. But besides that one minor intrusion, you're enclosed in solitude. Willows on every side of the tent pad create a cozy spot to spend the night.

## #24 Privacy Rating: A
**Reservable?** No. First-come, first-served.

Surrounded by aspens on three sides, #24 has the added advantage of being set back from the campground road. The neighbors to the left and right are both a good distance away and the aspens hide them from view. The stream is behind this site, although because the space was occupied while we visited we aren't sure whether you can see the water from the camp spot: from a distance, the vegetation by the stream looks thick.

## #31 Privacy Rating: A+
**Reservable?** No. First-come, first-served.

Tall, narrow, reedy plants that might be young willows enclose #31, which merits our seal of privacy approval. Behind the campsite, Convict Creek meanders through the aspens. The neighbors on the left and right are far away and vegetation hides them from view. The space across the street is made irrelevant by the fact #31 is pushed back far from the campground road. Those reedy plants surround the picnic table and tent pad, enclosing the area in privacy.

**#41 Privacy Rating: A+**
**Reservable?** No. First-come, first-served.

This site has a lot of privacy and a lot of personality. It was our favorite site at Convict Lake and one of the best in any Eastern Sierra campground. Sunken from the road and the willow-lined driveway, #41 is reached by six stairs that lead down to the picnic table, fire pit, and tent pad. Aspens and willows lining the left and right sides of the camp space create the illusion of an outdoor room where the back "wall" is a meadow. Best of all, the stream flows to the right of this campsite, and although it's not visible from the picnic table or tent pad, walk a short, 12-foot-long path and you'll soon be at the water's edge. The creek here is especially beautiful, creating a tranquil pond lined with water birch, willows, and a stately juniper.

Another campsite sits far across the meadow that's behind this site, but there's good distance between the two spaces. Plus, the willows and aspens enclosing #41 stop your across-the-meadow neighbor from becoming a visual nuisance. Beyond the meadow, there's a good view of a majestic aspen forest and above that a peek at the mountains near Convict Lake. You've won the equivalent of the camping lottery if you're lucky enough to snag this site. A big thank you to Bob, who graciously allowed us to look at this campsite and take photos while he was staying there.

**#57 Privacy Rating: A-**
**Reservable?** Yes. Visit **www.recreation.gov** for reservations.

**ADA Accessible Site**

This handicapped-accessible, sunny site is out in the open on a cul-de-sac, but it has no nearby neighbors on the left and the spaces to the right are far away. Between the willows you can see glimpses of the stream behind the site—and you'll hear it, too. This site also boasts postcard perfect views of Laurel Mountain's colorful cliffs. Beyond the stream and the aspens surrounding it is Convict Lake Road, which means you might hear a small amount of road noise. And during the 2015 season you might be a touch too close to the construction noise. But you'll probably be out and about during the day anyway.

**#60 Privacy Rating: A+**
**Reservable?** No. First-come, first-served.

With no neighbors visible on the left, right, or behind and with only the aspens and willows to keep you company, #60 is a delightful spot for anyone who likes privacy while

 camping. Vegetation screens most of this site off from view of the campground road, too. You'll also have good views of the mountains.

**#61 Privacy Rating: A**
**Reservable?** Yes. Visit **www.recreation.gov** for reservations.

**ADA Accessible Site**

Willows grow thickly on the left and right of this site, blocking any spaces on those sides from view. It's tucked back nicely from one loop of the campground road, although the other loop of the road passes close behind #61. Still, plenty of willows and other vegetation filter most of the road from view. You'll hear the creek from this campsite, although you can't see it.

**#63 Privacy Rating: A+**
**Reservable?** Yes. Visit **www.recreation.gov** for reservations.

**ADA Accessible Site**

The willow-lined driveway leads to a slightly elevated platform housing the picnic table, fire pit, and tent pad. Willows and aspens surround the platform on three sides, creating the illusion of an outdoor room. There are no neighbors visible on any side and there are no other spaces across the road from this one.

**#65 Privacy Rating: A+**
**Reservable?** Yes. Visit **www.recreation.gov** for reservations.

Surrounded by willows on three sides and pushed back from the campground road, this site has a ton of privacy. Your parked vehicle will hide #65 from view of the road. #65 is suitable for tents, pickup trucks with camper tops, and camper vans — no RVs or trailers.

**Words of Warning:** This site has no bear box.

**#66 Privacy Rating: A+**
**Reservable?** No. First-come, first-served.

Aspens and willows grow on three sides of this campsite, which is tucked back from the campground road. Your parked vehicle will also screen off a good part of the campsite from view of the road. This site is a little more open by the driveway, which has sagebrush to the right, but a line of aspens in front of the picnic table and fire pit screen them from sight.

**Words of Warning:** We weren't able to gain access to this site the day we visited because it was occupied, so there is the possibility that this site, like its neighbor #65, might not have a bear box.

**#81 Privacy Rating: B+**
**Reservable?** Yes. Visit **www.recreation.gov** for reservations.

**ADA Accessible Site**

Sitting in the sagebrush and rabbitbrush, #81 is more out in the open than the other sites we chose in this campground, but it's well-spaced from other campsites so it still feels private. There are no neighbors to the immediate left or behind the site. The bathrooms are to the left. There is a campsite across the street, but your gaze will be riveted toward the spectacular view of Laurel Mountain and the other peaks towering over Convict Canyon. However, the day we were there the people camped across the street used the F-word in every sentence, making us aware that a loud neighbor across the campground road could make a stay in this campsite unpleasant since the sound seemed to carry really well between the sites. Despite its open location, #81 has a tall pine that shades part of the space, although the picnic table will likely be in the sun for a good part of the day.

# MCGEE CREEK CANYON

**Directions:** From Mammoth Lakes drive south on Highway 395 for approximately 8 miles. Turn right at the McGee Creek exit and drive uphill on McGee Creek Road for about 2 miles to the campground on the left.

## What's It Like?

Most of the campsites here sit out in the sagebrush and rabbitbrush, with a handful of camp spaces nudging up against the aspens next to McGee Creek. What the campground lacks in privacy, it makes up for in its spectacular setting. It's a wonderful place to watch lightning crackling over Glass Mountain far to the east. And it's two miles away from McGee Creek Canyon trailhead, one of the most beautiful trails in the Eastern Sierra. This campground isn't heavily used during the week, so even if you're camped in a site that's close to an adjoining spot, you might get lucky and have no one staying next door.

Each of the campsites here has a ramada, a roof over the picnic table to provide shade. Wild rose bushes are sprinkled throughout the campground, adding splashes of color when they are blooming in June. We found three campsites here that meet our privacy qualifications (see campsite descriptions below).

## What's It Near?

• Hikes: Trek as far as you want to in McGee Creek Canyon, which boasts a spectacular wildflower display in June and early July and then puts on another colorful show in fall when the aspens don their colorful finery. There's a view of a waterfall about 2 miles in and Steelhead Lake is 6 miles from the trailhead.

• Horseback rides through McGee Creek Pack Station.

• Fishing in McGee Creek. Crowley Lake is another option for anglers — it's located off Highway 395 about a 20-minute drive from the campground.

• East Side Bake Shop, in McGee Creek Lodge about 10 minutes' drive from the campground,  serves homemade pastries, scones, sandwiches, baked enchiladas, quiche, pies, and special dinners on weekends accompanied by live music. We enjoyed our lunch here so much that we returned that same night for a lasagna dinner and to listen to a blues band.

• Crowley Lake General Store, about 15 minutes away from the campground, has surprisingly good pizza. They serve breakfast and lunch, too.

**Elevation:** 7,600 feet

**Toilets:** Flush

**Verizon Cell Service:** Yes, limited reception, which is usually best when facing east/southeast. Better luck with text messaging. Campsites #23 and #24 have the worst cell reception. But it's a short drive down the main road to pick up good reception.

**Takes Reservations?** Yes. Visit **www.recreation.gov** for reservations. Some campsites are first-come, first-served.

**Number of Campsites:** 28

**Bear Boxes?** Yes

# Campsites with the Most Privacy

**#1 Privacy Rating: C+**
**Reservable?** Yes. Visit **www.recreation.gov** for reservations.

Sitting among the sagebrush and rabbitbrush, this site is extremely exposed, but it has some advantages. We're including it because it's the best of all the exposed sites. It has no neighbors on the left, behind, or immediately across the street. Its only nearby neighbor is #2 to the right, but that site isn't too close. The ramada in your campsite will provide some privacy, but only when you're sitting at the picnic table. The campsite boasts spectacular views of Glass Mountain to the east and the mountains of McGee Creek Canyon to the west. At night, the sky above puts on a star-studded show.

**#26 Privacy Rating: B+**
**Reservable?** Yes. Visit **www.recreation.gov** for reservations.

Leprechaun green aspens to the rear of this campsite are a sharp contrast against the pale gray-green sagebrush and rabbitbrush covering most of #26. To reach the site, you travel along a 50-foot long path from the parking area. McGee Creek skips along through the aspens behind #26. The neighbor to the left (#27) is far enough away that it doesn't intrude upon your space. To the right sits #25, but it doesn't feel intrusive either. Plus, #25 is closer to the campground road whereas #26 is tucked back. A nice spot for an angler. In fact, be prepared for the possibility that fishermen will pass behind your campsite as they cast a line in the creek.

**#27 Privacy Rating: A-**
**Reservable?** Yes. Visit **www.recreation.gov** for reservations.

To reach this creekside campsite, stroll along a 35-foot path

leading from the parking area through the sagebrush and rabbitbrush to the aspen-lined banks of the stream. Compared to most other campsites at McGee Creek, which are out in the open and within full view of each other, this one is a gem. There is a campsite to the left, but it's closer to the road and the ramada in site #27 partially hides the view. The space to the right is visible, but due to the layout of this campsite and the distance between the two sites, #27 still has a private feel.

Above the aspen forest on the right is a spectacular view of the mountains rising above McGee Creek Canyon. Because #27 is so far back from the campground road, the space across the street is inconsequential. One tall pine, lonely among the aspens, grows in the space, providing welcome shade. The aspens growing to the rear of the campsite part to make way for McGee Creek, visible through the trees. An excellent site for an angler. Expect a fisherman or two walking through the outskirts of your campsite to stake out their space in the creek.

# ROCK CREEK CANYON

## Tuff Campground

**Directions:** The campground is located approximately 14 miles south from the intersection of Highway 395 and State Route 203 (Mammoth Lakes turnoff). Turn left (east) at Tom's Place on to Owen's Gorge Road. Where the paved road curves to the left, take the dirt road on the right. Tuff is about 0.2 mile from Highway 395 and is located on the opposite side of the highway from all the other campgrounds in Rock Creek Canyon. From Bishop, travel north on Highway 395 for 24 miles and turn right (east) at Tom's Place, following the road where it curves to the right.

**What's It Like?**

Interesting pink formations made from the rock known as tuff tower over sections of the campground. Tuff was deposited as ash when the Long Valley Caldera erupted 760,000 years ago and over the years hardened into rock. Some of the sites sit among the aspens and near Rock Creek while other spaces are out in the open in the sagebrush and rabbitbrush. Some of the campsites have views of the tuff formations. There are some peaceful sites here, if you know which ones to choose. Take a look at the descriptions below for the best choices.

**What's It Near?**

• Fishing for brown, rainbow, or golden trout in Rock Creek, Rock Creek Lake, and Crowley Lake and many other backcountry streams and lakes.

• Mountain biking on Lower Rock Creek Trail, one of the Eastern Sierra's best singletrack trails.

• Boating on Rock Creek Lake and Crowley Lake.

• Hiking in Little Lakes Valley, notable not only for its impressive High Sierra scenery, but also for being one of the few hikes in the Eastern Sierra where you don't have to huff and puff up a steep hill. A backdrop of 13,000-foot-peaks, including Bear Creek Spire and Pyramid Peak, serve as sentries over this lush, green, lake-studded valley.

To reach the valley from Mosquito Flat at the end of Rock Creek Road, you'll have to walk up a moderately steep hill for about a half mile, then the remaining 1.5 miles to Long Lake are mostly flat or gentle uphill. You'll pass a series of lakes including Mack, Heart, and Box Lakes. If you don't want to trek uphill, then end your journey at Long Lake. If you have more energy progress farther up the trail toward Chickenfoot Lake and Gem Lakes.

• A steep, 4.5-mile round trip excursion to Ruby Lake is worth your time, both for the views of Little Lakes Valley and the beauty of the lake itself. Ruby Lake is off of the Mono Pass trail.

• Other hikes: Hilton Lakes (9 miles round trip to the second lake, 8.75 miles round trip to the third lake, 9.75 miles round trip to the fourth lake), Davis Lake (10 miles round trip), and Owen's River Gorge (walk as far as you want to, but eventually the path will peter out).

• Horseback riding through Rock Creek Pack Station.

• Pie, pie, and more homemade pie at Rock Creek Lakes Resort Café. They also have a small, but tasty, breakfast and lunch menu. Just get there early, because the pie selection dwindles later in the afternoon, especially on weekends.

• Tom's Place Resort features a general store to stock up on camp supplies and tackle as well as a café serving breakfast, lunch, and dinner. Thursday and Saturday night they have a prime rib special. Don't forget to grab a milkshake or a slice of pie for dessert.

**Elevation:** 7,000 feet

**Toilets:** Vault

**Verizon Cell Service?** Yes

**Takes Reservations?** Yes. Visit **www.recreation.gov** for reservations. First-come, first-served sites are also available.

**Number of Campsites:** 34

**Bear Boxes?** Yes

**Campsites with the Most Privacy**

**#18 Privacy Rating: A-**
**Reservable?** Yes. Visit **www.recreation.gov** for reservations.

A nice little spot in the aspens and willows, #18 has no nearby neighbors to the left. Another spot sits to the right of this one, but the aspens and willows in between the two sites partially filter out the view of the neighbor. Two sections of the campground road are in front and behind this spot. To the rear of the site, a row of aspens shelters #18 from view of the road. In front of the campsite, across the road in a neighboring spot, there's a good view of an interesting tuff formation— Mother Nature sculpted the formation into what looks like rock faces.

**#23 Privacy Rating: B**
**Reservable?** Yes. Visit **www.recreation.gov** for reservations.

This sunny site in the sagebrush is out in the open, but only has one neighbor, about 24 feet to the left. Tall sagebrush and bitterbrush shoulders out some of the view of your neighbor, and unless a big RV pulls in on that side, #23 will still feel private. A hill rises up to the rear of the site and curves around to the right, and if you climb to the top of it you'll see some of the mountains in Rock Creek Canyon. Tall Jeffrey pines are sprinkled randomly on the hill and on the outskirts of the campsite, offering a tiny bit of reprieve from the sun. There are no spaces directly across the street, where you'll have a view of aspens. An electric line runs across the top of the hill behind #23, but a large pine does a good job of concealing the tall wooden electrical tower from view.

**#30 Privacy Rating: A+**
**Reservable?** Yes. Visit **www.recreation.gov** for reservations.

This site is the cream of the campground privacy crop. It's so private that you can't even see the campsite from the driveway. A short path through the willows and other vegetation leads to the site, which sits in the middle of a circle of aspens and willows. Through the vegetation, there is just the barest hint of a view of the neighbor to the left, but they're much closer to the road than #30, so your back will be to what little view you have of that spot.

Not only is the right side of #30 free of neighbors, but also on the other side of the vegetation the stream takes its time passing the grassy shores, forming a peaceful pond. Across the stream is a great view of one of the coolest tuff formations in the campground, an outcropping of ruddy colored rock studded with holes. Behind #30 there are no other campsites, and this spot is so well hidden from the road that it wouldn't matter if there was an entire neighborhood across the street.

### #33 Privacy Rating: A+
**Reservable?** Yes. Visit **www.recreation.gov** for reservations.

#33 is like a penthouse suite compared to other sites in the campground. It's huge! You can hear the stream murmuring from behind a thick hedge of willows to the rear of the site. This space is far away from the neighbor on the right, and it's sunken down from the campground road. The bathrooms are to the left of #33, and there's another neighbor on that side, but far enough away not to be a bother. The absence of neighbors directly across the street adds to the privacy of this spot.

A few tall pines shade the bear box, picnic table, and part of the campsite. And there's a nice view of a couple tall pillars of tuff across the creek. This is a really popular spot, especially in July and August, so you're going to have to fight for it on recreation.gov by making your reservations as early as you can, although you might get lucky and find an opening last minute, especially during the week.

## French Camp

**Directions:** The campground is located approximately 14 miles south from the intersection of Highway 395 and State Route 203 (Mammoth Lakes turnoff). Turn right (west) at Tom's Place on Rock Creek Canyon Road and follow the road about a half mile to the campground on the right. Or from

Bishop, travel north on Highway 395 for 24 miles, turn left (west) at Tom's Place, and follow the road about a half mile to the campground on the right.

## What's It Like?

You'll feel as if you're camping in the high desert mountains here, thanks to French Camp's location among the pinyon pines and junipers. The elevation here is a lot lower than the other campgrounds in Rock Creek Canyon, so it's hot here — but a 15-minute drive will have you relaxing up at 10,000 feet staring at distant snow-patches. Rock Creek flows next to the campground but none of the campsites are located streamside. The closest you can get is a campsite across the campground road from the creek. If you need an easy in-out to Highway 395, this and Tuff are the two most convenient campgrounds in Rock Creek Canyon.

## What's It Near?

• Fishing for brown, rainbow, or golden trout in Rock Creek, Rock Creek Lake, and Crowley Lake and many other backcountry streams and lakes.

• Mountain biking on Lower Rock Creek Trail, one of the Eastern Sierra's best singletrack trails.

• Boating or kayaking on Rock Creek Lake or Crowley Lake.

• Hiking in Little Lakes Valley, notable not only for its impressive High Sierra scenery, but also for being one of the few hikes in the Eastern Sierra where you don't have to huff and puff up a steep hill. A backdrop of 13,000-foot peaks, including Bear Creek Spire and Pyramid Peak, serve as sentries over this lush, green, lake-studded valley.

To reach the valley from Mosquito Flat at the end of Rock Creek Road, you'll have to walk up a moderately steep hill for about a half mile, then the remaining 1.5 miles to Long Lake are mostly flat with some gentle uphill. You'll pass a series of lakes including Mack, Heart, and Box Lakes. If you don't want to trek up hill, then end your journey at Long Lake. If you have more energy progress farther up the trail toward Chickenfoot Lake and Gem Lakes.

• A steep, 4.5-mile round trip excursion to Ruby Lake from Little Lakes Valley is worth your time, both for the views of the valley and the beauty of the lake itself.

• Other hikes: Hilton Lakes (9 miles round trip to the second lake, 8.75 miles round trip to the third lake, 9.75 miles round trip to the fourth lake), Davis Lake (10 miles round trip), and Owen's River Gorge (walk as far as you want to, but eventually the path will peter out).

• Horseback riding through Rock Creek Pack Station.

• Pie, pie, and more homemade pie at Rock Creek Lakes Resort Café. They also have a small, but tasty, breakfast and lunch menu. Get there early, because the pie selection dwindles later in the afternoon, especially on weekends.

• Tom's Place Resort, featuring a general store to stock up on camp supplies and tackle and a café serving breakfast, lunch, and dinner. Thursday and Saturday night they have a prime rib special. Don't forget to grab a milkshake or a slice of pie for dessert.

• Rock Creek Lodge near the Upper and Lower Pine Grove Campgrounds has groceries and serves breakfast.

**Elevation:** 7,500 feet

**Toilets:** Flush

**Verizon Cell Service?** Yes

**Takes Reservations?** Yes. Visit **www.recreation.gov** for reservations. Some campsites are first-come, first-served.

**Number of Sites:** 86

**Bear Boxes?** Yes

## Campsites with the Most Privacy

**#2 Privacy Rating: A**
**Reservable?** Yes. Visit **www.recreation.gov** for reservations.

You've got plenty of room to spread out in this large site, which will fit at least two big tents or several smaller ones. Site #3 is visible to the right from the front of the campsite but the main part of #2 is pushed so far back from #3 that the close presence of a neighbor doesn't seem to matter. Plus, trees partially screen out the view of #3. The picnic table and fire pit are located in a big, sunny clearing ringed by pinyons, junipers, and other pines. The clearing is removed far enough from the campground road that you can barely see #1 across the street. There are no neighbors to the left or behind. The bear box is close to the parking space, but far away from the picnic table, for good reason—it receives more shade. Adding a touch of scenic seasoning to this site is a view of the White Mountain Range to the east.

## #4 Privacy Rating: A-
**Reservable?** Yes. Visit **www.recreation.gov** for reservations.

Another spacious spot with room for several tents, #4 sits in a sunny clearing carved out from a forest of pinyons and other pines. It has no neighbors behind and the closest space to the right (#1) isn't visible. To the left, #6 is a good 30 feet away, and you'll only catch a glimpse of it through the pinyons and other pines. #4 is far enough back from the campground road that the space across the street, also back from the road, isn't in clear view.

## #16 Privacy Rating: A
**Reservable?** Yes. Visit **www.recreation.gov** for reservations.

To reach the picnic table of this small, rocky site, you'll pass under a bridge formed by the branches of two conifers reaching out to each other. In the heat of the afternoon, these trees also provide a shady spot to place your chair and they also keep the bear box cool. The space to the right is blocked by a hill, the neighbor to the left is also invisible. Boulders and pinyons march off into the distance behind the site. The only neighbor in view is the space across the street, but #16 is back enough from the campground road that the across-the-street neighbor isn't in your face.

## #68 Privacy Rating: A+
**Reservable?** No. First-come, first-served.

A beauty of a site across the campground road from Rock Creek, #68 is set among the Jeffrey pines and pinyons. The space to the right is far away and pinyon pines block it from view. The nearest space to the left is also a good distance away and not visible from here. The bathrooms are conveniently located behind #68, but the trees screen them from view. The bear box gets some shade, and although #68 is blasted by afternoon sun, plenty of trees in the site also offer some places to hide from the heat. With no near neighbors on any side, and plenty of elbow room, #68 is one of the most private spaces in the campground.

## #72 Privacy Rating: A+
**Reservable?** No. First-come, first-served.

Along with #68, this site is one of the best in the campground for privacy. A hill shields you from the neighbors to the right, there are no immediate neighbors to the left, and behind #72 all that's visible are bitterbrush and pinyons. Across the campground road, tall pines reach toward the sky and beyond that Rock Creek skips along past the campground.

#72 isn't as shady as #68 but a few pinyon pines shadow the bear box for part of the day. You might be able to squeeze your tent into a shady area, but that will place you a little close to the bear box. Otherwise, there's plenty of room for a tent in the sun.

### Iris Meadows Campground

**Directions:** From Mammoth Lakes, travel approximately 14

miles south. Turn right (west) at Tom's Place on Rock Creek Road and follow the road about 4 miles to the campground on the right. Or from Bishop, travel north on Highway 395 for 24 miles, turn left (west) at Tom's Place, and follow the road about 4 miles to the campground on the right.

**What's It Like?**

There are two sections to this campground. The sites in the meadow have a more open and exposed feel, even though some of them are located where the meadow meets the aspen forest. Based on the name of this campground these meadowside sites probably have a great view of the irises blooming in early summer. The sites we liked best were farther back on a spur off the main loop. These sites are settled in among the aspens and not as exposed to the campground road. However, their short driveways make them best suited for tents, pickups with camper tops, small trailers, and camper vans.

**Words of Warning:** In 2015, expect road construction on Rock Creek Road during the week. Delays up to 30 minutes are possible. Also, this campground is not suited for large RVs since maximum vehicle length is 26 feet.

**What's It Near?**

• Fishing for brown, rainbow, or golden trout in Rock Creek, Rock Creek Lake, and Crowley Lake and many other backcountry streams and lakes.

• Mountain biking on Lower Rock Creek Trail, one of the Eastern Sierra's best singletrack trails.

• Boating or kayaking on Rock Creek Lake or Crowley Lake.

• Hiking in Little Lakes Valley, notable not only for its impressive High Sierra scenery, but also for being one of the few hikes in the Eastern Sierra where you don't have to huff and puff up a steep hill. A backdrop of 13,000-foot peaks, including Bear Creek Spire and Pyramid Peak, serve as sentries over this lush, green, lake-studded valley.

To reach the valley from Mosquito Flat at the end of Rock Creek Road, you'll have to walk up a moderately steep hill for about a half mile, then the remaining 1.5 miles to Long Lake are mostly flat. You'll pass a series of lakes including Mack, Heart, and Box Lakes. If you don't want to trek up hill, then end your journey at Long Lake. If you have more energy progress farther up the trail toward Chickenfoot Lake and Gem Lakes.

• A steep, 4.5-mile round trip excursion to Ruby Lake from Little Lakes Valley is worth your time, both for the views of the valley and the beauty of the lake itself.

• Other hikes: Hilton Lakes (9 miles round trip to the second lake, 8.75 miles round trip to the third lake, 9.75 miles round trip to the fourth lake), Davis Lake (10 miles round trip), and Owen's River Gorge (walk as far as you want to, but eventually the path will peter out).

• Horseback riding through Rock Creek Pack Station.

• Pie, pie, and more homemade pie at Rock Creek Lakes Resort Café. They also have a small, but tasty, breakfast and lunch menu. Get there early, because the pie selection dwindles later in the afternoon, especially on weekends.

• Tom's Place Resort, featuring a general store to stock up on camp supplies and tackle and a café serving breakfast, lunch, and dinner. Thursday and Saturday night they have a prime rib special. Don't forget to grab a milkshake or a slice of pie for dessert.

• Rock Creek Lodge near the Upper and Lower Pine Grove Campgrounds has groceries and serves breakfast.

**Elevation:** 8,300 feet

**Toilets:** Flush

**Verizon Cell Service?** No

**Takes Reservations?** No. First-come, first served.

**Number of Campsites:** 14

**Bear Boxes?** Yes

### Campsites with the Most Privacy

**#6 Privacy Rating: A+**
**Reservable?** No. First-come, first-served.

This roomy site at the end of a cul-de-sac has it all: a streamside location next to Rock Creek, shade provided by junipers and lodgepole pines (including one granddaddy tree), and tons of privacy with no neighbors on any side. There's plenty of room here for two tents, although you might need to pitch one tent in the sun.

**#7 Privacy Rating: A+**
**Reservable?** No. First-come, first-served.

It's difficult to hide from the Sierra sun in this site, which is surrounded on two sides by low-growing aspens that don't provide a lot of shade. To the left of #7, aspens block the view of neighbors in that direction. You won't have any neighbors on the right. A hill stands watch from behind the campsite. If you like camping among the aspens, this is a peaceful site, but consider bringing a canopy to provide extra shade.

**#8 Privacy Rating: A+**
**Reservable?** No. First-come, first-served.

Aspens serve as your welcoming committee on the left and right as you pull into the driveway of this site. There are no neighbors to the left, and the space to the right isn't visible. #8 is tucked back from the campground road so you can't see any neighbors across the street. It gets a blast of afternoon sun, but a tall conifer on the hill immediately behind the site provides a shady place to pull up a chair.

## Big Meadow Campground

**Directions:** From Mammoth Lakes, travel approximately 14 miles south. Turn right (west) at Tom's Place on Rock Creek Road and follow the road about 4.5 miles to the campground on the right. Or from Bishop, travel north on Highway 395 for 24 miles, turn left (west) at Tom's Place, and follow the road about 4.5 miles to the campground on the right.

## What's It Like?

Most of the campsites in Big Meadow aren't suited for anyone who likes privacy. All but one of the campsites are strung together alongside or across from Rock Creek with no elbow room. However, there is one campsite in Big Meadow that gets our vote for being one of the most beautiful and private campsites in the Eastern Sierra (See campsite description below).

## What's It Near?

• Fishing for brown, rainbow, or golden trout in Rock Creek, Rock Creek Lake, and Crowley Lake and many other backcountry streams and lakes.

• Mountain biking on Lower Rock Creek Trail, one of the Eastern Sierra's best singletrack trails.

• Boating or kayaking on Rock Creek Lake or Crowley Lake.

• Hiking in Little Lakes Valley, notable not only for its impressive High Sierra scenery, but also for being one of the few hikes in the Eastern Sierra where you don't have to huff and puff up a steep hill. A backdrop of 13,000-foot peaks, including Bear Creek Spire and Pyramid Peak, serve as sentries over this lush, green, lake-studded valley.

To reach the valley from Mosquito Flat at the end of Rock Creek Road, you'll have to walk up a moderately steep hill for about a half mile, then the remaining 1.5 miles to Long Lake are mostly flat with some gentle uphill. You'll pass a series of lakes including Mack, Heart, and Box Lakes. If you don't want to trek up hill, then end your journey at Long Lake. If you have more energy progress farther up the trail toward Chickenfoot Lake and Gem Lakes.

• A steep. 4.5 mile round trip excursion to Ruby Lake from Little Lakes Valley is worth your time, both for the views of the valley and the beauty of the lake itself.

• Other hikes: Hilton Lakes (9 miles round trip to the second lake, 8.75 miles round trip to the third lake, 9.75 miles round trip to the fourth lake), Davis Lake (10 miles round trip), and Owen's River Gorge (walk as far as you want to, but eventually the path will peter out).

• Horseback riding through Rock Creek Pack Station.

• Pie, pie, and more homemade pie at Rock Creek Lakes Resort Café. They also have a small, but tasty, breakfast and lunch menu. Get there early, because the pie selection dwindles later in the afternoon, especially on weekends.

• Tom's Place Resort, featuring a general store to stock up on camp supplies and tackle and a café serving breakfast, lunch, and dinner. Thursday and Saturday night they have a prime rib special. Don't forget to grab a milkshake or a slice of pie for dessert.

• Rock Creek Lodge near the Upper and Lower Pine Grove Campgrounds has groceries and serves breakfast.

**Elevation:** 8,600 feet

**Toilets:** Flush

**Verizon Cell Service?** No

**Takes Reservations?** No, first-come, first-served.

**Number of Sites:** 11

**Bear Boxes?** Yes

## Campsite with the Most Privacy

**#9 Privacy Rating: A+**
**Reservable?** No. First-come, first-served.

One of the most beautiful campsites in the Eastern Sierra, #9 was a pleasant surprise compared to the other spaces in Big Meadow, which are jammed together along the stream. Located where the campground road dead ends, this streamside site has no neighbors on any side. The sunlight filters through the trees and bathes the campsite here and there in an almost fairytale-like glow. The stream, clearly visible from #9, is especially beautiful here, a combination of clear pools and miniature rapids bubbling over the rocks. A touch of greenery under the conifers adds more tranquility, and you'll have a glimpse of the rocky cliffs on the canyon walls.

You're going to have to have good campsite-grabbing karma to snatch up #9, especially on Fridays, when people are pouring into the canyon for the weekend. Since Big Meadow is on the way to East Fork Campground, which has more selections, it's worth stopping at Big Meadow first to see if you can snatch this spot.

**Words of Warning:** Camp hosts at another campground who stayed in this spot in the 1990s told me that during a particularly bad monsoonal rainstorm, the stream rose and the campsite flooded. If they hadn't put their chairs in their trailer before they went to bed, the chairs would have been washed downstream. I can only image what would have happened if they had been sleeping in a tent. Based on this story, if bad weather and flash flooding is predicted during your visit, this campsite may not be the best choice. Otherwise, it's a beautiful spot.

## East Fork Campground

**Directions:** From Mammoth Lakes, travel approximately 14 miles south. Turn right (west) at Tom's Place on Rock Creek Road and follow the road about 6 miles to the campground on the left. Or from Bishop, travel north on Highway 395 for 24 miles, turn left (west) at Tom's Place on Rock Creek Road, and follow the road about 6 miles to the campground on the left.

### What's It Like?

This campground is a privacy lover's paradise. Not only is there a large selection of private campsites, but because of the large number of sites in the campground—133—East Fork rarely fills up completely, even on weekends. The camp hosts told me that the only time the campground was full was on July 4 and they predicted it would also fill on Labor Day weekend. The campsites with the most privacy are found in the aspens away from Rock Creek. Most of the sites by the creek aren't very private, but we did find a few streamside sites to our liking.

**Words of Warning:** On weekdays through 2015, they are widening Rock Creek Road, so you might hear the rumble of road construction noise between 7 a.m. and 7 p.m. Still, it was very peaceful in this campground and the road construction noise never bothered us much when we camped there in 2014 and 2015.

**What's It Near?**

• Fishing for brown, rainbow, or golden trout in Rock Creek, Rock Creek Lake, and Crowley Lake and many other backcountry streams and lakes.

• Mountain biking on Lower Rock Creek Trail, one of the Eastern Sierra's best singletrack trails.

• Boating or kayaking on Rock Creek Lake or Crowley Lake.

• Hiking in Little Lakes Valley, notable not only for its impressive High Sierra scenery, but also for being one of the few hikes in the Eastern Sierra where you don't have to huff and puff up a steep hill. A backdrop of 13,000-foot peaks, including Bear Creek Spire and Pyramid Peak, serve as sentries over this lush, green, lake-studded valley.

To reach the valley from Mosquito Flat at the end of Rock Creek Road, you'll have to walk up a moderately steep hill for about a half mile, then the remaining 1.5 miles to Long Lake are mostly flat or gentle uphill. You'll pass a series of lakes including Mack, Heart, and Box Lakes. If you don't want to trek up hill, then end your journey at Long Lake. If you have more energy progress farther up the trail toward Chickenfoot Lake and Gem Lakes.

• A steep, 4.5-mile round trip excursion to Ruby Lake from Little Lakes Valley is worth your time, both for the views of the valley and the beauty of the lake itself.

• Other hikes: Hilton Lakes (9 miles round trip to the second lake, 8.75 miles round trip to the third lake, 9.75 miles round trip to the fourth lake), Davis Lake (10 miles round trip), and Owen's River Gorge (walk as far as you want to, but eventually the path will peter out).

• Horseback riding through Rock Creek Pack Station.

• Pie, pie, and more homemade pie at Rock Creek Lakes Resort Café. They also have a small, but tasty, breakfast and lunch menu. Get there early, because the pie selection dwindles later in the afternoon, especially on weekends.

• Tom's Place Resort, featuring a general store to stock up on camp supplies and tackle and a café serving breakfast, lunch, and dinner. Thursday and Saturday night they have a prime rib dinner. Don't forget to grab a milkshake or a slice of pie for dessert.

• Rock Creek Lodge near the Upper and Lower Pine Grove Campgrounds has groceries and serves breakfast.

**Elevation**: 9,000 feet

**Toilets:** Flush

**Verizon Cell Service?** No

**Takes Reservations?** Yes. Visit **www.recreation.gov** for reservations. Also a good selection of first-come, first-served sites.

**Number of Sites:** 133

**Bear Boxes?** Yes

# Campsites with the Most Privacy

**#1 Privacy Rating: A+**
**Reservable?** Yes. Visit **www.recreation.gov** for reservations.

This site comes with its own private miniature stream gurgling along on the left side of the site, wildflowers lining its banks. Surprisingly, the stream was still flowing when we were there in late August of a drought year so it's probably spring fed. There's an interesting phenomenon that happens with the stream. In the morning, there's a robust amount of water, but by the late afternoon and evening, the flow dwindles. The stream pours out of a metal culvert up by the road, but that only slightly mars the view.

Aspens and pines are your only neighbor to the right. Conifers and aspens hide most of the view of the space to the left, about 20 feet away. The only reason you can see that site at all is because up by the tent pad of #1 a path leads between the two sites, where the trees part to open up a view. Woods grow behind #1 and beyond that is Rock Creek Road. There are no neighbors immediately across the street either.

Unlike many of the camp spaces on this side of the road, this one has a fair amount of morning and late afternoon shade although the bear box is in the sun most of the day. This is a beautiful site, one that stayed in my mind long after we left the campground.

**Words of Warning**: #1's proximity to Rock Creek Road means you might hear road construction noise during the week beginning at 7 a.m. throughout 2015, depending on what part of the road they're working on during your visit. And even without the road construction, some cars start whizzing by the campsite on Rock Creek Road beginning around 5 a.m. — early morning anglers perhaps and workers at the resorts up canyon. Even so, I camped in #1 with my brother and sister-in-law in 2015 and felt rejuvenated after spending time here. I didn't want to leave.

**#2 Privacy Rating: A**
**Reservable?** Yes. Visit **www.recreation.gov** for reservations.

A shady spot that sits in the lodgepole pine forest and backs up to an aspen-lined meadow, #2 offers plenty of elbow room. Trees hide the view of the space on the right, and you'll have no neighbors on your left. Aspens gather between the parking area and campground road, adding a partial privacy screen, although you can still see much of the campsite from the road. The mini-stream that passes by #1 also travels to the left of #2, but you can't see the water from most of the campsite. #2 doesn't have the personality nor the almost complete privacy of #1, but it's an ideal home away from home just the same.

**Words of Warning**: The same warning applies here as it did to #1: Its proximity to Rock Creek Road means you might hear cars driving past early in the morning and road construction noise throughout 2015, depending on what part of the road they're working on when you're there. However, #2 is slightly farther away from Rock Creek Road, which might make a difference.

## #3 Privacy Rating: B+
**Reservable?** Yes. Visit **www.recreation.gov** for reservations.

Low-growing aspens march up the hill behind this site. Conifers and aspens conceal the space to the right (#1) from view and do double duty by providing some shade to the site—although the picnic table and bear box are in full sun. A path between #3 and #1 opens up a slight view of #1's tent pad, but even so good privacy still exists between the two campsites. The widely spaced aspens and conifers give this site a more open feel. To the left, about 24 feet away, if there's an RV or trailer parked in that neighboring site you will catch a glimpse of it through the aspens. #2 is across the street, but the two spaces are well-separated.

**Words of Warning:** It's close enough to Rock Creek Road that you might hear some early morning traffic driving past. Throughout 2015, you might also hear the road construction noise here, too.

## #5 Privacy Rating: B
**Reservable?** No. First-come, first-served.

Located to the left of #133, across a small, willow-dotted meadow, #5 is a serene spot with nice views of the stars at night and the mountains near Little Lakes Valley in the day. #133 is visible through a gap in the willows, but there's good spacing between the two spots. Pines hide the view of the neighbor to #5's left. Rock Creek, out of view, cuts through the willows and vegetation behind #5. The neighbors across the street are far away and mostly hidden behind trees. This site gets blasted with Sierra sun, but there is a shady spot to place a tent—although most people pitch their tent in a sunny clearing.

**Words of Warning:** #5 is also across the campground road from Rock Creek Road, meaning you might hear cars driving past early in the morning. And through 2015 you might hear road construction noise during the week from 7 a.m. to 7 p.m. depending on the road worker's location.

**#6 Privacy Rating: A+**
**Reservable?** No. First-come, first-served.

A path leads through low-growing aspens to this secluded spot. Aspens embrace the site on every side, so no neighbors are visible. Over the tops of the trees, you have a good view of the mountains by Little Lakes Valley. There's a nice spot for a tent among the aspens, although two smaller tents could find a home in this site. Like many of the spots on this side of the campground, shade is scarce. #6 is best suited for either tent campers or people with camper vans or pickup trucks with camper tops.

**Words of Warning:** #6 is also on the side of the campground closest to Rock Creek Road, meaning cars driving past early in the morning could create a minor disturbance. And through 2015 you might hear road construction noise during the week from 7 a.m. to 7 p.m. depending on the road worker's location.

**#8 Privacy Rating: A+**
**Reservable?** No. First-come, first-served.

This is an ideal spot for people who have a small trailer, pick up truck with a camper top, or camper van. Tent campers are out of luck here, though, because there's no room for a tent. Low-growing aspens surrounding the site block the view of any neighbors. This is another campsite with a nice view of the mountains near Little Lakes Valley. Shade is lacking here, too, so bring a canopy for the picnic table. Due to its location near Rock Creek Road, be prepared of the possibility of weekday road construction noise through 2015.

**Words of Warning:** #8 is farther back from Rock Creek Road compared to #1, but it's still close enough that you might hear cars driving past early in the morning. And through 2015 you might hear road construction noise during the week from 7 a.m. to 7 p.m. depending on the road worker's location.

**#10 Privacy Rating: A**
**Reservable?** No. First-come, first-served.

From where you park your vehicle, stroll up a short path to reach this spot. Just like its neighbor to the right, #10 also has no place for a tent, so this is another site suitable for a small trailer, truck with a camper top, or camper van. Unlike its more private neighbors #6 and #8, this site has a filtered view of the campground road through a curtain of trees, but you don't feel exposed and have no visible neighbors on any side. The view of the mountains by Little Lakes Valley is hidden from this site. But #10 does have something #6 and #8 don't have—shade over the picnic table and bear box compliments of a good-sized juniper tree. The aspens here are more scattered, giving the site a more open feel.

**#12 Privacy Rating: A+**
**Reservable?** No. First-come, first-served.

Like its immediate neighbors, #12 is reached by trekking along a short path from the driveway to the actual campsite. Some of the aspens gathering around this campsite are taller compared to the stunted ones in the other nearby sites, providing a little morning shade to the picnic table, bear box, and tent area. You should have room for a bigger tent and a smaller tent here so this is an ideal site for small families. This sheltered site has no views of any neighbors on any side.

## #27 Privacy Rating: A-
**Reservable?** Yes. Visit **www.recreation.gov** for reservations.

We gave this cozy spot in the aspens a slightly reduced privacy rating because even though you can't see any other campsites from the picnic table and fire pit, there is a camp space close to the right of #27. However, you won't even know it's there unless an RV pulls in and runs its generator. You have a glimpse of that site from where you place your tent—in a small meadow filled with sagebrush and grass behind #27. Despite the proximity of the space to the right, it feels like Mother Nature is enclosing you in a peaceful embrace. The aspens grow a bit taller here, so there's some shade.

## #30 Privacy Rating: A
**Reservable?** Yes. Visit **www.recreation.gov** for reservations.

Park in an alleyway of aspens and take a short path into this tranquil site carved out in a circle of trees. The only neighbor on the left is the bathroom, barely visible through the aspens, which are taller here than their stunted cousins across the street. The aspens shelter this site from view of any neighbors to the rear. There's some morning shade on the picnic table and bear box. A big piece of fallen wood adds character to the site.

## #35 Privacy Rating: A+
**Reservable?** Yes. Visit **www.recreation.gov** for reservations.

With aspens and conifers growing on every side, this site is a privacy lover's dream. The bathroom is to the left, but you can't see it. Your neighbors to the right are also blocked from view, and the forest serves as your only neighbor to the rear. There's a nice place to pitch your tent in partial shade. In fact, compared to many of the campsites on this side of the campground road, #35 is blessed with more shade, especially over the picnic table and bear box in early morning and late afternoon, thanks to the conifers and aspens that grow a little taller here. This isn't a good spot for an RV, but it's a beauty for tent campers and anyone with a small trailer, camper van, or pickup truck with a camper shell.

## #39 Privacy Rating: A+
**Reservable?** No. First-come, first-served.

Low-growing aspens surround this sunny site on the left and right, providing a peaceful privacy screen between you and any neighbors on either side. Behind #39, the aspens climb up a hillside, leaving you with perfect privacy in that direction as well. The trees also do a good job of shielding this spot from view of neighbors across the street.

This is a better choice for someone with a small trailer, camper van, or pickup truck with a camper top, because there's not much room to pitch a tent. Although, if you were really determined, you might be able to squeeze a small one- or two-person tent in a space among the aspens. You could also pitch your tent in the driveway, but it would be near the campground road, and with all the good choices in this campground for tent campers it's probably not worth the effort.

**#41 Privacy Rating: A+**
**Reservable?** Yes. Visit **www.recreation.gov** for reservations.

Pushed back from the campground road and with low-growing aspens gathering around the campsite on three sides, #41 boasts lots of privacy. There are neighbors on the left and right, but the greenery completely blocks them from view. This site also has a nice view of the hillside to the east.

**#46 Privacy Rating: A+**
**Reservable?** Yes. Visit **www.recreation.gov** for reservations.

This site, suitable for tents, camper vans, or pickup trucks with a camper shell, is bundled in privacy thanks to the aspens and conifers obliterating views of any neighbors on the left or right. It also has no rear neighbors and the restroom and water spigot is across the street. It has a nice view of the hillside on the east side of Rock Creek Canyon. The trees shade the picnic table. There's room for two small tents pitched on 8 X 8 pads. Lots of aspens screen this site from view of the campground road. One minor disadvantage: the bear box is at the far end of the campsite driveway, far away from the picnic table.

**#49 Privacy Rating: B+**
**Reservable?** Yes. Visit **www.recreation.gov** for reservations.

No neighbors are visible to the left of this site. If you're standing up, you can see the space to the right (#48), but the low-growing aspens partially hide the view of that neighbor as well as the site across the street (#50). An aspen-covered hill behind the site leads up to Rock Creek Road, but because this site is sunken farther down than sites #1 through #12, road noise might be more muffled. Aspens and conifers on the east side of the site provide some morning shade. Although there's plenty of room for a tent, this is a good spot for an RV with lots of space to park a large vehicle up to 55 feet long. #49 is also near the bathrooms.

**#59 Privacy Rating: B-**
**Reservable?** No. First-come, first-served.

While not the most private site in the campground, #59 does have one huge advantage: Rock Creek flows within view about 40 feet behind the camp space. Located on a little plateau overlooking the creek, #59 has no neighbors on the right or behind it. However, the driveway for another space sits about 15 feet away to the left, although low-growing vegetation partially filters the view of any car parked there. If an RV pulls into that site, it might feel a bit more intrusive, but the neighboring site's driveway is staggered back from #59 so it's not to the immediate left. And a campsite is visible across the campground road. But aim your chair at the creek and you'll never know you have neighbors on the other sides. A path meanders along the creek between #59 and the stream, so from time to time you might see people ambling along behind your site. A great spot for an angler.

**#62 Privacy Rating: A+**
**Reservable?** No. First-come, first-served.

This is an absolutely beautiful camp space, one of the best in the Eastern Sierra for privacy and personality. After parking your vehicle, you'll stroll about 20 feet along an aspen-lined path to the site. Aspens and lodgepole pines encircle the site, concealing it from view of the campground road. You'll see nothing but trees on three sides. To the right, through the trees, there's just a hint of a view of a distant neighbor, depending upon where you're standing in the campsite. There's plenty of space for two tents, making this an ideal spot for families and friends. At sunset, look up and you can admire the alpenglow on the ridge above the canyon. The creek across the campground road will sing you a lullaby at night. For now, the one disadvantage is that #62 has a smaller bear box. But the camp managers tell us they're going to replace it soon with a standard-sized food locker.

## #86 Privacy Rating: A
**Reservable?** No. First-come, first-served.

As far as privacy is concerned, this site is the best streamside space in the campground. You can pitch your tent near the stream behind #86. Nature cushions this space on all sides with no neighbors to the immediate left and Rock Creek in full view from the campsite. The neighboring space to the right is far away and the two sites are staggered, so that #86 is farther back from the road. Thanks to this tucked-back location under the lodgepole pines, neighbors across the street are a non-issue. This is an ideal site for an angler, since you can cast a line right from your campsite. A streamside trail between #86 and the creek means you might have to put up with an occasional hiker or angler trekking past, which is the only reason we didn't give this beautiful spot an A+ rating.

## #99 Privacy Rating: B
**Reservable?** No. First-come, first-served.

We haven't given this the best privacy rating in the campground, but we really enjoyed our three-night stay in this shady spot. A space to the immediate right is about 24 feet away, but low-growing aspens and tall pines growing on a little hill filter out part of the view. Aspens and conifers serve as a see-through curtain partially blocking the space to the left. A path connecting these two spaces opens up a gap in the forest between the sites, providing more of a view of our neighbor than we liked from certain spots in our campsite, but it doesn't feel overly intrusive because the sites are well-spaced.

Behind the site, grass grows in a marshy area filled with bushes, and beyond that is Rock Creek, which serenades anyone staying in this site, although you can't actually see the water from here. One of the camp hosts is directly across the street, but from the fire pit and the tent area you can't see the host's RV thanks to tall, conveniently placed conifers. Another ideal spot for an angler, since a short path leads to the creek. The restrooms also are a short walk away — in fact you have your choice of two bathroom buildings a convenient stroll away. And, the water spigot is across the street.

**#133 Privacy Rating: B-**
**Reservable?** No. First-come, first-served.

Sitting out in a willow-speckled meadow, #133 is the ideal choice for anyone who doesn't like anything to interfere with the view of the stars at night. There's also a nice vista of the mountains looking toward Little Lakes Valley. The only really close neighbor sits about 30 feet away to the left partially visible through a gap in the willows. This campsite is across the campground road from a grouping of several campsites that sit out in the sagebrush. Those sites tend to be a hub of activity, especially on weekends. Although #133 is off by itself and is separated from those other sites by willows and some other vegetation, it is still close to the action across the road, which may bother some people.

Yet, there are no neighbors behind the site, nor to the right, and the bathrooms are across the street. Willows conceal the creek to the right of the site. A solitary conifer provides the only shade over a spot where a small tent can be pitched for anyone who doesn't want their tent roasting in the sun. This spacious spot also has room for a total of three or more tents. The picnic table at this site is funky—metal instead of wood and wobbly. And it's sunny here, so bringing a canopy to provide extra shade is a good idea.

## Lower Pine Grove Campground

**Directions:** From Mammoth Lakes, travel approximately 14 miles south. Turn right (west) at Tom's Place on Rock Creek Road and follow the road about 8 miles to the campground on the left. Or from Bishop, travel north on Highway 395 for 24 miles, turn left (west) at Tom's Place on Rock Creek Road, and follow the road about 8 miles to the campground on the left.

### What's It Like?

Lower Pine Grove is more like a parking lot than a campground—what Patrick calls condo camping. We could not find any campsites with privacy here.

### What's It Near?

• Fishing for brown, rainbow, or golden trout in Rock Creek, Rock Creek Lake, and Crowley Lake and many other backcountry streams and lakes.

• Mountain biking on Lower Rock Creek Trail, one of the Eastern Sierra's best singletrack trails.

• Boating or kayaking on Rock Creek Lake or Crowley Lake.

• Hiking in Little Lakes Valley, notable not only for its impressive High Sierra scenery, but also for being one of the few hikes in the Eastern Sierra where you don't have to huff and puff up a steep hill. A backdrop of 13,000-foot peaks, including Bear Creek Spire and Pyramid Peak, serve as sentries over this lush, green, lake-studded valley.

To reach the valley from Mosquito Flat at the end of Rock Creek Road, you'll have to walk up a moderately steep hill for about a half mile, then the remaining 1.5 miles to Long Lake are mostly flat or gently uphill. You'll pass a series of lakes including Mack, Heart, and Box Lakes. If you don't want to trek up hill, then end your journey at Long Lake. If you have more energy progress farther up the trail toward Chickenfoot Lake and Gem Lakes.

• A steep, 4.5-mile round trip excursion to Ruby Lake from Little Lakes Valley is worth your time, both for the views of the valley and the beauty of the lake itself.

• Other hikes: Hilton Lakes (9 miles round trip to the second lake, 8.75 miles round trip to the third lake, 9.75 miles round trip to the fourth lake), Davis Lake (10 miles round trip), and Owen's River Gorge (walk as far as you want to, but eventually the path will peter out).

• Horseback riding through Rock Creek Pack Station.

• Pie, pie, and more homemade pie at Rock Creek Lakes Resort Café. They also have a small, but tasty, lunch menu. Get there early, because the pie selection dwindles later in the afternoon, especially on weekends.

• Tom's Place Resort features a general store to stock up on camp supplies and tackle and a café serving breakfast, lunch, and dinner. Thursday and Saturday night they have a prime rib special. Don't forget to grab a milkshake or a slice of pie for dessert.

• Rock Creek Lodge near the Upper and Lower Pine Grove Campgrounds has groceries and serves breakfast.

**Elevation:** 9,300 feet

**Toilets:** Vault

**Verizon Cell Service?** No

**Takes Reservations?** No. First-come, first-served.

**Number of Sites:** 11

**Bear Boxes?** Yes

### Campsites with the Most Privacy

None.

## Upper Pine Grove Campground

**Directions:** From Mammoth Lakes, travel approximately 14 miles south. Turn right (west) at Tom's Place on Rock Creek Road and follow the road about 8 miles to the campground on the left. Or from Bishop, travel north on Highway 395 for 24 miles, turn left (west) at Tom's Place on Rock Creek Road, and follow the road about 8 miles to the campground on the left.

**What's It Like?**

The sites here are more widely spaced and less like a parking lot compared to Upper Pine Grove's lower neighbor. The campground sits under the pines and aspens next to a serene meadow. The tent pads in this campground are especially nice. Still, we could find only one spot that met our qualifications (see campsite description below).

**Words of Warning:** Large RVs and trailers not recommended here.

### What's It Near?

• Fishing for brown, rainbow, or golden trout in Rock Creek, Rock Creek Lake, and Crowley Lake and many other backcountry streams and lakes.

• Mountain biking on Lower Rock Creek Trail, one of the Eastern Sierra's best singletrack trails.

• Boating or kayaking on Rock Creek Lake or Crowley Lake.

• Hiking in Little Lakes Valley, notable not only for its impressive High Sierra scenery, but also for being one of the few hikes in the Eastern Sierra where you don't have to huff and puff up a steep hill. A backdrop of 13,000-foot peaks, including Bear Creek Spire and Pyramid Peak, serve as sentries over this lush, green, lake-studded valley.

To reach the valley from Mosquito Flat at the end of Rock Creek Road, you'll have to walk up a moderately steep hill for about a half mile, then the remaining 1.5 miles to Long Lake are mostly flat or gently uphill. You'll pass a series of lakes including Mack, Heart, and Box Lakes. If you don't want to trek up hill, then end your journey at Long Lake. If you have more energy progress farther up the trail toward Chickenfoot Lake and Gem Lakes.

• A steep, 4.5-mile round trip excursion to Ruby Lake from

Little Lakes Valley is worth your time, both for the views of the valley and the beauty of the lake itself.

• Other hikes: Hilton Lakes (9 miles round trip to the second lake, 8.75 miles round trip to the third lake, 9.75 miles round trip to the fourth lake), Davis Lake (10 miles round trip), and Owen's River Gorge (walk as far as you want to, but eventually the path will peter out).

• Horseback riding through Rock Creek Pack Station.

• Pie, pie, and more homemade pie at Rock Creek Lakes Resort Café. They also have a small, but tasty, lunch menu. Get there early, because the pie selection dwindles later in the afternoon, especially on weekends.

• Tom's Place Resort, featuring a general store to stock up on camp supplies and tackle and a café serving breakfast, lunch, and dinner in an old-fashioned diner atmosphere. Thursday and Saturday night they have a prime rib dinner. Don't forget to grab a milkshake or a slice of pie for dessert.

• Rock Creek Lodge near the Upper and Lower Pine Grove Campgrounds has groceries and serves breakfast.

**Elevation:** 9,400 feet

**Toilets:** Vault

**Verizon Cell Service?** No

**Takes Reservations?** No. First-come, first-served.

**Number of Sites:** 8

**Bear Boxes?** Yes

**#7 Privacy Rating: A+**
**Reservable?** No. First-come, first-served.

This spot sparkles compared to the rest of the sites in the campground. It's a beautiful site set back from the campground road in the conifers and aspens. No other sites are visible from #7. To reach the sunken tent pad, you stroll down three steps from the platform housing the picnic table, fire pit, and bear box, where you can pitch your home away from home surrounded by tranquil greenery, low-growing aspens, and towering pines.

## Rock Creek Lake Campground

**Directions:** From Mammoth Lakes, travel approximately 14 miles south. Turn right (west) at Tom's Place on Rock Creek Road and follow the road about 9 miles to the campground on the left. Or from Bishop, travel north on Highway 395 for 24 miles, turn left (west) at Tom's Place on Rock Creek Road, and follow the road about 9 miles to the campground on the left.

## What's It Like?

Rock Creek Lake Campground has a funky layout. The sites are spread out throughout a parking lot that is also used by day use visitors. Unlike many campgrounds, where the campsites are dispersed along a campground road, here the sites sit off the parking lot. The spaces we liked best were some of the walk-in sites, which are far away from the commotion of the parking lot.

## What's It Near?

• Fishing for brown, rainbow, or golden trout in Rock Creek, Rock Creek Lake, and Crowley Lake and many other backcountry streams and lakes.

• Mountain biking on Lower Rock Creek Trail, one of the Eastern Sierra's best singletrack trails.

• Boating or kayaking on Rock Creek Lake or Crowley Lake.

• Hiking in Little Lakes Valley, notable not only for its impressive High Sierra scenery, but also for being one of the few hikes in the Eastern Sierra where you don't have to huff and puff up a steep hill. A backdrop of 13,000-foot peaks, including Bear Creek Spire and Pyramid Peak, serve as sentries over this lush, green, lake-studded valley.

To reach the valley from Mosquito Flat at the end of Rock Creek Road, you'll have to walk up a moderately steep hill for about a half mile, then the remaining 1.5 miles to Long Lake are mostly flat or gently uphill. You'll pass a series of lakes including Mack, Heart, and Box Lakes. If you don't want to trek up hill, then end your journey at Long Lake. If you have more energy progress farther up the trail toward Chickenfoot Lake and Gem Lakes.

• A steep, 4.5-mile round trip excursion to Ruby Lake from Little Lakes Valley is worth your time, both for the views of the valley and the beauty of the lake itself.

• Other hikes: Hilton Lakes (9 miles round trip to the second lake, 8.75 miles round trip to the third lake, 9.75 miles round trip to the fourth lake), Davis Lake (10 miles round trip), and Owen's River Gorge (walk as far as you want to, but eventually the path will peter out).

• Horseback riding through Rock Creek Pack Station.

• Pie, pie, and more homemade pie at Rock Creek Lakes Resort Café. They also have a small, but tasty, lunch menu. Get there early, because the pie selection dwindles later in the afternoon, especially on weekends. Rock Creek Lake Campground is the nearest campground to the café.

• Tom's Place Resort features a general store to stock up on camp supplies and tackle and a café serving breakfast, lunch, and dinner. Thursday and Saturday night they have a prime rib special. Don't forget to grab a milkshake or a slice of pie for dessert.

• Rock Creek Lodge near the Upper and Lower Pine Grove Campgrounds has groceries and serves breakfast.

**Elevation:** 9,600 feet

**Toilets:** Flush

**Verizon Cell Service?** No

**Takes Reservations?** No. First-come, first-served.

**Number of Campsites:** 28

**Bear Boxes?** Yes

## Campsites with the Most Privacy

**#6 Privacy Rating: B**
**Reservable?** No. First-come, first-served.

This site has a spectacular view of Bear Creek Spire and the other mountains towering up over Little Lakes Valley. It also captures a partial view of Rock Creek Lake. The sunny site is out in the open, with some low-growing aspens gathering around on two sides. Of all the walk-in sites in this cluster, this one has the most privacy, although another site across the trail is in clear view of it, which is why we gave it a B rating. Still, that's the only other campsite rubbing shoulders with #6. The downside? It's about a 30-yard trek to the bathroom from here and a hike from your car to lug up your gear (if the wheelbarrows mentioned in #25 below exist, I'm not sure they could make it to this site, because the path up to it is rocky). But the views from #6 and its isolation from the hustle and bustle of the parking lot make the walk worth it.

**#20 Privacy Rating: A+**
**Reservable?** No. First-come, first-served.

This campsite is an unexpected surprise because it's near the parking lot and yet retains its privacy. From the parking lot, follow a short, aspen-lined path to the campsite, which is encased in yet more aspens on every side with a few small pines mingling in between. No neighbors are visible on any side. It's near the bathrooms, too.

## #21 Privacy Rating: A-
**Reservable?** No. First-come, first-served.

The last campsite in a series of walk-in spaces, #21 is a long trek from the parking lot. You access the site along a trail that meanders through the willows, over a bridge, and then into a pine forest. You do have to walk by three other spaces to reach the spot. But once you get there you can only partially see one neighbor through the trees in front of the site. Aspens to the right of the campsite rustle in the breeze and lodgepole pines grow to the left. Behind the space, there's a view of a mountain. It's located across the trail from Rock Creek, which you can see and hear from the campsite. It's also a short walk to where Rock Creek tumbles over a pretty cascade.

**Helpful Tip:** I have heard rumors that they have wheelbarrows in the parking lot to help you lug your stuff to this and the other walk in sites but we saw no signs of them when we were there. You can also bring your own cart to wheel in your gear because it's quite a walk from the parking lot to this and the other five sites in this walk-in cluster.

## #25 Privacy Rating: C+
**Reservable?** No. First-come, first-served.

To reach this and the other walk-in sites in this group, you take a path through the willows and cross the creek on a tranquil bridge. On the other side of the creek, you reach your new home away from home, a spacious spot with a large, soft and sandy tent pad. Conifers stand like guardians around the tent area. There's a good amount of shade, especially around the borders of the campsite.

#24 is really close on the left, but some vegetation partially filters it from view, and if you only have one tent you can pitch it a good distance away from the neighbor. The stream is nearby although you don't have a good view of it from the campsite. You might have some angler traffic walking near or in your site, since the stream and the trail are both nearby. Out of all the sites in this group of walk-in spaces, #25 is the closest to the parking area and therefore closest to the bathrooms, which are still almost an 1/8-mile hike away.

**Helpful Tip:** We have heard rumors that they have wheelbarrows in the parking lot to help you lug your stuff to this and the other walk in sites but we saw no signs of them when we were there. You can also bring your own cart to wheel in your gear because it's quite a hike from the parking lot to this and the other five sites in this walk-in cluster.

**#26 Privacy Rating: A**
**Reservable?** No. First-come, first-served.

#26 is slightly more off the trail compared to #25 and therefore feels more private. It's a large sandy spot with a beautiful tent pad. Behind the site is a granite outcropping that provides some texture and contrasts nicely with the low-growing aspens fringing the campsite. Some conifers on the campsite's outskirts offer some shade. #25 is the only neighbor within sight but the distance between the two spaces is good. Another advantage? This site is near a sandy beach on the stream, ideal for either fishing, dipping your toes in the water, or sitting with a good book.

**Helpful Tip:** We have heard rumors that they have wheelbarrows in the parking lot to help you lug your stuff to this and the other walk in sites but we saw no signs of them when we were there. You can also bring your own cart to wheel in your gear because it's quite a hike from the parking lot to this and the other five sites in this walk-in cluster.

# BISHOP CREEK CANYON

## Bitterbrush Campground

**Directions:** From the intersection of Highway 395 and West Line Street (Highway 168) in Bishop, travel west on West Line Street for about 13 miles to the campground on the left.

### What's It Like?

Bitterbrush Campground is the first National Forest Service campground in Bishop Creek Canyon. At a lower elevation than the other campgrounds, it stays open all winter, since it is often just below snow level or is covered in only small amounts of snow. During the winter, there is no water or trash service. The campsites are all out in the open in the sagebrush and bitterbrush with some sites near aspen-lined Bishop Creek, although none of the sites are actually in the aspens. We found only one camp space here that met our criteria (see description below), but in the winter and shoulder seasons, no matter which site you choose you probably won't have many (if any) neighbors.

### What's It Near?

• Fishing for rainbow, brown, brook, and Alpers trout in Bishop Creek, Intake 2, North Lake, South Lake, and Lake Sabrina.

• Boating, kayaking, and canoeing on Intake 2, North Lake, South Lake, and Lake Sabrina.

• Hikes: Blue Lake (6 miles round trip), Donkey Lake (8 miles round trip), Marie Louise Lake (4 miles round trip to lower lake), Chocolate Lakes (6 miles round trip to Upper Chocolate Lake), Treasure Lakes (6 miles round trip to lakes 1 and 2, 7.7 miles round trip to upper lakes), Long Lake (4 miles round trip), Bishop Lake (8.5 miles round trip), Bishop Pass (11.4

miles round trip), Tyee Lakes (7.6 miles round trip to Tyee Lake 5), Green Lake (6 miles round trip), Brown Lake (3 miles round trip), and Horton Lakes (7.6 miles round trip if you have a 4 X 4 with high clearance that can reach the locked gate at the trailhead, 8.3 miles round trip with a passenger car).

• Horseback riding through Rainbow Pack Outfitters.

• Cardinal Village Resort serves breakfast and lunch until 3 p.m. and dinner on the deck on Mondays and Tuesdays from mid-June until mid-August (reservations recommended). Be sure to try their homemade salsa. They serve all you can eat pizza every Saturday evening in summer.

• Bishop Creek Lodge has a small store with limited groceries and camping and fishing supplies. Stop in their restaurant for gourmet pizzas, burgers, Yukon gold crosscut French fries, chili, and steaks. Brave customers can venture to the bar to try a Duck Fart signature drink. Top off your meal with pie or a milkshake.

• Lake Sabrina Boat Landing Café serves breakfast and lunch on weekends in summer accompanied by a spectacular view of Lake Sabrina and the Sierra Crest in the background. They're famous for their homemade pies with homemade vanilla ice cream.

• The South Fork Café at Parchers Resort features a self-serve breakfast Monday through Friday. They also have a scrumptious breakfast buffet on Saturday and Sunday including an all-you-can-eat waffle bar, scrambled eggs, biscuits n' gravy, bacon, sausage, fresh fruit, quiche, and homemade baked goods such as sticky buns, French toast bakes, and more.

**Elevation:** 7,350

**Toilets:** Vault

**Verizon Cell Service:** 1 bar

**Takes Reservations?** No. First-come, first-served.

**Number of Campsites:** 30

**Bear Boxes?** Yes

### Campsite with the Most Privacy

**#27 Privacy Rating: A**
**Reservable?** No. First-come, first-served.

Well-spaced from its neighbors, with the creek flowing behind it, #27 is a gem compared to the rest of the sites in the campground. It's perched on a plateau above the creek, although you can't see the water from the campsite. Conifers fringe the space, providing a little shade. Aspens grow by the creek, adding a splash of color in fall. Bitterbrush partially screens off the view of the neighbor to the left, plus that neighboring space is pushed forward more toward the campground road whereas #27 is farther back. There are no neighbors to the immediate right.

A couple of campsites are eked out from the sagebrush and bitterbrush across the street, but if you turn your chair toward the creek you will feel as if you have the campground to yourself. Looking up canyon, you can see the tops of the jagged peaks peering out over the barren hill that runs alongside Bishop Creek Canyon.

**Words of Warning:** The seat of the picnic table at this site is warped and bent so bring good camp chairs with you.

## Big Trees Campground

**Directions:** From Bishop, travel west on West Line Street, which turns into Highway 168, for about 14 miles to the campground on the left.

**What's It Like?**

I really wanted to find some sites with privacy here. I looked at the campground when Patrick was resting in the tent, recovering from a late-summer flu. The campground is located far away from the main highway, far below in the canyon, so for that reason it has a secluded feel. And it's on the banks of Bishop Creek, under tall Jeffrey pines (hence, the name Big Trees). But every campsite is either out in the open in the sagebrush or jammed up next to each other by the creek. If you're looking for campsites with privacy don't bother to make the long drive from the main road.

**What's It Near?**

• Fishing for rainbow, brown, brook, and Alpers trout in Bishop Creek, Intake 2, North Lake, South Lake, and Lake Sabrina.

• Boating, kayaking, and canoeing on Intake 2, North Lake, South Lake, and Lake Sabrina.

• Hikes: Blue Lake (6 miles round trip), Donkey Lake (8 miles round trip), Marie Louise Lake (4 miles round trip to lower lake), Chocolate Lakes (6 miles round trip to Upper Chocolate Lake), Treasure Lakes (6 miles round trip to lakes 1 and 2, 7.7 miles round trip to upper lakes), Long Lake (4 miles round trip), Bishop Lake (8.5 miles round trip), Bishop Pass (11.4 miles round trip), Tyee Lakes (7.6 miles round trip to Tyee Lake 5), Green Lake (6 miles round trip), Brown Lake (3 miles round trip), and Horton Lakes (7.6 miles round trip if you have a 4 X 4 with high clearance that can reach the locked gate at the trailhead, 8.3 miles round trip with a passenger car).

• Horseback riding through Rainbow Pack Outfitters.

• Cardinal Village Resort serves breakfast and lunch until 3 p.m. and dinner on the deck on Mondays and Tuesdays from mid-June until mid-August (reservations recommended). Be sure to try their homemade salsa. They serve all you can eat pizza every Saturday evening in summer.

• Bishop Creek Lodge has a small store with limited groceries and camping and fishing supplies. Stop in their restaurant for gourmet pizzas, burgers, Yukon gold crosscut French fries, chili, and steaks. Brave customers can venture to the bar to try a Duck Fart signature drink. Top off your meal with pie or a milkshake.

• Lake Sabrina Boat Landing Café serves breakfast and lunch on weekends in summer accompanied by a spectacular view of Lake Sabrina and the Sierra Crest in the background. They're famous for their homemade pies with homemade vanilla ice cream.

• The South Fork Café at Parchers Resort features a self-serve breakfast Monday through Friday. They also have a scrumptious breakfast buffet on Saturday and Sunday including an all-you-can-eat waffle bar, scrambled eggs, biscuits n' gravy, bacon, sausage, fresh fruit, quiche, and homemade baked goods such as sticky buns, French toast bakes, and more.

**Elevation:** 7,500 feet

**Toilets:** Flush

**Verizon Cell Service?** No

**Takes Reservations?** No. First-come, first-served.

**Number of Sites:** 16

**Bear Boxes?** Yes

### Campsites with the Most Privacy
None.

## Upper and Lower Intake 2 Campground

**Directions:** From the intersection of Highway 395 and West Line Street (Highway 168) in Bishop, travel west on West Line Street for about 16 miles to the campground on the left.

**What's It Like?**

Lower Intake 2 has five walk-in sites sitting peacefully under an aspen forest. Four of the sites are close together and are so visible to each other that we ruled them out of consideration for this book. However, one of the sites definitely met our privacy qualifications (see below).

Upper Intake 2 is the epitome of what Patrick calls condo camping—all the spaces are jammed up next to each other in what looks more like a parking lot than a campground.

**What's It Near?**

• Fishing for rainbow, brown, brook, and Alpers trout in Bishop Creek, Intake 2, North Lake, South Lake, and Lake Sabrina.

• Boating, kayaking, and canoeing on Intake 2, North Lake, South Lake, and Lake Sabrina.

• Hikes: Blue Lake (6 miles round trip), Donkey Lake (8 miles round trip), Marie Louise Lake (4 miles round trip to lower lake), Chocolate Lakes (6 miles round trip to Upper Chocolate Lake), Treasure Lakes (6 miles round trip to lakes 1 and 2, 7.7 miles round trip to upper lakes), Long Lake (4 miles round trip), Bishop Lake (8.5 miles round trip), Bishop Pass (11.4 miles round trip), Tyee Lakes (7.6 miles round trip to Tyee Lake 5), Green Lake (6 miles round trip), Brown Lake (3 miles round trip), and Horton Lakes (7.6 miles round trip if you have a 4 X 4 with high clearance that can reach the locked gate at the trailhead, 8.3 miles round trip with a passenger car).

• Horseback riding through Rainbow Pack Outfitters.

• Cardinal Village Resort serves breakfast and lunch until 3 p.m. and dinner on the deck on Mondays and Tuesdays from mid-June until mid-August (reservations recommended). Be sure to try their homemade salsa. They serve all you can eat pizza every Saturday evening in summer.

• Bishop Creek Lodge has a small store with limited groceries and camping and fishing supplies. Stop in their restaurant for gourmet pizzas, burgers, Yukon gold crosscut French fries, chili, and steaks. Brave customers can venture to the bar to try a Duck Fart signature drink. Top off your meal with pie or a milkshake.

• Lake Sabrina Boat Landing Café serves breakfast and lunch on weekends in summer accompanied by a spectacular view of Lake Sabrina and the Sierra Crest in the background. They're famous for their homemade pies with homemade vanilla ice cream.

• The South Fork Café at Parchers Resort features a self-serve breakfast Monday through Friday. They also have a scrumptious breakfast buffet on Saturday and Sunday including an all-you-can-eat waffle bar, scrambled eggs, biscuits n' gravy, bacon, sausage, fresh fruit, quiche, and homemade baked goods such as sticky buns, French toast bakes, and more.

**Elevation:** 8,200 feet

**Toilets:** Flush

**Verizon Cell Service?** Intermittent

**Takes Reservations?** No. First-come, first-served.

**Number of Sites:** 13

**Bear Boxes?** Yes

### Campsite with the Most Privacy

**#1 Privacy Rating: A**
**Reservable?** No. First-come, first-served.

To reach this walk-in site, stroll along a short, private path through a thick forest of aspens, which render this site invisible from view of the campground road. The aspens open up to a lakeside meadow, where your campsite awaits. A peekaboo view of Intake 2 Lake through the willows infuses some personality into #1.

There's a large tent pad, but campers with smaller tents often prefer to pitch them closer to the aspens fringing the meadow in order to take advantage of the shade. That's where the bear box is, too. There are no spaces to the left of this one. A couple of the walk-in spaces to the right are partially camouflaged by tall aspens, but the fact you catch a glimpse of those campsites is the only reason we didn't give this space an A+.

You have to park across the street from this spot, but the parking is only about ten feet away from the little path that leads to the site. And you can temporarily park your car by the path when you're unloading.

The proximity to the lake makes this a nice spot for anglers. But if you don't fish, be aware that anglers might wander around the outskirts of this campsite as they look for a place to cast their line into the lake.

## Bishop Park Campground

**Directions:** From Highway 395 in Bishop, travel west on West Line Street (Highway 168) for about 17 miles to the campground on the right.

**What's It Like?**

Resting alongside the Middle Fork of Bishop Creek, this campground has a mixed bag of campsites, some that are in the aspens and lodgepole and Jeffrey pines next to the creek, and other more open campsites in the sagebrush. Many of the sites by the creek are packed in next to each other, but there are a few beautiful campsites here (see campsite descriptions below).

## What's It Near?

• Fishing for rainbow, brown, brook, and Alpers trout in Bishop Creek, Intake 2, North Lake, South Lake, and Lake Sabrina.

• Boating, kayaking, and canoeing on Intake 2, North Lake, South Lake, and Lake Sabrina.

• Hikes: Blue Lake (6 miles round trip), Donkey Lake (8 miles round trip), Marie Louise Lake (4 miles round trip to lower lake), Chocolate Lakes (6 miles round trip to Upper Chocolate Lake), Treasure Lakes (6 miles round trip to lakes 1 and 2, 7.7 miles round trip to upper lakes), Long Lake (4 miles round trip), Bishop Lake (8.5 miles round trip), Bishop Pass (11.4 miles round trip), Tyee Lakes (7.6 miles round trip to Tyee Lake 5), Green Lake (6 miles round trip), Brown Lake (3 miles round trip), and Horton Lakes (7.6 miles round trip if you have a 4 X 4 with high clearance that can reach the locked gate at the trailhead, 8.3 miles round trip with a passenger car).

• Horseback riding through Rainbow Pack Outfitters.

• Cardinal Village Resort serves breakfast and lunch until 3 p.m. and dinner on the deck on Mondays and Tuesdays from mid-June until mid-August (reservations recommended). Be sure to try their homemade salsa. They serve all you can eat pizza every Saturday evening in summer.

• Bishop Creek Lodge has a small store with limited groceries and camping and fishing supplies. Stop in their restaurant for gourmet pizzas, burgers, Yukon gold crosscut French fries, chili, and steaks. Brave customers can venture to the bar to try a Duck Fart signature drink. Top off your meal with pie or a milkshake.

• Lake Sabrina Boat Landing Café serves breakfast and lunch on weekends in summer accompanied by a spectacular view of Lake Sabrina and the Sierra Crest in the background.
They're famous for their homemade pies with homemade vanilla ice cream.

• The South Fork Café at Parchers Resort features a self-serve breakfast Monday through Friday. They also have a scrumptious breakfast buffet on Saturday and Sunday including an all-you-can-eat waffle bar, scrambled eggs, biscuits n' gravy, bacon, sausage, fresh fruit, quiche, and homemade baked goods such as sticky buns, French toast bakes, and more.

**Elevation:** 8,400 feet

**Toilets:** Flush

**Verizon Cell Service?** Intermittent

**Takes Reservations?** No. First-come, first-served.

**Number of Sites:** 21

**Bear Boxes?** Yes

## Campsites with the Most Privacy

### #4 Privacy Rating: A+
**Reservable?** No. First-come, first-served.

A circle of aspens gather around this tranquil, tent-only site, located in a small meadow. To reach #4, stroll along a short path that's about 18 feet away from the parking area across the campground road. There are no campsites to the left and the space to the right isn't visible. The aspens hide most of the site from view of the campground road as well as the site

across the street. Bishop Creek flows behind #4, although you can't see it through the aspens. A big conifer delivers shade. If you like your privacy when camping, it doesn't get any better than this.

**#6 Privacy Rating: A**
**Reservable?** No. First-come, first-served.

Another nice site, this one has a view through the trees of Bishop Creek flowing behind the camp space. This shady spot is pushed far back from the campground road. There's a site right in front of it, but the pines do a good job of filtering out most of the view of your forward neighbor. Plus, #6 is tucked back far enough that you've got plenty of elbow room. You can't see the campsites to the left or right, either. As with #4, you'll have to park across the campground road from this spot, but it's not too far of a walk.

**#15 Privacy Rating: A**
**Reservable?** No. First-come, first-served.

Well-spaced from its neighbor to the left, this creekside campsite is down a hill from the main road. There are no neighbors to the immediate right, although when I was there I could see an RV parked in one of the spaces far away. This site also has a good view of the mountains lining Bishop Creek Canyon. I would choose #4 or #6 over #15, but given its location next to the stream it's not a bad spot.

## Sabrina Campground

**Directions:** From the intersection of Highway 395 and West Line Street (Highway 168) in Bishop, travel west on West Line Street for about 18 miles to the campground on the right.

**What's It Like?**

I love camping in the aspens. And Sabrina Campground offers plenty of opportunity to surround yourself with a shimmering curtain of green quaking leaves. The Middle Fork of Bishop Creek wanders past about half of the campsites, while the other half are in the aspens or pines across the campground road from the stream. *Sunset Magazine* has included this campground on their best campgrounds list.

**What's It Near?**

• Fishing for rainbow, brown, brook, and Alpers trout in Bishop Creek, Intake 2, North Lake, South Lake, and Lake Sabrina.

• Boating, kayaking, and canoeing on Intake 2, North Lake, South Lake, and Lake Sabrina.

• Hikes: Blue Lake (6 miles round trip), Donkey Lake (8 miles round trip), Marie Louise Lake (4 miles round trip to lower lake), Chocolate Lakes (6 miles round trip to Upper Chocolate Lake), Treasure Lakes (6 miles round trip to lakes 1 and 2, 7.7 miles round trip to upper lakes), Long Lake (4 miles round trip), Bishop Lake (8.5 miles round trip), Bishop Pass (11.4 miles round trip), Tyee Lakes (7.6 miles round trip to Tyee Lake 5), Green Lake (6 miles round trip), Brown Lake (3 miles round trip), and Horton Lakes (7.6 miles round trip if you have a 4 X 4 with high clearance that can reach the locked gate at the trailhead, 8.3 miles round trip with a passenger car).

• Horseback riding through Rainbow Pack Outfitters.

• Cardinal Village Resort serves breakfast and lunch until 3 p.m. and dinner on the deck on Mondays and Tuesdays from mid-June until mid-August (reservations recommended). Be sure to try their homemade salsa. They serve all you can eat pizza every Saturday evening in summer.

• Bishop Creek Lodge has a small store with limited groceries and camping and fishing supplies. Stop in their restaurant for gourmet pizzas, burgers, Yukon gold crosscut French fries, chili, and steaks. Brave customers can venture to the bar to try a Duck Fart signature drink. Top off your meal with pie or a milkshake.

• Lake Sabrina Boat Landing Café serves breakfast and lunch on weekends in summer accompanied by a spectacular view of Lake Sabrina and the Sierra Crest in the background. They're famous for their homemade pies with homemade vanilla ice cream.

• The South Fork Café at Parchers Resort features a self-serve breakfast Monday through Friday. They also have a scrumptious breakfast buffet on Saturday and Sunday

———

including an all-you-can-eat waffle bar, scrambled eggs, biscuits n' gravy, bacon, sausage, fresh fruit, quiche, and homemade baked goods such as sticky buns, French toast bakes, and more.

**Elevation:** 9,000 feet

**Toilets:** Vault

**Verizon Cell Service?** Intermittent

**Takes Reservations?** No. First-come, first-served.

**Number of Sites**: 18

**Bear Boxes?** Yes

### Campsites with the Most Privacy

**#10 Privacy Rating: A**
**Reservable?** No. First-come, first-served.

Aspens on three sides bestow upon this site plenty of privacy. You can just barely see the picnic table and fire pit from the campground road. There's a neighboring site on the left, but the trees do a good job of cancelling out its presence. Behind the site, above the aspens, is a nice view of the canyon wall to the south.

**#14 Privacy Rating: A**
**Reservable?** No. First-come, first-served.

There are no neighbors visible on the left or right, but you'll have plenty of aspens to keep you company along with some tall boulders. The aspens do a good job of sheltering this site from view of the campground road and neighbors across the street. Plus, #14 is set back a little from the road. Plenty of room here for a motorhome, although long RVs aren't recommended in this campground.

**#15 Privacy Rating: A-**
**Reservable?** No. First-come, first-served.

I camped in this site five years ago and felt at peace here. Low-growing aspens hide the view of the neighbor to the left. Above the aspens rises a view of the ridge on the northwest side of the canyon. To the right of the site, a thick forest of aspens quiver in the breeze. Behind #15, stairs lead down to a small streamside meadow, where deer sometimes graze in the evening. This site is about eight paces away from Bishop Creek, but you can't see the creek from the camp space. Down the stairs and to the right, there's a sandy beach by a bend in the creek where anglers like to hang out.

The fire pit and picnic table are in clear view of the campground road when you're out and about, but your parked vehicle will provide added privacy. It's a sunny site, so you might consider bringing a canopy for the picnic table. Another plus: No neighbors immediately across the street—only the bathroom. This site is best suited for tent campers or pickup trucks with camper tops, camper vans, or small trailers.

**#18 Privacy Rating: A+**
**Reservable?** No. First-come, first-served.

We camped at this roomy spot and felt like we were in our own world. One night, an RV ran its generator until after 10 p.m. but we couldn't even hear it from #18—and this is a small campground. We only heard the generator when we walked to the bathroom.

#18 is the last campsite in the campground. It has a neighbor on only one side — across the street in the middle of the cul de sac. And that neighbor is completely invisible from #18 due to vegetation and low-growing aspens on the outskirts of both sites. Bushes and low-growing aspens surround #18, hiding it from view of the campground road. To the right about 40 feet away, up an incline, is the road to Lake Sabrina. To the left is North Lake Road, so no neighbors on that side either. Anglers will sometimes park in a pullout about 20 feet behind #18, which subtracts only a little bit from the privacy of this campsite.

Tall pines provide some shade. And with two tent pads #18 can fit two large tents or a total of four small tents.

Some nice views from #18 add a touch of scenic spice. To the right of the site is a view of a rust-colored mountain that lights up nicely as the sun sets. In front of #18 admire a view of the Sierra crest, which is marred only slightly by an electrical wire intersecting the view. There's an especially nice view of the stars at night.

## North Lake Campground

**Directions:** From Highway 395 in Bishop, travel west on West Line Street (Highway 168) for about 18 miles. Turn right on North Lake Road and travel about 2.3 miles to the campground.

## What's It Like?

If you like getting away from it all, this is your campground. To reach it, you have to drive up a steep, curvy road with spectacular views of Bishop Creek Canyon along the way. You won't be alone here because anglers gather around North Lake and backpackers use the road to access the trailheads into the backcountry. But you will be surrounded by serenity away from all the activity of the main part of Bishop Creek Canyon.

The campground itself is not near the lake—it's about a half-mile drive past the lake. The campsites rest under the Jeffrey and lodgepole pines or are nestled in the aspens next to the North Fork of Bishop Creek. Unfortunately, except for two campsites with perfect privacy (see description below), the rest of the sites in the campground are pressed up against each other. The campground is at 9,500 feet so make sure you're well acclimated before you set up camp here.

**Words of Warning**: Trailers and RVs are not allowed in this campground.

## What's It Near?

• Fishing for rainbow, brown, brook, and Alpers trout in Bishop Creek, Intake 2, North Lake, South Lake, and Lake Sabrina.

• Boating, kayaking, and canoeing on Intake 2, North Lake, South Lake, and Lake Sabrina.

• Hikes closest to North Lake: Lamarck Lake (5.2 miles round trip to lower lake. 6.4 miles round trip to upper lake), Wonder Lakes (6.75 miles to second lake), Loch Leven Lake (4.6 miles round trip), Piute Lake (7 miles round trip), Piute Pass (9.4

miles round trip). All mileages are from North Lake Campground.

• Other hikes: Blue Lake (6 miles round trip), Donkey Lake (8 miles round trip), Marie Louise Lake (4 miles round trip to lower lake), Chocolate Lakes (6 miles round trip to Upper Chocolate Lake), Treasure Lakes (6 miles round trip to lakes 1 and 2, 7.7 miles round trip to upper lakes), Long Lake (4 miles round trip), Bishop Lake (8.5 miles round trip), Bishop Pass (11.4 miles round trip), Tyee Lakes (7.6 miles round trip to Tyee Lake 5), Green Lake (6 miles round trip), Brown Lake (3 miles round trip), and Horton Lakes (7.6 miles round trip if you have a 4 X 4 with high clearance that can reach the locked gate at the trailhead, 8.3 miles round trip with a passenger car).

• Horseback riding through Rainbow Pack Outfitters.

• Cardinal Village Resort serves breakfast and lunch until 3 p.m. and dinner on the deck on Mondays and Tuesdays from mid-June until mid-August (reservations recommended). Be sure to try their homemade salsa. They serve all you can eat pizza every Saturday evening in summer.

• Bishop Creek Lodge has a small store with limited groceries and camping and fishing supplies. Stop in their restaurant for gourmet pizzas, burgers, Yukon gold crosscut French fries, chili, and steaks. Brave customers can venture to the bar to try a Duck Fart signature drink. Top off your meal with pie or a milkshake.

• Lake Sabrina Boat Landing Café serves breakfast and lunch on weekends in summer accompanied by a spectacular view of Lake Sabrina and the Sierra Crest in the background. They're famous for their homemade pies with homemade vanilla ice cream.

• The South Fork Café at Parchers Resort features a self-serve breakfast Monday through Friday. They also have a scrumptious breakfast buffet on Saturday and Sunday including an all-you-can-eat waffle bar, scrambled eggs, biscuits n' gravy, bacon, sausage, fresh fruit, quiche, and homemade baked goods such as sticky buns, French toast bakes, and more.

**Elevation:** 9,500 feet

**Toilets:** Vault

**Verizon Cell Service?** No

**Takes Reservations?** No. First-come, first-served.

**Number of Sites:** 11

**Bear Boxes?** Yes

### Campsites with the Most Privacy

**#1 Privacy Rating: A+**
**Reservable?** No. First-come, first-served.

A delightful campsite that sits between two miniature streams lined with greenery and a smattering of wildflowers. It has no neighbors on any side. Plenty of conifers shade the site and to its left the trees give way to a sunny meadow, beyond which a distant mountain rises up toward the sky. There's a nice tent pad, but there's also room for another tent or two higher up in the site.

**#2 Privacy Rating: A+**
**Reservable?** No. First-come, first-served.

You're going to have to earn your privacy if you want to camp in this walk-in site. We estimated it's about 20 yards from the parking area to site #2, so it's a good idea to bring a cart to haul all your gear. Still, it's worth the walk, especially if #1 is already taken. It's near Bishop Creek, which you can't see but which makes its presence known by its melodious sound. There's also a miniature stream flowing to the left of the campsite. Plenty of conifers shade the spot and some green understory and aspens add even more tranquility. There are no campsites on any side. It's also near the trail to Lamarck Lakes.

## Forks Campground

**Directions:** From Highway 395 in Bishop, travel west on West Line Street (Highway 168), for about 15 miles. Turn left on South Lake Road and drive ¼ mile to the campground on the right.

**What's It Like?**

Named for its location near where the South Fork and Middle Fork of Bishop Creek merge together, Forks Campground is home to campsites that are either completely exposed out in the sagebrush, resting under widely spaced pines, or on the banks of Bishop Creek. There aren't a lot of spaces with privacy here—but as you'll see from our description below, two campsites made the cut.

**What's It Near?**

• Fishing for rainbow, brown, brook, and Alpers trout in Bishop Creek, Intake 2, North Lake, South Lake, and Lake Sabrina.

• Boating, kayaking, and canoeing on Intake 2, North Lake, South Lake, and Lake Sabrina.

• Hikes: Blue Lake (6 miles round trip), Donkey Lake (8 miles round trip), Marie Louise Lake (4 miles round trip to lower lake), Chocolate Lakes (6 miles round trip to Upper Chocolate Lake), Treasure Lakes (6 miles round trip to lakes 1 and 2, 7.7 miles round trip to upper lakes), Long Lake (4 miles round trip), Bishop Lake (8.5 miles round trip), Bishop Pass (11.4 miles round trip), Tyee Lakes (7.6 miles round trip to Tyee Lake 5), Green Lake (6 miles round trip), Brown Lake (3 miles round trip), and Horton Lakes (7.6 miles round trip if you have a 4 X 4 with high clearance that can reach the locked gate at the trailhead, 8.3 miles round trip with a passenger car).

• Horseback riding through Rainbow Pack Outfitters.

• Cardinal Village Resort serves breakfast and lunch until 3 p.m. and dinner on the deck on Mondays and Tuesdays from mid-June until mid-August (reservations recommended). Be sure to try their homemade salsa. They serve all you can eat pizza every Saturday evening in summer.

• Bishop Creek Lodge has a small store with limited groceries and camping and fishing supplies. Stop in their restaurant for gourmet pizzas, burgers, Yukon gold crosscut French fries, chili, and steaks. Brave customers can venture to the bar to try a Duck Fart signature drink. Top off your meal with pie or a milkshake.

• Lake Sabrina Boat Landing Café serves breakfast and lunch on weekends in summer accompanied by a spectacular view of Lake Sabrina and the Sierra Crest in the background. They're famous for their homemade pies with homemade vanilla ice cream.

• The South Fork Café at Parchers Resort features a self-serve breakfast Monday through Friday. They also have a scrumptious breakfast buffet on Saturday and Sunday including an all-you-can-eat waffle bar, scrambled eggs, biscuits n' gravy, bacon, sausage, fresh fruit, quiche, and homemade baked goods such as sticky buns, French toast bakes, and more.

**Elevation:** 7,800 feet

**Toilets:** Flush and Vault

**Verizon Cell Service?** Limited

**Takes Reservations?** No. First-come, first-served.

**Number of Sites:** 21

**Bear Boxes?** Yes.

### Campsites with the Most Privacy

**#17 Privacy Rating: A**
**Reservable?** No. First-come, first-served.

Compared to most of the other campsites in this campground, which are more like parking spaces eked out of the sagebrush, this site is a pleasant surprise. It's tucked back from the road, so its only nearby neighbor, the site across the street, doesn't seem all that close. Some vegetation to the left of the camp space entrance partially blocks it from view of the campground road, and your parked vehicle will eliminate the rest of the view. To the right, sagebrush and other high desert vegetation gives #17 a more open feel. A couple of tall pines near the bear box and picnic table do their best to interfere with the heat of the sun. Behind the site, there's a pleasant view up a canyon toward a mountain peak. #17 is for tents, pickup trucks with a camper top, a camper van, or a small trailer.

**#20 Privacy Rating: B**
**Reservable?** No. First-come, first-served.

At first, I knocked this one off our list. I could see the campers there too well from the road. But then I began to appreciate its location in the pines and the fact that compared to many of the sites in this campground it has a lot of elbow room and a lot more shade. There are no visible neighbors behind it and the spaces on either side aren't too close.

## Four Jeffrey Campground

**Directions:** From Highway 395 in Bishop turn west on West Line Street (State Route 168) and drive approximately 15 miles. Turn left on South Lake Road and travel 1 mile to the campground on the left.

**What's It Like?**

You'll understand why this campground got its name when you see the tall Jeffrey pines near the entrance. But you'll leave most of the pines behind when you enter the campground, where campsites either sit in the sagebrush or under aspens closer to the stream. The sites in the sagebrush aren't very private, but they do have nice views of Table Mountain and other massive mountain peaks.

**Disclaimer:** Patrick had a family emergency the day we visited this campground, so we were unable to view all of it. However, the camp host told us that the sites we looked at are the most private (see our campsite descriptions below). Visit the campground updates section of our website at

**www.ilovetheeasternsierra.com** where we will post more information about this campground the next time we visit.

## What's It Near?

• Fishing for rainbow, brown, brook, and Alpers trout in Bishop Creek, Intake 2, North Lake, South Lake, and Lake Sabrina.

• Boating, kayaking, and canoeing on Intake 2, North Lake, South Lake, and Lake Sabrina.

• Hikes: Blue Lake (6 miles round trip), Donkey Lake (8 miles round trip), Marie Louise Lake (4 miles round trip to lower lake), Chocolate Lakes (6 miles round trip to Upper Chocolate Lake), Treasure Lakes (6 miles round trip to lakes 1 and 2, 7.7 miles round trip to upper lakes), Long Lake (4 miles round trip), Bishop Lake (8.5 miles round trip), Bishop Pass (11.4 miles round trip), Tyee Lakes (7.6 miles round trip to Tyee Lake 5), Green Lake (6 miles round trip), Brown Lake (3 miles round trip), and Horton Lakes (7.6 miles round trip if you have a 4 X 4 with high clearance that can reach the locked gate at the trailhead, 8.3 miles round trip with a passenger car).

• Horseback riding through Rainbow Pack Outfitters.

• Cardinal Village Resort serves breakfast and lunch until 3 p.m. and dinner on the deck on Mondays and Tuesdays from mid-June until mid-August (reservations recommended). Be sure to try their homemade salsa. They serve all you can eat pizza every Saturday evening in summer.

• Bishop Creek Lodge has a small store with limited groceries and camping and fishing supplies. Stop in their restaurant for gourmet pizzas, burgers, Yukon gold crosscut French fries, chili, and steaks. Brave customers can venture to the bar to try a Duck Fart signature drink. Top off your meal with pie or a milkshake.

• Lake Sabrina Boat Landing Café serves breakfast and lunch on weekends in summer accompanied by a spectacular view of Lake Sabrina and the Sierra Crest in the background. They're famous for their homemade pies with homemade vanilla ice cream.

• The South Fork Café at Parchers Resort features a self-serve breakfast Monday through Friday. They also have a scrumptious breakfast buffet on Saturday and Sunday including an all-you-can-eat waffle bar, scrambled eggs, biscuits n' gravy, bacon, sausage, fresh fruit, quiche, and homemade baked goods such as sticky buns, French toast bakes, and more.

**Elevation:** 8,100 feet

**Toilets:** Flush

**Verizon Cell Service?** Intermittent

**Takes Reservations?** Yes. Visit **www.recreation.gov** for reservations. Some sites are first-come, first-served.

**Number of Sites:** 106

**Bear Boxes?** Yes

### Campsites with the Most Privacy

**#1 Privacy Rating: A+**
**Reservable?** Yes. Visit **www.recreation.gov** for reservations.

Surrounded by aspens and one solitary pine, this site has no neighbors to the right, and the neighbors to the left are invisible thanks to the trees. Bishop Creek is behind the space, although aspens and thick vegetation interfere with the view of the water. The space is sunken down just slightly from the road, which adds to its privacy, and as an added bonus there are no spaces immediately across from it.

**#10 Privacy Rating: A-**
**Reservable?** Yes. Visit **www.recreation.gov** for reservations.

This site has lots of neighbors across the street, but the picnic table and fire pit are pushed back from the campground road, inserting some good distance between you and your across-the-street neighbors. Plus, a few aspens in front of the site create a partial privacy screen. The aspens make your neighbors to the left and right invisible. Aspens behind the site hide Bishop Creek from view.

**#12 Privacy Rating: A**
**Reservable?** Yes. Visit **www.recreation.gov** for reservations.

#12 is set back from the campground road and far away from the one neighbor across the street. On three sides of the site, aspens quake in the breeze. The trees hide any view of the neighbors on either side. A couple of aspens in front of the picnic table add a splash of privacy there and the only neighbor behind the camp space is the forest.

**#14 Privacy Rating: A**
**Reservable?** Yes. Visit **www.recreation.gov** for reservations.

Fringed by aspens on three sides, #14 is sheltered from view of anyone to the left or right. There's a neighbor across the street, but the aspens, your parked vehicle, and the distance between #14 and the road means the presence of your across-the-street neighbor won't matter.

**#16 Privacy Rating: A+**
**Reservable?** Yes. Visit **www.recreation.gov** for reservations.

Far back from the campground road in a rectangular nook carved out of the aspen forest, #16 is a shady site with tons of privacy. Aspens on the left and right hide the view of any neighbors in those directions. Behind the site, tall aspens reach up toward the sky. This site is just slightly farther away from the creek than the other spaces we've mentioned. It has no neighbors directly across the street.

**#17 Privacy Rating: A**
**Reservable?** Yes. Visit **www.recreation.gov** for reservations.

Because #17 is a little higher than the campground road and therefore slightly more visible than some of the other spots and because it's just slightly closer to the campground road than space #16, we gave this an A rating. But it's still a very private spot thanks to a thick forest of aspens on three sides. A line of aspens also grow in front of the site, partially filtering it from view of the campground road. It has no neighbors across the street, and no neighbors are visible on the left or right.

## Willow Campground

**Directions:** From Bishop and Highway 395, travel west on West Line Street (State Route 168) for approximately 15 miles. Turn left on South Lake Road and drive approximately 5 miles to the campground on the left.

**What's It Like?**

This cozy campground, suitable only for tents, camper vans, and pickup trucks with camper shells, is a haven surrounded by willows and aspens. It is the closest campground to South Lake.

## What's It Near?

• Fishing for rainbow, brown, brook, and Alpers trout in Bishop Creek, Intake 2, North Lake, South Lake, and Lake Sabrina.

• Boating, kayaking, and canoeing on Intake 2, North Lake, South Lake, and Lake Sabrina.

• Hikes: Blue Lake (6 miles round trip), Donkey Lake (8 miles round trip), Marie Louise Lake (4 miles round trip to lower lake), Chocolate Lakes (6 miles round trip to Upper Chocolate Lake), Treasure Lakes (6 miles round trip to lakes 1 and 2, 7.7 miles round trip to upper lakes), Long Lake (4 miles round trip), Bishop Lake (8.5 miles round trip), Bishop Pass (11.4 miles round trip), Tyee Lakes (7.6 miles round trip to Tyee Lake 5), Green Lake (6 miles round trip), Brown Lake (3 miles round trip), and Horton Lakes (7.6 miles round trip if you have a 4 X 4 with high clearance that can reach the locked gate at the trailhead, 8.3 miles round trip with a passenger car).

• Horseback riding through Rainbow Pack Outfitters.

• Cardinal Village Resort serves breakfast and lunch until 3 p.m. and dinner on the deck on Mondays and Tuesdays from mid-June until mid-August (reservations recommended). Be sure to try their homemade salsa. They serve all you can eat pizza every Saturday evening in summer.

• Bishop Creek Lodge has a small store with limited groceries and camping and fishing supplies. Stop in their restaurant for gourmet pizzas, burgers, Yukon gold crosscut French fries, chili, and steaks. Brave customers can venture to the bar to try a Duck Fart signature drink. Top off your meal with pie or a milkshake.

• Lake Sabrina Boat Landing Café serves breakfast and lunch on weekends in summer accompanied by a spectacular view of Lake Sabrina and the Sierra Crest in the background. They're famous for their homemade pies with homemade vanilla ice cream.

• The South Fork Café at Parchers Resort features a self-serve breakfast Monday through Friday. They also have a scrumptious breakfast buffet on Saturday and Sunday including an all-you-can-eat waffle bar, scrambled eggs, biscuits n' gravy, bacon, sausage, fresh fruit, quiche, and homemade baked goods such as sticky buns, French toast bakes, and more.

**Elevation**: 9,000 feet

**Toilets:** Vault

**Verizon Cell Service?** No

**Takes Reservations?** No. First-come, first-served.

**Number of Sites:** 8

**Bear Boxes?** Yes

### Campsites with the Most Privacy

**#1 Privacy Rating: A+**
**Reservable?** No. First-come, first-served.

Bordered on two sides by aspens and punctuated at the far end with lichen-covered boulders, this is a peaceful and private site. There are no spaces across the campground road, and its only neighbor—#2 to the right—isn't visible.

**#2 Privacy Rating: A+**
**Reservable?** No. First-come, first-served.

Aspens hug the left and right sides of this campsite and giant boulders loom up behind. No neighbors are visible on any side. A site definitely worth grabbing.

**#8 Privacy Rating: A+**
**Reservable?** No. First-come, first-served.

Another beauty of a spot, although sunnier than #1 and #2. A hill, decorated with some low-growing aspens, rises up behind the space. To the left and right are yet more aspens— no neighbors in sight.

# WHITE MOUNTAINS – ANCIENT BRISTLECONE PINES

## Grandview Campground

**Directions:** From Big Pine travel east on Highway 168 for about 12 miles. Turn left on White Mountain Road and drive 5 miles to the campground on the left.

**What's It Like?**

If you like camping under the stars, you'll love Grandview Campground, set among the pinyon pines and junipers of the White Mountains. Its location far from civilization means the campground is a stargazer's paradise. Astronomers gather here and often stay up all night to watch the show in the night sky.

The spaces in the upper part of the campground have more privacy than the ones down below in the main part of the campground. Our biggest beef with many of the sites in the lower section is that their fire pits and picnic tables are really close to the campground road. The lower part of the campground, which backs up to a meadow, is usually more popular with astronomers. On weekends, this campground fills up fast, so you're going to want to get here early on a Friday or start your weekend early and stake out your spot on Thursday.

The campground is free, but they request a $5 donation to help with maintenance costs.

**Words of Warning**: There is no water at this campground and there aren't any streams nearby to filter water. It's a half hour's drive to civilization from here so be certain to bring your own water.

Also, a ranger told us that there's talk of putting more campsites in the upper part of the campground. This could change the vibe there considerably. The decision hasn't been made yet, and we hope if they do add campsites that they are well-spaced from their neighbors. To stay informed about any changes at this campground, visit the campground updates page at www.ilovetheeasternsierra.com and sign up for our email list on the website.

**What's It Near?**

• A lookout on the road to the visitor's center provides impressive views of the imposing wall of the Sierra, which stares back at you from across the Owen's Valley.

• Two groves of Bristlecone Pines, the oldest-living things on Earth, are a half hour to an hour's drive away. The Patriarch Grove, 12 miles northwest of the visitor's center, is more isolated up a bumpy dirt road that is accessible by passenger car. We found this grove to be the more interesting of the two, surrounded by spectacular scenery. However, the oldest trees are growing in the Schulman Grove, lower down by the visitor's center.

• This is the closest established campground to the trailhead to 14,246-foot White Mountain Peak. Out of all the Fourteeners in California, this has the easiest access, although the 7-mile hike to the top is no walk in the park. The trail—really a dirt road—starts at 12,000 feet, so there's a 2,246 foot elevation gain. Compare that to the 6,500 feet of elevation gain hiking up to California's most famous Fourteener, Mt. Whitney. The hike becomes five miles on two days of the year in July, August, or early September when the White Mountain Research Center keeps its annual tradition of opening up the gate at the trailhead, allowing you to park two miles up the road at the research center. Visit **www.wmrc.edu**, click on general info, and then news to find out what dates the gate will open in a given year.

• A short trail leads from the visitor's center to The Mexican Mine.

• The Grandview Mine is about a mile drive on a dirt road that departs from the campground. High-clearance, 4WD vehicles recommended. You'll see ancient mining relics and great views of the Sierra.

• Plenty of dirt roads for mountain biking, some with spectacular views of the Sierra.

**Elevation:** 8,600 feet

**Toilets:** Vault

**Verizon Cell Service?** No

**Takes Reservations?** No. First-come, first-served.

**Number of Sites:** 23

**Bear Boxes?** Not needed. No bears in the White Mountains.

**Campsites with the Most Privacy**

**#10 Privacy Rating: A**
**Reservable?** No. First-come, first-served.

The only site with privacy in the lower part of the campground, it sits off by itself, pushed far back against a sagebrush meadow. Trees partially block it from view of the campground road, so it doesn't feel as exposed as some of the sites in this section. Although this is a very sunny spot, the branches of one juniper offer some relief. No neighbors across the street and proximity to the bathrooms are additional advantages.

**#20 Privacy Rating: A**
**Reservable?** No. First-come, first-served.

With lots of separation between #20 and its neighbors, this site is one of a number of nice spots in the upper section of the campground. You can barely see a couple of other sites from here through the junipers and pinyons surrounding them. More trees serve as a backdrop to this site. A sunny spot in the morning and afternoon, #20 has one tall juniper shading a nice area for a tent. Also an ideal spot for a trailer or RV, thanks to the pull through.

**#21 Privacy Rating: A-**
**Reservable?** No. First-come, first-served.

Sitting on an island in the middle of four branches of the campground road, this spot is surprisingly private for its location. We stayed here on a trip to celebrate our first wedding anniversary. The junipers and pinyons that surround much of the campsite partially shelter it from view from the campground road. You have a glimpse of the picnic table of site #20 from here, but the two sites are far away from each other. The lack of any other nearby neighbors made us feel as if we were cushioned in solitude. It's also near a bathroom, located behind a wall of pinyon pines and junipers to the right of the site.

**#22 Privacy Rating: A+**
**Reservable?** No. First-come, first-served.

At the end of a spur in the campground road, this site is surrounded by solitude, with no neighbors visible in any direction. A large pinyon relieves the site from the sun. A dead tree lies like a fallen wooden soldier behind the space, adding a touch of personality. A blooming cactus behind the campsite looks like it might add a splotch of color in the summer. A pull-through loop for a driveway makes this a good spot for a trailer, although campers with a tent will appreciate it, too.

**#23 Privacy Rating: A+**
**Reservable?** No. First-come, first-served.

This is a gem of a campsite, with an uphill sea of pinyons and junipers stretching out behind it. Even though #21 is across the street, you can't see it from the picnic table or fire pit of #23 due to ample distance between the sites and a curtain of trees screening the view. No neighbors are visible on any side. It's far back from the campground road, too. We recommend hiking up the hill behind this campsite. As you climb to the top, you'll find views of the Sierra to the west, and mountains bordering Death Valley to the east. The day we hiked the hill, a storm was breaking up, and the ribbons of light rippled across the mountains to the east as the sun broke through the clouds.

# BIG PINE CREEK CANYON

## Sage Flat Campground

**Directions:** From Big Pine turn west on Crocker Street and travel 9.2 miles to campground on your left.

## What's It Like?

This campground has a main busy section sandwiched between two small, more tranquil areas. Despite its name, much of the campground is in an aspen and conifer forest next to Big Pine Creek. The main part of the campground is very open, with spaces near each other under the pines and very little underbrush. But we did find some nice spots away from all the action.

## What's It Near?

• North Fork Trail Hikes: Lon Chaney's cabin (5.5 miles round trip), Second Lake (9.5 miles round trip), loop hike to Second through Seventh Lake (13.1 miles round trip), Palisade Glacier View (21 miles round trip). I have hiked to Second Lake and can say it holds a place in my heart as one of the most beautiful lakes in the Eastern Sierra. It's fed by a glacier, which turns the  water to turquoise. Temple Crag creates an imposing backdrop.

• South Fork Trail Hikes: Brainerd Lake (11 miles round trip), Finger Lake (uphill 500 feet cross-country from Brainerd Lake).

• Fishing for rainbow trout in Big Pine Creek and in Glacier Lodge's trout pond.

• Horseback riding through Glacier Pack Train.

• Glacier Lodge has a fish cleaning station, limited fishing and camping supplies, ice, and showers.

**Elevation:** 7,400 feet

**Toilets:** Vault

**Verizon Cell Service?** No

**Takes Reservations?** No. First-come, first-served.

**Number of Campsites:** 28

**Bear Boxes?** Yes

## Campsites with the Most Privacy

**#2 Privacy Rating: B+**
**Reservable?** No. First-come, first-served.

Near the campground entrance and pay station, #2 is surrounded by greenery, which partially filters the view of the spaces to the left and right. It's close to Big Pine Creek — which flows behind the site — but not right on the banks. There's no one across the street. This section of the campground is tranquil, thanks to its location apart from the commotion of the rest of the campground.

**Words of Warning:** There was no number marker on this campsite. It was between #1 and #3. Since there was no cone or anything blocking the site, we presume it is open. The camp host wasn't around during our visit, so we couldn't ask.

**#3 Privacy Rating: B+**
**Reservable?** No. First-come, first-served.

Sunken down from the road slightly, this site is similar to #2, with a partial view of your neighbors to the left and right through a curtain of vegetation. The view of the stream

behind the site is obscured by greenery. Its lack of neighbors across the street and its location in this more tranquil section of the campground, make this spot an ideal choice.

**#25 Privacy Rating: B+**
**Reservable?** No. First-come, first-served.

This site is well-spaced from its neighbors to the left and right and vegetation and trees filter views of any nearby campsites. No other camp spaces across the street, either. It's located away from the more energetic main section of the campground, giving it a quiet vibe.

**#26 Privacy Rating: B+**
**Reservable?** No. First-come, first-served.

On a cul-de-sac loop away from the more crowded section of the campground, this site is near the stream and well spaced from its neighbors. A canopy of aspens provide some shade.

**#27 Privacy Rating: A+**
**Reservable?** No. First-come, first-served.

A beautiful shady site with Big Pine Creek splashing along

behind it in clear view, #27's nearest neighbor—#28—is out of sight behind greenery. There are no neighbors across the street and #26 is far enough away to the left to ensure it doesn't ruin your privacy. This is by far the best site in the campground for privacy.

**#28 Privacy Rating: A**
**Reservable?** No. First-come, first-served.

This site, which punctuates the end of the cul de sac loop, is nearly as good as #27, with one disadvantage—the main road up Big Pine Creek Canyon is to the right just a bit farther than a stone's throw away. However, the road isn't terribly busy, so I wouldn't hesitate to stay in this streamside spot. It has only one neighbor, #27 to the left, but greenery obscures the view. Half in the sagebrush, half in the trees, it's a sunnier spot than #27, but it still has plenty of shade. Aspens provide a peaceful backdrop.

## Upper Sage Flat

**Directions:** From Big Pine turn west on Crocker Street and travel 9.8 miles to campground on your left.

**What's It Like?**

This campground is more befitting of its name than its lower neighbor, with a lot of the sites out in the open sage and rabbitbrush. Jeffrey pines and aspens gather closer to the stream, providing some shade in streamside spots. This campground has a very busy feel to it, but there are some campsites that we feel are worthy of this book (see below for descriptions).

## What's It Near?

• North Fork Trail Hikes: Lon Chaney's cabin (5.5 miles round trip), Second Lake (9.5 miles round trip), loop hike to Second through Seventh Lake (13.1 miles round trip), Palisade Glacier View (21 miles round trip). I have hiked to Second Lake and can say it holds a place in my heart as one of the most beautiful lakes in the Eastern Sierra. It's fed by a glacier, which turns the water to turquoise. Temple Crag creates an imposing backdrop.

• South Fork Trail Hikes: Brainerd Lake (11 miles round trip), Finger Lake (uphill 500 feet cross-country from Brainerd Lake).

• Fishing for rainbow trout in Big Pine Creek and in Glacier Lodge's trout pond.

• Horseback riding through Glacier Pack Train.

• Glacier Lodge has a fish cleaning station, limited fishing and camping supplies, ice, and showers.

**Elevation:** 7,600 feet

**Toilets:** Vault

**Verizon Cell Phone Service?** No

**Takes Reservations?** Yes. Visit **www.recreation.gov** for reservations. A small number of sites are first-come, first-served.

**Number of Campsites:** 20

**Bear Boxes?** Yes

# Campsites with the Most Privacy

**#8 Privacy Rating: B+**
**Reservable?** Yes. Visit **www.recreation.gov** for reservations.

Set back from the campground road with the stream immediately behind it, #8 is well-spaced from its neighbors, especially compared to some of the sites in this campground. There is a space to #8's left, but there's plenty of elbow room between the two spots and vegetation helps filter the view. Conifers provide some shade near the rear of the site. This is an ideal spot for an angler.

**#10 Privacy Rating: A+**
**Reservable?** Yes. Visit **www.recreation.gov** for reservations.

You're going to have to fight for this spot when making reservations on recreation.gov because it's popular—and rightly so. At the end of a cul de sac, it has no neighbors behind, to the left, or right. It has a wonderful view of the creek—which ambles along to the right of the site—and of a cute little pedestrian bridge. Another great home away from home for an angler.

**#11 Privacy Rating: B**
**Reservable?** No, First-come, first-served.

Another streamside spot that's reasonably well-spaced from its neighbors on the left and right. Big Pine Creek marches along behind the site. It's not as nice as #8 or #9 because it's more exposed, but it's a step above many of the spaces in the campground.

**#18 Privacy Rating: A+**
**Reservable?** Yes. Visit **www.recreation.gov** for reservations.

This is a sweet spot set well-back from the campground road.

The stream—visible from the site—skips over a miniature cascade immediately behind #18. Set up your camp chair by the conifer-lined banks and read, daydream, or fish. Plenty of trees provide shade over the camp space. There are neighbors to the right, but they're closer to the campground road while

#18 is pushed farther back. Plus, vegetation partially hides those neighbors from view. There are no immediate neighbors on the left or across the street.

**Big Pine Creek Campground**

**Directions:** From Big Pine turn west on Crocker Street and travel 10.7 miles to campground on your left.

**What's It Like?**

Many campgrounds have a hub of activity and other sections that feel more peaceful and quiet. But all of Big Pine Creek Campground feels peaceful and quiet. Spaces sit under the pines and in the willows and aspens. Many sites are located next to Big Pine Creek. Of the three campgrounds in Big Pine Creek canyon, this one has the most tranquil atmosphere. The tent pads here are especially nice. Unfortunately, the few first-come, first-served sites in this campground are not the most private. You'll have to make reservations to grab one of the really good spots described below.

**What's It Near?**

• North Fork Trail Hikes: Lon Chaney's cabin (5.5 miles round trip), Second Lake (9.5 miles round trip), loop hike to Second through Seventh Lake (13.1 miles round trip), Palisade Glacier View (21 miles round trip). I have hiked to Second Lake and can say it holds a place in my heart as one of the most beautiful lakes in the Eastern Sierra. It's fed by a glacier, which turns the water into turquoise. Temple Crag creates an imposing backdrop.

• South Fork Trail Hikes: Brainerd Lake (11 miles round trip), Finger Lake (uphill 500 feet cross-country from Brainerd Lake).

• Fishing for rainbow trout in Big Pine Creek and in Glacier Lodge's trout pond.

• Horseback riding through Glacier Pack Train.

• Glacier Lodge has a fish cleaning station, limited fishing and camping supplies, ice, and showers.

**Elevation:** 7,700 feet

**Toilets:** Vault

**Verizon Cell Phone Service?** No

**Takes Reservations?** Yes. Visit **www.recreation.gov** for reservations. Only a few sites are first-come, first served.

**Number of Campsites:** 30

**Bear Boxes?** Yes

# Campsites with the Most Privacy

**#10 Privacy Rating: A+**
**Reservable?** Yes. Visit **www.recreation.gov** for reservations.

Mother nature created a room where the walls are tall bushes. A short path lined with vegetation leads into #10. There are no neighbors to the immediate left and willows obliterate the view of the neighbor to the right. No neighbors behind it either and greenery curtains off any view of #11 across the street. This spot is bathed in sunlight in the afternoon so you might want to bring a canopy to put over the picnic table.

**#11 Privacy Rating: A+**
**Reservable?** Yes. Visit **www.recreation.gov** for reservations.

Low-growing aspens and tall bushes surround this site on three sides. Site #10 across the street also is blocked from view. #11 is a dream come true for anyone who wants privacy while camping. To the rear of the site, behind the trees, mountains soar up in the distance.

**#13 Privacy Rating: A+**
**Reservable?** Yes. Visit **www.recreation.gov** for reservations.

Another site enclosed in aspens and bushes with not even a

peek of a neighbor to the left or right, #13 is an ideal place to spend the night. Aspens serve as a backdrop to the campsite. Similar to #10 and #11, but this site is just a bit closer to the bathrooms.

## #14 Privacy Rating: A
**Reservable?** Yes. Visit **www.recreation.gov** for reservations.

This site shares a driveway with #15 on the right, but once you walk into the campsite you'll forget you have a neighbor on that side. At least, you won't be able to see #15, because you're tucked back from the road more, and Mother Nature conveniently placed some bushes and trees to block the view. What you *can* see is a glimpse of a serene meadow behind the campsite. Plenty of greenery to the left also hides the view of anyone in that direction. From some places in #14, there's a view of the mountains, although you can't see the glaciers from here.

## #15 Privacy Rating: A-
**Reservable?** Yes. Visit **www.recreation.gov** for reservations.

Connected at the hip to #14 by a shared driveway that eventually splits apart to the two campsites, #15 is still a very private spot thanks to the bushes and trees in front of site #14. This site is higher up than #14 on a small hill, giving it a better view of the willow-filled meadow behind it. A few tall pines graciously offer shade, but the picnic table and bear box are bathed in afternoon sun. There are no neighbors to the right or behind it and no neighbors directly across the street. We gave this site a slightly lower privacy rating than #14 because #15 is in clear view of the neighbors in #14 when they park their car in the shared driveway. If the folks staying in #14 were to park a big trailer in the driveway, you will feel observed. In fact, if a trailer were to park in the driveway, #15 might seem more like a B campsite. Like #14, this site has a good view of the mountains, although the glaciers are just out of sight, obscured from view by tall conifers on the other side of the campground.

**#16 Privacy Rating: A-**
**Reservable?** Yes. Visit **www.recreation.gov** for reservations.

This tent-only site has personality. Three stairs lead from the main part of the campsite to the tent pad, which is almost completely encircled by tall greenery and willows. The plants bend over the place for the tent, creating what we call a tent cave. It almost feels like you're sleeping in a room where the walls are plants. Other than the shady tent cave, this is a very sunny spot. If you're going to spend time here mid-day, we suggest setting up a canopy over the picnic table. The picnic table and fire pit are closer to the campground road than we like, but this space is on a spur loop away from the rest of the camp and the road won't see much traffic. Plus, there are no other spots across the street.

**#17 Privacy Rating: A+**
**Reservable?** Yes. Visit **www.recreation.gov** for reservations.

In a world of its own at the end of a cul de sac loop, this is a sweet spot. The driveway is surrounded on either side by greenery and tall pines behind the site provide shade. #17 has no immediate neighbors on any side—including across the campground road. #18 is to the right, but it's far away and vegetation shields it from view.

### #19 Privacy Rating: A+
**Reservable?** Yes. Visit **www.recreation.gov** for reservations.

Off by itself, #19 has no neighbors to the left, right, behind, or across the street. Immediately to the left, you have a peek-a-boo view of the stream through thick vegetation. The tent pad is next to and slightly above the stream, which will sing you a lullaby at night. As an added bonus, the picnic table and bear box are surrounded by wild roses, which will add a splash of color in late June to early July. There's a view of the mountains but the glaciers aren't visible from here. This is a very open, sunny site that boasts lots of privacy.

### #21 Privacy Rating: A-
**Reservable?:** Yes. Visit **www.recreation.gov** for reservations.

A shady, streamside spot, well-spaced from its neighbors, this is a popular site due to the creek— partially visible through the willows—splashing around behind the camp space. Low-growing vegetation in the front of the site partially filters the view of the campground road, although it doesn't block it from sight completely. There are no immediate neighbors on the right and the space to the left is far away and hidden by vegetation. Greenery in front of the camp partially filters the view of the neighbor across the street. Most of the time, you're going to be looking at the creek anyway.

### #22 Privacy Rating: B
**Reservable?** Yes. Visit **www.recreation.gov** for reservations

Recreation.gov calls this a choice site due to its location next to the stream, but from a privacy perspective it's not the best site in the campground. There's nothing but a small meadow between #22 and it's neighbor on the left, #24. The spaces aren't close together but they're within full view of each other and just close enough to knock down the privacy rating. I camped in #24 the year I was acclimating to climb to the top of Mount Whitney and when there were neighbors in #22 I did feel rather exposed. However, #22's location, with the stream flowing behind it and the fact that greenery hides its neighbor to the right from view make this spot worthy of including in this book. #22 also has a neighbor across the way (#23) but their fire pit and table are back far enough from the campground road that they don't steal your privacy.

---

**Are You Enjoying This Book? Write a Review on Amazon.com**

Your input is important to us. Write a review on Amazon and let us know if we've succeeded in helping you find a peaceful campsite.

# INDEPENDENCE CREEK CANYON

## Upper and Lower Gray's Meadow

**Directions:** From Independence, travel 6 miles west on Market Street to the campground on the right.

**What's It Like?**

This campground gets overshadowed by its dramatic high-altitude sibling up the road (Onion Valley Campground), but Gray's Meadow possesses a more subtle beauty. It sits under the black oaks and in the willows and sagebrush on the banks of Independence Creek. Some of the campsites have views of Mount Williamson. You'll have a good choice of campsites with privacy here. Because of its lower elevation, Gray's Meadow can roast in the summer, but many of the campsites have a lot of shade to help cool you off.

**Words of Warning:** Watch out for rattlesnakes here. Sightings are rare, but it's a good idea to watch where you're walking, just in case.

**What's It Near?**

• This is the nearest established campground to the Shepherd's Pass trailhead. Even if you don't want to tackle the strenuous hike to the pass, traveling a mile to four miles up the trail will lead you past a wildflower-lined stream to a hefty climb up switchbacks with views of Mount Williamson. Anyone not traveling on to the pass can end the hike within view of a cataract splashing its way down the canyon or simply stop after the first mile before the trail starts heading steeply up hill.

• Manzanar National Historic Site is about a ten-minute drive away from the campground, 5 miles south of Independence on Highway 395. Manzanar was where the government relocated Japanese Americans against their will during World War II, a sobering reminder out of the past.

• Hikes that depart from nearby Onion Valley: Gilbert Lake (4.6 miles round trip), Kearsarge Pass (9.6 miles round trip), Matlock Lake (6.8 miles round trip), Robinson Lake (a steep 3.4 miles round trip). Kearsarge Pass is one of my favorite hikes of all time. I can still remember the joy I felt when I crested the ridge and caught my first glimpse of the snow-capped peaks undulating off into the distance with Kearsarge Lakes glimmering below. It's also one of the easiest passes to hike to in the Eastern Sierra, although it's no walk in the park.

• Horseback riding through Onion Valley Pack Train.

• Fishing in Independence Creek. Best place to fish is from just above the Upper Gray's Meadow Campground down to the Inyo-county operated Independence Creek Campground. This is where the Department of Fish and Game stocks the creek.

**Elevation:** 6,000 feet

**Toilets:** Flush

**Verizon Cell Phone Service?** No.

**Takes Reservations?** Yes. Visit **www.recreation.gov** for reservations. Some sites are first-come, first-served.

**Number of Campsites:** 52

**Bear Boxes?** Yes

# Campsites with the Most Privacy

## Upper Gray's Meadow

**#1 Privacy Rating: A**
**Reservable?** Yes. Visit **www.recreation.gov** for reservations.

A thick forest of willows and black oaks to the left and right of #1 embrace the campsite and give it a lot of privacy, and a little shade, too. The space to the left is completely hidden from view, and there are no spaces to the right. Both #1 and the neighboring site across the street are pushed so far back from the road that they're not interfering with each other.

**#2 Privacy Rating: A+**
**Reservable?** No. First-come, first-served.

This is another nice site enclosed with willows and black oaks on three sides. It has no neighbors to the left, and the site to the right is invisible through the thick foliage near #2's picnic table and fire pit—although you do have a slight view of that campsite from your parking area. Mother Nature built a green wall of privacy behind the site using lots of willows and black oaks. Because it's far back from the road and so is the campsite across the street, you don't have to worry about anyone in that direction either.

**#4 Privacy Rating: A**
**Reservable?** No. First-come, first-served.

Willows hug the right side of the campsite with no other spaces beyond that anywhere in the vicinity. On the left, there's a filtered view of #2's parking area through the vegetation. Behind the campsite, a sea of willows undulates toward a partial view of the Sierra. A couple of black oaks punctuating the rear of the site provide some shade. This one also has a nice tent pad. #4 is more suitable for tents, camper vans, pickups with camper tops, and very small trailers.

### #10 Privacy Rating: B+
**Reservable?** Yes. Visit **www.recreation.gov** for reservations.

This site has a lot of personality thanks to its location under a tree cave, where the willows droop over the site, creating a roof of greenery. It has no neighbors to the immediate left, behind, or across the street, where Lone Pine Creek flows. You can't see the creek from the site, but you can hear it. The reason we gave this a B+ rating is because the neighbors to the right are closer than we would have liked. Still, the trees partially obscure them from view, and when you're in your willow cave you probably won't notice them much.

### #12 Privacy Rating: A
**Reservable?** Yes. Visit **www.recreation.gov** for reservations.

With no neighbors visible to the left, right, or behind, #12 has a good cushion of privacy. Willows do a good job of hiding the view of the neighbor across the street. One advantage of this site is that you can see the creek passing by to the right— and you can hear it, too. #12 is very shady and pleasant. The maximum vehicle length here is only 25 feet, so this site is best suited for a tent, a pickup truck with a camper top, a camper van, or a small trailer.

### #19 Privacy Rating: A+
**Reservable?** Yes. Visit **www.recreation.gov** for reservations.

This is one of the most private campsites in the Eastern Sierra. It's sunken down far from the campground road and you wouldn't know it was there if it wasn't for the camp space number. A thick forest of willows and other trees enclose the site on all sides so it feels like you're in a room with walls made of greenery and a blue sky ceiling. And it's near the stream, too, although you can't see it from the campsite. However, its biggest advantage—its location sunken down far from the road—is also its biggest disadvantage because to reach the campsite from the parking area you have to lug all your stuff down 16 steep stairs. We'd be willing to get the extra exercise in order to camp in a space with this much privacy, but it's your call.

## #21 Privacy Rating: A+
**Reservable?** Yes. Visit **www.recreation.gov** for reservations.

#21 is a cozy spot pushed back from the campground road. Willow surround the picnic table and fire pit. No neighbors are visible on either side or behind and there are no campsites across the street, either. The willows and a pine to the right of the driveway provide some shade. It's also near the bathroom.

## #32 Privacy Rating: B+
**Reservable?** No. First-come, first-served.

The massive wall of the Inyo Mountains rise up to the east of this campsite, so set your chair out in the evening and watch the setting sun paint them with color. Mighty Mount Williamson also is within view. #32 is a high desert campsite, with plenty of sagebrush and rabbitbrush. But it does have one large Jeffrey pine and a tall deciduous tree to provide a little shade. Tall desert vegetation—what looks like bitterbrush—partially conceals a neighbor visible to the right, about 24 to 30 feet away. There are no immediate neighbors to the left and none directly across the street, either. If it wasn't for the neighbor to the right, this would be an A+ campsite.

## #33 Privacy Rating: A+
**Reservable?** Yes. Visit **www.recreation.gov** for reservations.

Located where the sagebrush meets the willows, pines, and black oaks, #33 boasts spectacular views of the Inyo

Mountains to the east. To the west, Mount Williamson, the second highest peak in California, soars up towards the sky. No neighbors are visible on three sides and the only neighbor in sight is down the campground road far away. Out of view behind the willows next to #33, Independence Creek serenades anyone who camps here. There's some shade, especially if you gravitate toward the fringes of the camp space, but mid-day expect a good dose of sun.

**#34 Privacy Rating: B**
**Reservable?** No. First-come, first-served.

Unlike many of the other sites in this campground that are tucked into the willows, this one is more out in the open among the sagebrush and rabbitbrush. However, a smattering of tall pines provide some shade. There's a space behind this one but it's about 40 to 50 feet away, so it doesn't feel as if the people there are breathing down your neck. On the left, there's a space about 42 feet away—also a good distance. The space across the street isn't in view and there are no neighbors visible to the immediate right. This is a nice spot for stargazers, and the location opens up views of the mountains you don't have from a lot of the other sites.

**#35 Privacy Rating: A+**
**Reservable?** Yes. Visit **www.recreation.gov** for reservations.

The willows open up a little nook into which this campsite fits neatly. The willows also hide the picnic table from view of the campground road. You can see no spaces on any side, and there's no one across the street. Some morning and late afternoon shade keep the Sierra sun at bay. Overall, a very private space.

**#37 Privacy Rating: A+**
**Reservable?** Yes. Visit **www.recreation.gov** for reservations.

A shady spot sheltered from view of the campground road, #37 delivers a lot of privacy in a peaceful setting with no neighbors in sight to the left or right and no other spots across the campground road. Tall willows drape over the picnic table and tent area. Black oaks and willows on the right and willows on the left shade the campsite. The road to Onion Valley swerves by to the right of the driveway, but vegetation screens out most of the view of the road and the picnic table and tent area are so far away from the road that this shouldn't pose an issue.

**#38 Privacy Rating: A+**
**Reservable?** No. First-come, first-served.

You pull into a willow-lined alley to reach this site. Shaped like a rectangular room with willow walls, shady #38 is pushed back from the road. Thanks to the thick greenery, no neighbors are visible to the left, right, or behind, and there are no spaces across the street. Willows drape over the tent area, creating a cozy little "cave" where you can spend the night. The creek is across the street.

**#39 Privacy Rating: A+**
**Reservable?** Yes. Visit **www.recreation.gov** for reservations.

Almost a twin to its neighbor #38, this campsite also sits among the willows, which line up like sentinels on either side of the driveway and behind the campsite. As with #38, willows in this camp space drape over the tent area, providing a shady spot to call home. Unlike #38, #39 also has just a peek of a mountain view over the willows. There are no neighbors to the left, right, or behind, and the stream flows across the street.

**#40 Privacy Rating: A-**
**Reservable?** Yes. Visit **www.recreation.gov** for reservations.

This spacious, streamside campsite isn't as private as some of the other spots in this campground. It's visible from the campground road, although some bushes provide a partial privacy screen and it's back just far enough from the road that it doesn't feel like anyone driving by is right in your face. A neighbor is visible on the right, although they're a good distance away, about 48 feet. However, #40 has the advantage of having Independence Creek directly behind it, which you can glimpse through gaps in the greenery growing on the banks. Black oaks spread their branches overhead to block out a lot of the sun.

**Words of Warning:** because of this campsite's location, other campers arriving at night might shine their headlights at you as they enter the campground. With only 16 campsites in this lower section, there won't be a ton of cars driving in, so perhaps this won't be much of an issue, but we wanted to warn you it is a possibility.

**#50 Privacy Rating: A-**
**Reservable?** Yes. Visit **www.recreation.gov** for reservations.

Carved out of the sagebrush and rabbitbrush, #50 has a more open feel, but its location far from the campground road and the fact it has no nearby neighbors give it a lot of privacy. You can see the neighbors to the right, but they're about 50 feet away. To reach the picnic table and fire pit from the driveway, you wander along a 20-foot path lined with sagebrush and rabbitbrush, A big black oak provides shade to what would otherwise be a sun-blasted high-desert campsite. This campsite also has a good view of the Sierra and Mount Williamson.

**#51 Privacy Rating: A+**
**Reservable?** Yes. Visit **www.recreation.gov** for reservations.

This roomy campsite has it all. It's shady thanks to a forest of black oaks. It's next to the creek. It has a partial view of the Inyo Mountains to the east. And the only visible neighbor is so far away to the right that you have more than enough elbow room. There is a neighbor across the street, but #51 is set far enough back, meaning there's good distance between the two spaces. Besides, the view of the Inyo Mountains in the opposite direction will likely capture your attention.

## Onion Valley Campground

**Directions:** From Independence, turn west on Market Street and travel 15 miles to the campground.

**What's It Like?**

Onion Valley is one of the most magical places in the Sierra. If you've never been here before, try to arrive in daylight because the drive up the road to Onion Valley is an adventure in itself. At first, the road shoots straight toward the mountains, with a full-on view of the wall of the High Sierra in front of you. As the road curls back and forth around sharp curves and you climb higher, spectacular views of Independence and the Inyo Mountains open up to the east. You'll feel a moment of joy when you first arrive in the valley and see the waterfalls and the majestic mountain peaks.

The most private campsites are located in the aspens, while other sites under the pines have more shade but less privacy. Some of the walk-in sites are the most private. You can park your car next to these sites to unload, but you'll have to move your vehicle to the parking lot about 1/16 mile away.

**Words of Warning**: The road up to Onion Valley is not recommended for large motorhomes and the campground is only suitable for tents, camper vans, and pickup trucks with camper shells.

Onion Valley is located at 9,200 feet above sea level, so if you're coming from sea level drink lots of water before you arrive and during your visit. And take it easy the first day there. If you show any signs of altitude sickness (severe headache, nausea) go down to a lower elevation. Gray's Meadow, lower down on the road to Onion Valley, is a peaceful lower-elevation campground (6,000 feet) where you can acclimate for a couple nights before moving up the road.

---

## What's It Near?

• Hikes: Gilbert Lake (4.6 miles round trip), Kearsarge Pass (9.6 miles round trip), Matlock Lake (6.8 miles round trip), Robinson Lake (a steep 3.4 miles round trip). Kearsarge Pass is one of my favorite hikes of all time. I can still remember the joy I felt when I crested the ridge and caught my first glimpse of the snow-capped peaks undulating off into the distance with Kearsarge Lakes glimmering below. It's also one of the easiest passes to hike to in the Eastern Sierra, although it's no walk in the park.

• Hardy hikers can also tackle the trail to Golden Trout Lakes or Dragon Peak Lakes, each about a 5.6-mile round-trip hike. The trail climbs steeply uphill next to the waterfall — the one with the rusty orange stripe behind it. When you get to the meadow above the falls the trails to Golden Trout Lakes and Dragon Peak Lakes become fainter so it's a good idea to get a topo map before undertaking the journey.

• Horseback riding through Onion Valley Pack Train.

• Fishing in one of the many backcountry lakes mentioned above.

**Elevation:** 9,200 Feet

**Toilets:** Vault

**Verizon Cell Phone Service?** Spotty. Best reception is usually on the Kearsarge Pass trail within view of Independence, and you're more likely to be able to access text messages there rather than make calls.

**Takes Reservations?** Yes. Visit **www.recreation.gov** for reservations. Some sites are first-come, first-served.

**Number of Campsites:** 29

**Bear Boxes?** Yes

## Campsites with the Most Privacy

### #2 Privacy Rating: A-
**Reservable?** Yes. Visit **www.recreation.gov** for reservations.

Aspens surround this site on three sides. It has a partial view of one of the waterfalls. People can see into this campsite as they walk or drive past, so it's not as private as #6 or #7, but it's not completely out in the open thanks to the aspens and its location pushed back from the campground road. Overall, a peaceful space.

### #3 Privacy Rating: B-
**Reservable?** Yes. Visit **www.recreation.gov** for reservations.

This site has no immediate neighbors to the left or right, giving it a semblance of privacy. #1 is behind #3 but plenty of vegetation hides the view. You have a glimpse of one of the waterfalls from this campsite, and it has the advantage of a tall pine shading part of it. #2 is across the street, but that site is back so far from the campground road that having a neighbor there doesn't rain on your privacy parade. If this site has a flaw, it's that it's nearer the campground road than many of the campsites, which is why we marked down its privacy rating.

### #5 Privacy Rating: A
**Reservable?** No. First-come, first-served.

This is a spacious spot, well spaced from other campsites. The only nearby neighbor is campsite #6 across the street, but #6 is so well hidden from the campground road it feels like you have no nearby neighbors at all. There's room here for two tents. And from places in the campsite, both waterfalls are visible. The one disadvantage is that #5 is elevated from the road, so you're on display more than in some of the camp spaces. Still, there's some low-growing aspens and other vegetation surrounding the campsite, so it's not completely exposed.

**Words of Warning**: This is a walk-in site, but you can park your car right next to it and unload all your stuff before moving your car to the parking lot about 1/16 mile away.

### #6 Privacy Rating: A+
**Reservable?** No. First-come, first-served.

This campsite is more like a hotel room where the walls are aspens. A short path leads from the campground road through low-growing aspens to the campsite. The site is mostly hidden from the road and is tied with #7 as having the most privacy in the campground. I like this site better later in the summer, when the waterfall under the rusty orange stripe on the mountain has dried up, because from #6 you have a much better view of the cascade draining from Robinson Lake, and that cascade is still flowing later in the season. Earlier in the season, I like staying in campsites where you can see both waterfalls, such as #7 or #8. Still, this is a beauty of a campsite for anyone who likes privacy, with no neighbors visible on any side.

**Words of Warning**: This is a walk-in site, but you can park your car right next to it and unload all your stuff before moving your car to the parking lot. I have stayed in this campsite before, and the fact I had to park my car about 1/16 mile away didn't bother me. It was a small price to pay for a very private spot.

**#7 Privacy Rating: A+**
**Reservable?** No. First-come, first-served.

This cozy spot has a lot of charm. You can see both waterfalls from here, and earlier in the season, a miniature stream trickles along next to the campsite. This space is barely visible from the campground road with a lot of vegetation mostly hiding it from view. People hiking along the Robinson Lake trail, which runs to the right of the campsite on the other side of some willows, may catch a glimpse of you. However, that trail is lightly used.

With no neighbors to the immediate left, no neighbors behind you, and #8 to the right mostly hidden behind a willow screen, this campsite is a privacy lover's dream. The site across the street (#5) is far away and vegetation hides it from view. It is a small campsite, with the picnic table and bear box squeezed into a space between the willows. Patrick was able to fit his four-person tent in here, but it was a tight fit. This site is really better suited for a two-person tent. I have always had a soft spot in my heart for #7. I love being able to set up the tent where I can unzip the back window and look out at the waterfall. Patrick expected that waterfall to be closer to the campground (it's actually on the far side of the canyon), but in years when it's roaring it's quite the sight even from a distance.

**Words of Warning**: This is a walk-in site, but you can park your car right next to it and unload all your stuff before moving your car to the parking lot. I have stayed in this campsite before, and the fact I had to park my car about 1/16 mile away didn't bother me. It was a small price to pay for a very private spot.

**#8 Privacy Rating: A+**
**Reservable?** Yes. Visit **www.recreation.gov** for reservations.

#8 is really a spectacular campsite and from a privacy perspective, the best reservable spot in this campground. It's not completely surrounded by aspens like some of the other campsites and therefore feels more open, but its neighbors are so far away that it doesn't matter. The openness of the campsite also affords a view of both the major waterfalls, the top of a small cascade on Independence Creek, and an expansive view of the mountains to the east. This site also is back from the road a little ways to infuse it with more privacy. If you hit it at the right time, you'll find yourself surrounded by flowers I call snowball flowers but that are really either ranger's buttons or poison angelica. From the picnic table, beyond a grove of low-growing aspen, there's a great view of the cascade tumbling down the hillside from Robinson Lake.

The trail to Robinson Lake is next to this campsite, but most people hike the Kearsarge Pass trail and the Robinson Lake trail is lightly used in comparison. #7 is beyond some willows on the other side of the trail, but the willows do a good job of concealing it from view.

**Words of Warning**: This is a walk-in site, but you can park your car right next to it and unload all your stuff before moving your car to the parking lot. I have stayed in this campsite before, and the fact I had to park my car about 1/16 mile away didn't bother me. It was a small price to pay for a very private spot.

## #9 Privacy Rating: A-
**Reservable?** No. First-come, first-served.

Not as private as some of the other sites that are tucked away in the aspens, #9 is still a nice spot due to its distance from other campers. There are no immediate neighbors on the left or right. #10 is across the street but a ways down the campground road. Behind the site is a view of the cascade tumbling down from Robinson Lake, and you can also see the other waterfall across the valley from here. It's out in the sagebrush with a more open feel, but there are a few low-growing aspens at the front of the site to just barely interrupt the view of it from the campground road. For people who want to have their car parked right in their camp space, this is a good alternative to #8 since it has a similar view of the waterfalls.

## #14 Privacy Rating: B
**Reservable?** No. First-come, first-served.

Sitting under some pines, #14 has more shade than the sites located in the aspens. It has no immediate neighbors to the left or behind it, and the neighbors to the right and across the street aren't so close as to disqualify this one from the book. You can see the waterfall that drains out of Golden Trout Lakes from here (the one with the rust-colored stripe in the granite above it), but the cascade pouring down from Robinson Lake isn't visible. There's a good view of the mountains here, too.

## #27 Privacy Rating: B+
**Reservable?** Yes. Visit **www.recreation.gov** for reservations.

The first time I ever stayed at Onion Valley, I made reservations at this campsite not knowing which sites were the best. As soon as I pulled into the site, while I was looking around thinking it wasn't a bad spot, the camp host walked over from his site across the street and said, "No! No! I have a much better spot for you. It has a view of both waterfalls and its own little stream."

He was referring to site #7, and as soon as I saw that site I was in love. So I took the host's advice and moved there. However, I still think #27 isn't a bad spot. Reserved spots in this campground tend to get snapped up quickly so if you want to make reservations here and #8 and #2 are taken, this is a good substitute. It has more privacy than site #3 (also reservable). #27 is encircled by low-growing aspens, which are just high enough to bestow some privacy. There are no other campsites to its left, right, or behind. Your vehicle and the aspens partially hide from view your only close neighbor, the camp host immediately across the street.

# LONE PINE – MOUNT WHITNEY

# Tuttle Creek Campground

**Directions:** From Highway 395, travel west of Lone Pine on Whitney Portal Road for 3.5 miles. Turn left on Horseshoe Meadow Road and drive 1.5 miles south to campground on the right.

## What's It Like?

Located in the high desert with only a smattering of small trees, Tuttle Creek has dramatic views of Mount Williamson, Lone Pine Peak, and Mount Whitney to the west and the Inyo Mountains to the east. It's very hot here in summer thanks to the campground's lower elevation, which is why Tuttle Creek is best suited for camping in September through May. However, it's also the closest campground to the Cottonwood trailheads—at least the closest campground where you can stay more than one night. So it's convenient from that aspect. And if you plan to leave your campsite early in the morning to head for the mountains and arrive back here in the evening, you'll miss the worst of the heat. Because the campsites are located in the sagebrush and rabbitbrush, privacy here means having your neighbor far enough away that you have some elbow room. Tuttle Creek Campground is open all year. It's only $5 per night to stay here, so it's a great deal.

**Words of Warning:** Water is only available in this campground from March through October.

**Disclaimer:** Patrick and I had the flu when we visited this campground and the heat was really getting to us. So we only looked at one of the two loops.

## What's It Near?

• The hike to the historic stone house (3.7 miles round trip or

2.2 miles round trip if you have a high clearance 4WD vehicle) departs from near Tuttle Creek Campground.

• The interesting rock formations of the Alabama Hills, including a short hike to the Mobius Arch.

• Hikes departing from Cottonwood Pass including South Fork Lake (11.2 miles round trip), Cirque Lake (12.2 miles round trip), Chicken Spring Lake (8.2 miles round trip), Cottonwood Lakes (11.8 miles round trip), Mount Langley (23 miles round trip by way of New Army Pass).

• Hikes departing from Whitney Portal, including Lone Pine Lake (6 miles round trip), Mount Whitney (21 miles round trip), Grass Lake (9.9 miles round trip), Camp Lake (10.2 miles round trip), and Meysan Lake (11 miles round trip).

• The lower access point to the Whitney Portal National Recreation Trail, which starts from Lone Pine Campground. This little-used, scenic trail is best done as a car shuttle hike with one car up at Whitney Portal and another at Lone Pine Campground. (This is not to be confused with the trail up to Mount Whitney).

• Fishing for rainbow, brown, brook and the world famous Alpers trout in Lone Pine Creek and at the pond by Whitney Portal.

• The Lone Pine Film History Museum, which celebrates the movies filmed in the Alabama Hills, Lone Pine, Death Valley, and the Eastern Sierra, is about a 15-minute drive from the campground.

• Manzanar National Historic Site is about a 25-minute drive away from the campground, north on Highway 395 between Lone Pine and Independence. Manzanar was where the government relocated Japanese Americans against their will during World War II, a sobering reminder out of the past.

• Good choices for restaurants in Lone Pine include: Alabama Hills Café and Bakery, the Merry-Go-Round, and Bonanza Mexican Restaurant.

• Whitney Portal Store serves giant pancakes for breakfast and juicy burgers for lunch and dinner.

**Elevation:** 5,120 feet

**Toilets:** Vault

**Verizon Cell Service?** Check our campground updates section at **www.ilovetheeasternsierra.com** for more information.

**Takes Reservations?** No. First-come, first-served.

**Number of Sites:** 83

**Bear Boxes?** No.

### Campsites with the Most Privacy

**#7 Privacy Rating: A-**
**Reservable?** No. First-come, first-served.

There are no neighbors to the immediate left of this campsite—only a stunning view of the Sierra. The bathrooms are off in that direction, too, not too close but they interrupt the view of the mountains slightly. To the right, there's

another campsite about 18 feet away. Behind #7 the desert stretches out toward the horizon, where it meets the imposing granite wall of the Sierra. One little tree in this campsite offers a hint of shade.

**#24 Privacy Rating: A**
**Reservable?** No. First-come, first-served.

This site has a spectacular view of the Inyo Mountains to the east. Watch cloud shadows drift over the mountains or admire the late afternoon and evening light spotlight the interesting geology of the barren slopes. There are no other sites visible to the right and a hill to the left partially eliminates the view of the neighbors in that direction. You also have a glimpse of the massive wall of the Sierra through some trees on the left.

**#27 Privacy Rating: A+**
**Reservable?** No. First-come, first-served.

The mighty wall of the Eastern Sierra dominates the view immediately behind this tent-only, walk-in site. To the right, a boulder-covered hill conveniently blocks the view of the walk-in site on that side. A good 60 feet of sagebrush and rabbitbrush sit between #27 and the neighbors on the left, giving you lots of space. Plus, there are no neighbors across the road either. As far as high desert campsites go, this one's a beauty. Even though it's a walk-in site, it's a short walk from where you park to the camp space.

**#28 Privacy Rating: A-**
**Reservable?** No. First-come, first-served.

This space would be almost as nice as #27 except that it has some campsites in view behind it. Still, those sites are far enough away that you don't feel as if they're breathing down your neck. The space to the right (#27) also is far away — about 60 feet. The absence of spaces to the immediate left or across the street provides good privacy on those sides. It's hard to know which way to look when you're standing in #28, because there are some amazing views of the Sierra to the west and Inyo Mountains to the east. Tiny Tuttle Creek, fringed by a bright patch of greenery, cuts through the parched ground behind the campsite, a nice surprise in the desert. One tree provides a touch of shade.

**#29 - #81**
As I mentioned earlier, we had a bad flu when we were here, so we weren't able to look at the rest of the campsites. You might find a campsite you like between #29 and #82. Check our website **www.ilovetheeasternsierra.com** under Campground Updates since we plan to return here to look at the rest of the campsites and will post the sties we like best on that page.

## Lone Pine Campground

**Directions:** From Highway 395 in Lone Pine, head west on Whitney Portal Road for 6 miles to the campground on left.

## What's It Like?

This is high-desert camping at its best. Campsites are located among the sagebrush and scattered deciduous trees alongside Lone Pine Creek. Many sites boast spectacular views of Mount Whitney and Lone Pine Peak to the west and the Inyo Mountains to the east, although the views of the Sierra from here are nowhere near as dramatic as they are from Tuttle Creek Campground. Large boulders are strewn about the campground. Despite its lack of tall trees and bushes, this campground has a handful of spaces with privacy (see our campsites description below).

**Words of Warning:** This campground is at 5,800 feet and it can get hot in the day! When I was setting up my tent here at 3 p.m. in July, the temperature was 92 degrees. However, if you plan to spend lots of time up in the Whitney Portal or Cottonwood Pass areas, you'll probably be up in the mountains during the hottest part of the day.

Keep an eye out for rattlesnakes. Sightings are rare, but it's a good idea to watch where you're walking.

## What's It Near?

• The interesting rock formations of the Alabama Hills, including a short hike to the Mobius Arch.

• Hikes departing from Cottonwood Pass including South Fork Lake (11.2 miles round trip), Cirque Lake (12.2 miles round trip), Chicken Spring Lake (8.2 miles round trip), Cottonwood Lakes (11.8 miles round trip), Mount Langley (23 miles round trip by way of New Army Pass).

• Hikes departing from Whitney Portal, including Lone Pine Lake (6 miles round trip), Mount Whitney (21 miles round trip), Grass Lake (9.9 miles round trip), Camp Lake (10.2 miles round trip), and Meysan Lake (11 miles round trip).

• The lower access point to the Whitney Portal National Recreation Trail starts from this campground. This little-used, scenic trail is best done as a car shuttle hike with one car up at Whitney Portal and another at Lone Pine Campground. (This is not to be confused with the trail up to Mount Whitney).

• Fishing for rainbow, brown, brook and the world famous Alpers trout in Lone Pine Creek and at the pond by Whitney Portal.

• The Lone Pine Film History Museum, which celebrates the movies filmed in the Alabama Hills, Lone Pine, Death Valley, and the Eastern Sierra, is about a 15-minute drive from the campground.

• Manzanar National Historic Site is about a 25-minute drive away from the campground, north on Highway 395 between Lone Pine and Independence. Manzanar was where the government relocated Japanese Americans against their will during World War II, a sobering reminder out of the past.

• Good choices for restaurants in Lone Pine include: Alabama Hills Café and Bakery, the Merry-Go-Round, and Bonanza Mexican Restaurant.

• Whitney Portal Store serves giant pancakes for breakfast and juicy burgers for lunch and dinner.

**Elevation:** 5,800 feet

**Toilets:** Vault

**Verizon Cell Service?** One bar. You can get full cell phone service about a mile or so down the Whitney Portal Road.

**Takes Reservations?** Yes. Visit **www.recreation.gov** for reservations. Some sites are first-come, first-served.

**Number of Campsites:** 43

**Bear Boxes?** Yes

## Campsites with the Most Privacy

**#20 Privacy Rating: B+**
**Reservable?** Yes. Visit **www.recreation.gov** for reservations.

I stayed here during my first attempt to summit Mount Whitney. A streamside site with a neighbor on only one side (to the left), #20 is a peaceful spot. It's a little close to the campground road, but the fact there are no neighbors across the street means it still feels private. A large boulder does a good job of erasing most of the view of the neighbor to the left. You can't actually see Lone Pine Creek from here, even though it's behind and below the site, but it's a hop, skip, and a jump down a short path to the water's edge. There's a spectacular glimpse of Mt. Whitney through the leaves of some trees. A couple of deciduous trees provide some shade, although this is still a very sunny spot. I camped in this spot in 2011, and although it wasn't the most private campsite I've ever camped in, for all the reasons mentioned above I found it quite pleasant.

**#21 Privacy Rating: A+**
**Reservable?** No. First-come, first-served.

This site near the creek is sheltered nicely from its neighbors. Boulders on the left completely cancel out the view of #20. There are no campsites directly across the street, although you can see a campsite down the road a little ways. On the right, deciduous trees and willows hide the view of the neighbor on that side. There's a great view of Mt. Whitney from here and you can also see some of the Inyo Mountains towering over a rocky hill across the stream. You can't actually see Lone Pine Creek from the campsite, but a short path down a hill leads to the water. The bad news? There isn't a ton of room here for a large tent. So this site is best suited for people with two-person tents, a camper van, or a pickup with a camper shell. And there's no shade, since the space is carved out of the sagebrush, rabbitbrush, and other low-growing vegetation.

**#22 Privacy Rating: A-**
**Reservable?** Yes. Visit **www.recreation.gov** for reservations.

This site's defining characteristic is its great view of the Inyo Mountains to the east of Lone Pine. We marked it down from an A+ to an A- because you can see the neighbor to the right. But some tall sagebrush partially hides them from view, and that site is closer to the campground road while #22 is pushed back. You can't see any neighbors to the left and because you're back farther, the campsite across the street doesn't intrude on your privacy. This site also has more shade than many of the other sites, including a place to pitch a tent in the shadows. It's near the stream, but you can't see the water from the campsite.

**#26 Privacy Rating: A+**
**Reservable?** Yes. Visit **www.recreation.gov** for reservations.

 This is another campsite with spectacular views of the Inyo Mountains to the east. It has no nearby neighbors to the left, right, or behind it. The bathrooms are

across the street. It's a spacious spot with a fair amount of shade. The description on recreation.gov says it's full shade, but we would call it partial shade. Only a small amount of vegetation partially screens it from the campground road, but with its lack of nearby neighbors, it's a great spot.

**#33 Privacy Rating: A+**
**Reservable?** No. First-come, first-served.

Vegetation does a good job of partially blocking this site from view of the campground road. There are no nearby neighbors to the left or right, behind the site is a hill with scrubby vegetation, and the neighbor across the street is set back from the campground road, so there's plenty of space between you and them. Some deciduous trees offer a way to escape the intense Sierra sun. Through the trees, there's a filtered view of the Inyo Mountains, not as spectacular as in #26, but something to add a bit of spice to the site.

## Whitney Portal Family Campground

**Directions:** From Highway 395 in Lone Pine, head west on Whitney Portal Road for 12 miles to the campground on the left.

## What's It Like?

Whitney Portal Family Campground is by no means just for families—single people and couples are welcome here, too. The campground sits under the pines on the shores of Lone Pine Creek, with some campsites located streamside. Small, white boulders are almost as prolific as the pine cones here. Campsites with privacy are sprinkled throughout the campground, while other spaces are too close for comfort. Read our descriptions below to discover the best spots.

**What's It Near?**

• The interesting rock formations of the Alabama Hills, including a short hike to the Mobius Arch. A great stop on your way to or from Whitney Portal.

• Hikes departing from Whitney Portal, including Lone Pine Lake (6 miles round trip), Mount Whitney (21 miles round trip), Grass Lake (9.9 miles round trip), Camp Lake (10.2 miles round trip), and Meysan Lake (11 miles round trip).

• The upper access point to the Whitney Portal National Recreation Trail starts from this campground. This little-used, scenic trail is best done as a car shuttle hike with one car up at Whitney Portal and another at Lone Pine Campground. (This is not to be confused with the trail up to Mount Whitney).

• Fishing for rainbow, brown, brook and the world famous Alpers trout in Lone Pine Creek and at the pond by Whitney Portal.

• The Lone Pine Film History Museum, which celebrates the movies filmed in the Alabama Hills, Lone Pine, Death Valley, and the Eastern Sierra, is about a 30-minute drive from the campground in Lone Pine. Stop by on your way up to the Portal or on your way back home.

• Manzanar National Historic Site is about a 40-minute drive away from the campground, north on Highway 395 between Lone Pine and Independence. Manzanar was where the government relocated Japanese Americans against their will during World War II, a sobering reminder out of the past.

• Good choices for restaurants in Lone Pine include: Alabama Hills Café and Bakery, the Merry-Go-Round, and Bonanza Mexican Restaurant.

• Whitney Portal Store serves giant pancakes for breakfast and juicy burgers for lunch and dinner.

**Elevation:** 8,100 feet

**Toilets:** Vault

**Verizon Cell Service?** Two bar.

**Takes Reservations?** Yes. Visit **www.recreation.gov** for reservations. Some sites are first-come, first-served.

**Number of Campsites:** 43

**Bear Boxes?** Yes

### Campsites with the Most Privacy

**#1 Privacy Rating: B-**
**Reservable?** No. First-come, first-served.

At first we didn't think this site was worthy of including in the book because it seemed like it's too close to its neighbor on the left. However, scattered pines intervene between the two campsites. On the right, about 35 feet away, the group campground begins, so you will have a neighbor on that side, too. Still, the site is located down a small hill, which shelters it from the campground road and the hill conceals your view of the people across the street. Despite the fact it has neighbors on the left and right, it's still a spacious spot under the pines. The creek flows behind it, and although you can't see it, you can hear it serenading you throughout the day and night. A trail passes by this campsite to the rear, so from time to time you might have passersby walking along the borders of your campsite.

## #22 Privacy Rating: A
**Reservable?** No. First-come, first-served.

I stayed in this shady campsite the year I hiked to the top of Mt. Whitney and I loved this spot! Lone Pine Creek borders the left side of the camp space, a peaceful sight as you eat at the picnic table or sit by an early evening campfire. No neighbors are visible to the right of #22 or behind it. Your parked vehicle will block most of the view of the campsite across the street. Plus, that neighbor is back from the road just enough to give you tons of privacy.

If this site has a flaw, it's the fact the tent pad is closer to the campground road than we like to see. However, I crawled into my sleeping bag at 7:30 p.m. the night before hiking to Whitney and never heard any cars drive by or saw any headlights in my tent. The tent pad's proximity to the campground road was the only reason we didn't give this site an A+. Even so, I'd stay here again in an instant. This site is also a great choice for anglers. It's not a good site for a big motorhome—best suited for tents, camper vans, pickup trucks with a camper top, or a very, very small trailer.

## #23 Privacy Rating: A-
**Reservable?** Yes. Visit **www.recreation.gov** for reservations.

This one's pushed back from the campground road. Some low-growing vegetation and boulders give it even more privacy from any campsites across the street. Big pines provide shade to this tent-only site. No neighbors are visible to the left, and the bathrooms are to the right, on the other side of the site's driveway, close enough if you need to go badly but far enough away to provide some good separation. One flaw? The main road to Whitney Portal is behind this site up a steep hill. Because people start hiking the Mount Whitney trail at all hours, there's going to be traffic on the road all night long. Still, the campsite is far enough down from the road that you shouldn't be bothered by headlights shining into your tent, and the site's sunken location might minimize some of the road noise.

**#39 Privacy Rating: A+**
**Reservable?** Yes. Visit **www.recreation.gov** for reservations.

Sunken down from the campground road and away from the main part of the campground, this tent-only campsite boasts tons of privacy. It faces the opposite direction from its nearest neighbor to the right, which isn't really visible anyway, and it has no neighbors on any other side, including across the street. It's perched above Lone Pine Creek, so you have a view of the water tumbling through the vegetation on its way down the canyon. Pines provide shade although the sun sneaks through in spots. It's a steep walk down to the site from the campground road and the creek isn't easily accessible from here, so although Patrick and I really liked this campsite, if you want to fish from your site, #22 might suit you better.

# DEATH VALLEY

## Panamint Springs Resort

**Directions:** From Lone Pine, turn left on Highway 136, which turns into Highway 190 east. Panamint Springs Resort is about 50 miles away from Lone Pine on Highway 190 (campground is on the left, general store and restaurant on the right).

### What's It Like?

Death Valley isn't known for having a lot of campsites with privacy. Because it's such a big park, sometimes you may need to compromise on privacy in order to stay near the landmark you want to visit. Panamint Springs is located near Darwin Falls and the hike to Panamint Dunes. If you plan on visiting either of those two natural wonders it may be worth staying at this campground even if most of the spaces are packed in next to each other in a parking lot. If you're lucky, you might even be able to reserve site #12 (see campsite description below). Panamint Springs also has a big advantage in the spring, summer, and early fall when temperatures in the Furnace Creek area are roasting. Panamint Springs is located at about 2,000 feet above sea level, so temperatures here are typically 10 to 15 degrees cooler than Furnace Creek.

### What's It Near?

• Hiking to Darwin Falls (2 miles round trip). This is a very popular hike, so expect lots of people, unless you decide to get adventurous and continue on to the hidden upper falls. The falls run all year long.

• Hiking to the Panamint Dunes (9 miles round trip).

• Amazing views from nearby Father Crowley Point.

• The restaurant at Panamint Springs Resort serves pizza,

salads, and 100 percent Angus Beef burgers. Choose from more than 150 beers.

• The Panamint Springs Resort General Store has limited groceries and camping supplies.

**Elevation:** 1,926 feet

**Toilets:** Flush

**Verizon Cell Service?** No. The resort offers extremely limited Internet service to send messages to friends and family to let them know you are safe, but asks that you don't use it for any other reason.

**Takes Reservations?** Yes. Visit **www.panamintsprings.com** for reservations.

**Number of Campsites:** 63

**Bear Boxes?** Not needed in Death Valley.

### Campsite with the Most Privacy

**#12 Privacy Rating: A**
**Reservable?** Yes. Visit **www.panamintsprings.com** for reservations.

Site #12 outshines all the other campsites in this campground. The last space on the Western end of the campground, it sits by itself with no other nearby campsites on any side. To one side, you'll have plenty of mesquite bushes as neighbors along with some rusty old equipment that looks like it dates back to the mining days. The campground road sits on the right side of the campsite. There is a space across the road, but several six-foot-tall trees partially screen out the view of that neighbor. The campsite also boasts a view of Panamint Valley

 where you can glimpse the sand dunes baking in the sun. In front of the campsite, you'll have a view of crinkled, dry mountains beyond the resort.

**Words of Warning:** We could see no numbers on many of the campsites and the woman behind the front desk couldn't tell us for sure if this was site #12. From the map of the campground and the aerial photo online it looks like it is #12, but the map shows #12 as being on the opposite side of the road from where it really is. When you make reservations tell them you want the campsite that's farthest to the west, off by itself with no immediate neighbors on any of the sides, with a pull-through and confirm that it is indeed site #12. Also, know that this is a RV site with a hook-up, but the resort produces electricity through generators and therefore the electricity might not be suitable for newer RVs. The resort may be willing to rent this site to tent campers, especially if the campground isn't full.

### Emigrant Campground

**Directions:** From Lone Pine, turn left on Highway 136, which turns into Highway 190 east. Past Panamint Springs Resort, climb over the pass, and start dropping down into Death Valley itself. The campground is near the turnoff to Emigrant

Canyon Road on the left. If you reach Stovepipe Wells you've gone too far.

## What's It Like?

This small, tent-only campground isn't known for its privacy. The 10 spaces sit out in the open off of a parking lot. Its one advantage? It's located at 2,100 feet above sea level, meaning it's 10 to 15 degrees cooler than Furnace Creek.

## What's It Near?

• Hikes to Nemo Canyon (7.2 miles round trip), Wildrose Peak (8.4 miles round trip), and Telescope Peak (14 miles round trip).

• A drive to Aguereberry Point, where you'll find a spectacular view looking out over the Panamint Mountains and Badwater Basin. You'll need a high-clearance 4WD vehicle.

• The Charcoal Kilns and the hike to Wildrose Peak.

• Hikes near Stovepipe Wells: Mosaic Canyon (3.6 miles round trip), Marble Canyon (17 miles round trip without a high-clearance 4WD vehicle, 14.8 miles round trip if you have a 4WD), and Grotto Canyon (4 miles round trip). Mosaic Canyon is one Death Valley sight you won't want to miss. The 750-million to 900-million-year-old rocks here are infused with interesting texture and colors.

• Take a stroll to the top of the Mesquite Dunes. Admire their curved shapes and the wavy ripples in the sand and marvel at the way the mesquite plants thrive in this harsh environment.

**Elevation:** 2,100 feet

**Toilets:** Flush

**Verizon Cell Service?** No.

**Takes Reservations?** No. First-come, first-served.

**Number of Campsites:** 10

**Bear Boxes?** Not needed in Death Valley.

### Campsites with the Most Privacy

None.

### Wildrose Campground

**Directions:** From Lone Pine, turn left on Highway 136, which turns into Highway 190 east. Past Panamint Springs Resort, climb over the pass, and begin dropping down into Death Valley itself. Turn right on Emigrant Canyon Road (if you reach Stovepipe Wells you've gone too far) and follow it about 21 miles to Wildrose Campground on the left.

**What's It Like?**

Campsites at Wildrose Campground sit in the outskirts of a parking lot among the desert vegetation. All the sites are out in the open and joined at the hip with their neighbors. It does have a spectacular view looking back down Wildrose Canyon to the West, but as far as privacy is concerned, you won't find much of it here. Camping here is free, and unlike Thorndike and Mahogany Flat Campgrounds up the road, water is available. If it's privacy you want you're better off trying your luck at grabbing a spot at the two campgrounds up the road.

## What's It Near?

• Hikes to Nemo Canyon (7.2 miles round trip), Wildrose Peak (8.4 miles round trip), and Telescope Peak (14 miles round trip).

• A short drive to the Charcoal Kilns.

• A drive to Aguereberry Point, where you'll find a spectacular view looking out over the Panamint Mountains and Badwater Basin. You'll need a high-clearance 4WD vehicle.

**Elevation:** 4,100 feet

**Toilets:** Vault

**Verizon Cell Service?** No

**Takes Reservations?** No

**Number of Campsites**: 23

**Bear Boxes?** Not needed in Death Valley.

### Campsites with the Most Privacy

None.

### Thorndike Campground

**Directions:** From Lone Pine, turn left on Highway 136, which turns into Highway 190 east. Pass Panamint Springs Resort, climb over the pass, and start dropping down into Death Valley itself. Turn right on Emigrant Canyon Road and follow it for about 20.9 miles, where the road turns into Mahogany Flat Road. Continue straight ahead past Wildrose

Campground and the charcoal kilns at 7.1 miles. The campground is about about 0.7 miles past the charcoal kilns on the left. Passenger cars can make it to the campground with careful driving.

**What's It Like?**

This small campground is our favorite campground in the entire park. Many of the spaces here have tons of privacy and are a breath of high-altitude fresh air compared to the campsites at Furnace Creek and other places in Death Valley. The campsites are located under the pinyon pines and junipers and many of the sites have stunning views of Wildrose Peak. Thorndike Campground is named for John Thorndike, a miner in the early 1900s who wanted to build a resort atop Telescope Peak. His plans never materialized, but he did build some cabins at the site of what today is Thorndike Campground. The cabins are long gone, and in their place are some peaceful campsites. Even better, this campground is free. Although it's a small campground, we've had good luck finding spaces here. One year we arrived on a Saturday morning on Easter weekend and had no trouble finding a campsite. The spaces here are not numbered. Because this is a high-altitude campground, it's only open from around March through November, depending on snow. And nights here can be quite cold even in March and April.

**Words of Warning:** There is no potable water here, so bring plenty of your own.

**What's It Near?**

• Hikes to Nemo Canyon (7.2 miles round trip), Wildrose Peak (8.4 miles round trip), and Telescope Peak (14 miles round trip).

• A short drive to the Charcoal Kilns.

———

• A drive to Aguereberry Point, where you'll find a spectacular view looking out over the Panamint Mountains and Badwater Basin. You'll need a high-clearance 4WD vehicle.

**Elevation:** 7,400 feet

**Toilets:** Vault

**Verizon Cell Service?** No.

**Takes Reservations?** No. First-come, first-served.

**Number of Sites:** 6

**Bear Boxes?** Not needed in Death Valley.

### Campsites with the Most Privacy

**1st Space on the Right**
**Privacy Rating: B**
**Reservable?** No. First-come, first-served.

Another campsite sits immediately behind this one, but your gaze is drawn in the opposite direction anyway, at a view of Wildrose Peak, so you won't face to the rear very often. A couple of junipers and a pinyon pine spread their bows over a nice nook for the tent and also screen out the campsite from view of Mahogany Flat Road, to the right of the campsite. The spot is also perched slightly above the road so that you only see the tops of cars driving past. There are no other sites to the left or in front of this one. To the left, across the campground road, is another campsite, but it's behind a couple of tall junipers. We felt at peace here when we camped in this space a number of years ago.

### 1st Space on the Left
**Privacy Rating: A**
**Reservable?** No. First-come, first-served.

With a nice view of Wildrose Peak in front and no neighbors breathing down your neck on any side, this campsite is a gem. Another space sits behind this one, but it's on the other side of a screen of tall vegetation, so you'll only catch a glimpse of the people camped there. A couple of tall junipers partially shelter this site from view of the campground road and the neighbors across the street, while at the same time providing a nice shady nook for the tent. It has no neighbors to the left or in front. The bathrooms are conveniently located in front of the campsite, just off to the side, so you don't have to look at them while you admire the view of Wildrose Peak. We camped in this site one Easter weekend and loved it.

### 2nd Space on the Left
**Privacy Rating: A**
**Reservable?** No. First-come, first served.

You won't have the uninterrupted view of Wildrose Peak from here since the 1st space on the left is between you and the view. But this is a nice spot from a privacy perspective, all the same. To the left of the campsite is another space, but a wall of vegetation serves as a privacy screen so you only have a hint of a neighboring presence on that side. To the right is another campsite, but the two sites are well-spaced and vegetation between them filters the view. There are no neighbors behind the campsite and the neighboring space across the street is far enough away to ensure you still have your privacy.

### 3rd Space on the Left
**Privacy Rating: A+**
**Reservable?** No. First-come, first-served.

Off by itself and pushed back a little from the campground

road, this spot is a beauty. On the right and behind the campsite, only the junipers will keep you company. To the left, another site sits a very long stone's throw away, and vegetation cancels out most of the view of that neighbor. The neighboring sites across the street are a good distance away. You won't have the unobstructed view of Wildrose Peak that some of the other sites in this campground have, but you will have a lot of privacy.

## Mahogany Flat Campground

**Directions:** From Lone Pine, turn left on Highway 136, which turns into Highway 190 east. Pass Panamint Springs Resort, climb over the pass, and start dropping down into Death Valley itself. Turn right on Emigrant Canyon Road and follow it for about 20.9 miles, where the road turns into Mahogany Flat Road. Continue straight ahead past Wildrose Campground and the charcoal kilns at 7.1 miles. The campground is about 1.6 miles past the charcoal kilns. You need a four-wheel drive, high-clearance vehicle to reach this campground.

**What's It Like?**

We could not make it up to Mahogany Flat because we have read in a number of places that a high-clearance, four-wheel drive vehicle is needed to reach it. We started up toward the campground with our Toyota Matrix hatchback, which is 4WD, but not high clearance, but I became nervous about going any farther due to the rocks and ruts on the road. When I asked a ranger if the spaces here have good privacy, she said, "Depends on the campsite." This campground is free. Be certain to visit the campground updates section of **www.ilovetheeasternsierra.com**, because we hope to eventually make it to this campground and post on the website the best campsites.

**Words of Warning:** There is no potable water at this campground so be certain to bring plenty of your own.

**What's It Near?**

• Hikes to Nemo Canyon (7.2 miles round trip), Wildrose Peak (8.4 miles round trip), and Telescope Peak (14 miles round trip).

• A short drive to the Charcoal Kilns.

• A drive to Aguereberry Point, where you'll find a spectacular view looking out over the Panamint Mountains and Badwater Basin. You'll need a high-clearance 4WD vehicle. This is a longer drive from Mahogany Flat Campground, but you can visit this scenic spot on the way to or from the campground.

**Elevation:** 8,200 feet

**Toilets:** Vault

**Verizon Cell Service?** No

**Takes Reservations?** No. First-come, first-served.

**Number of Sites:** 10

**Bear Boxes?** Not needed in Death Valley.

### Campsites with the Most Privacy

See "What's It Like?" above.

## Stovepipe Wells Campground

**Directions:** From Lone Pine, turn left on Highway 136, which turns into Highway 190 east. Travel 78.6 miles to the campground on the left.

**What's It Like?**

Even though this campground is really a parking lot filled with RVs, it has the advantage of being near some of Death Valley's most interesting attractions. If you stay in one of the tent spaces in the mesquite on the edges of the parking lot, you can face your chair out to the desert and ignore the RVs parked behind you. If you stay here mid-week during the slow times of the year, it's more peaceful and the parking lot isn't as full. Because Death Valley is a big park and it's easy to go through a lot of gasoline driving from one attraction to another, if you want to catch the first or last light on the Mesquite Dunes or if you want to hike to Mosaic Canyon, Marble Canyon, or Titus Canyon, this is the closest campground to those points of interest.

**What's It Near?**

• Hikes: Mosaic Canyon (3.6 miles round trip), Marble Canyon (17 miles round trip without a high-clearance 4WD vehicle, 14.8 miles round trip if you have a 4WD), Grotto Canyon (4 miles round trip). Mosaic Canyon is one Death Valley sight you won't want to miss. The 750-million to 900-million-year-old rocks here are infused with interesting texture and colors.

• Take a stroll to the top of the Mesquite Dunes. Admire their curved shapes and the wavy ripples in the sand and marvel at the way the mesquite plants thrive in this harsh environment.

• Walk or wheel your way into Titus Canyon Narrows with a 4WD. This is a spectacular slot canyon with towering limestone walls polished by the occasional flash flood. A surprising number of wildflowers sprinkled the canyon floor with color the spring I hiked Titus Canyon. It's a 2-mile hike to the end of the narrows, but if you want to visit Klare Springs with its petroglyphs and occasional big horn sheep sightings, you'll need to trek another 4 miles up the road.

**Elevation:** Sea level

**Toilets:** Flush

**Verizon Cell Service?** No

**Takes Reservations?** No. First-come, first-served.

**Number of Sites:** 190

**Bear Boxes?** Not needed in Death Valley.

## Campsites with the Most Privacy

The tent sites on the outskirts of the parking lot.

## Furnace Creek Campground

**Directions:** From Lone Pine, turn left on Highway 136, which turns into Highway 190. Drive 103 miles to the campground on the right.

**What's It Like?**

A large campground, Furnace Creek is full of activity. Tamarisk trees shade many of the campsites. Most of the campsites here are starved for privacy. But the fact the campground has a lot of trees does put it one step above many of the other campgrounds in Death Valley, where spaces are completely exposed. Excluding Panamint Springs Resort, this is the only campground that takes reservations in all of Death Valley. Despite its advantages, we could only find three campsites here that met our privacy criteria (see campsite descriptions below).

**What's It Near?**

• Badwater, the lowest spot in North America at 282 feet below sea level, is a 17 ½ mile drive away.

• Zabriskie Point is a short drive away from the campground. Take the walk up the paved path to the lookout and admire the view of the badlands below the point, the salt flats beyond, and 11,049 Telescope Peak in the distance.

• Hikes to Natural Bridge (2 miles round trip), Golden Canyon/Gower Gulch Loop (6.5 mile loop), and Desolation Canyon (5.2 miles round trip). The Mosaic Canyon hike (3.6 miles round trip) is about a 25-minute drive from here, past Stovepipe Wells.

• Hike to the top of Mesquite Flat Sand Dunes, about a 20-minute drive away from the campground.

• The Salt Creek Interpretive Trail (1/2 mile total) wanders past a little stream filled with Salt Creek pupfish. You can spot hundreds of them swimming in the creek in spring. They're dormant the rest of the year.

• Follow the Artist's Drive past a display of colorful rocks.

• Travel the 25 miles to Dante's View, where you can look 5,755 feet straight down to the salt flats of Badwater. When it's hot at Furnace Creek, the cool temperatures up at Dante's View offer a respite.

• Dine at the elegant Inn at Furnace Creek for breakfast, lunch, or dinner. The dining room overlooks the salt flats and the Panamint Mountains. There's a "resort attire" dress code for dinner—no t-shirts or tank tops. The architecture of the Inn at Furnace Creek is stunning, with rock walls and terraces.

• A more casual dining option is the Ranch at Furnace Creek, which has a number of restaurants including The Wrangler, 49'er Café, Corkscrew Saloon, and The 19th Hole.

• Challenge the 18-hole Furnace Creek Golf Course, the world's lowest golf course at 214 feet below sea level.

**Elevation:** 196 feet below sea level

**Toilets:** Flush

**Verizon Cell Service?** Yes

**Reservations:** Yes. Visit **www.recreation.gov** for reservations. Only a few campsites are first-come, first-served.

**Number of Sites:** 136

**Bear Boxes?** Not needed in Death Valley.

# Campsites with the Most Privacy

**#56 Privacy Rating: B+**
**Reservable?** Yes. From October 15 to April 15. Visit **www.recreation.gov** for reservations.

In a campground where most of the sites are out in the open and within inches of each other, this one stands out. It has no neighbors nearby on the left, and low-growing tamarisk trees on that side help shelter the site from view of the road. On the right, taller tamarisk trees provide a shady spot to pitch the tent and create a wall of vegetation mostly eliminating the view of any sites on that side. The neighbor across the street is far enough away and the trees in #56 help screen this site from view. What keeps this from being a perfect spot is the fact you can see the site immediately behind this one, but trees sprinkled here and there filter the view a little and the two spaces are just far enough apart to give #56 some elbow room.

**#115 Privacy Rating: B+**
**Reservable?** Yes. From October 15 to April 15. Visit **www.recreation.gov** for reservations.

**ADA Accessible Site — Should only be reserved by people who have disabilities.**

Tamarisk trees grow to the left, right, and behind, infusing some shade into the outskirts of this campsite, although the picnic table is in the sun. The only visible neighbor is behind #115, and you'll catch a glimpse of them through the trees. This is a walk-in campsite, but it's within a few steps of the parking area. That makes it convenient but it also means all the other walk-in campers will park in front of your campsite, creating a lot of activity within full view. Even so, this is one of the best campsites in the campground.

**#122 Privacy Rating: B**
**Reservable?** Yes. From October 15 to April 15. Visit **www.recreation.gov** for reservations.

This is a walk-in, tent-only campsite, although the parking area is immediately in front of it, so you won't have to walk far. A scraggly batch of tamarisk trees form a loose semi-circle around the campsite. The only nearby neighbor is to the right, a very long stone's throw away, but trees between the two spaces cancel out some of the view. Catch a glimpse of the Panamint Range through the trees behind the campsite. The one disadvantage is cars will pull into the parking spaces in front of #122, and since it's a very open campsite, this nearby hustle and bustle steals away some of the privacy. But compared to many of the sites in this campground, this spot isn't bad.

## Texas Springs Campground

**Directions:** From Lone Pine, turn left on Highway 136, which turns into Highway 190. Drive 103.5 miles to the campground on the left. Texas Springs is just past the main hub of Furnace Creek.

## What's It Like?

The tent section of Texas Springs Campground (section A) has some campsites that outshine the other "condo camping" spaces in the campground. Texas Springs Campground is located next to a tiny, spring-fed creek, which runs behind some of the campsites. Tamarisk trees in some areas provide shade to some of the campsites, but many spaces are out in the open. The upper section of the campground, which is more like a parking lot filled with RVs, has views of interesting rock formations.

## What's It Near?

• Badwater, the lowest spot in North America at 282 feet below sea level, is a 17½-mile drive away.

• Zabriskie Point is a short drive away from the campground. Take the walk up the paved path to the lookout and admire the view of the badlands below the point, the salt flats beyond, and 11,049 Telescope Peak in the distance.

• Hikes to Natural Bridge (2 miles round trip), Golden Canyon/Gower Gulch Loop (6.5 mile loop), and Desolation Canyon (5.2 miles round trip). The Mosaic Canyon hike (3.6 miles round trip) is about a 25-minute drive from here, past Stovepipe Wells.

• Hike to the top of Mesquite Flat Sand Dunes, about a 20-minute drive away from the campground.

• The Salt Creek Interpretive Trail (1/2 mile total) wanders past a little stream filled with Salt Creek pupfish. You can spot hundreds of them swimming in the creek in spring. They're dormant the rest of the year.

• Follow the Artist's Drive past a display of colorful rocks.

• Travel the 25 miles to Dante's View, and look 5,755 feet straight down to the salt flats of Badwater. When it's hot at Furnace Creek, the cool temperatures up at Dante's View offer a respite.

• Dine at the elegant Inn at Furnace Creek for breakfast, lunch, or dinner. The dining room overlooks the salt flats and the Panamint Mountains. There's a "resort attire" dress code for dinner — no t-shirts or tank tops. The architecture of the Inn at Furnace Creek is stunning, with rock walls and terraces.

• A more casual dining option is the Ranch at Furnace Creek, which has a number of restaurants including The Wrangler, 49'er Café, Corkscrew Saloon, and The 19th Hole.

• Challenge the 18-hole Furnace Creek Golf Course, the world's lowest golf course at 214 feet below sea level.

**Elevation:** Sea level

**Toilets:** Flush

**Verizon Cell Service?** Yes

**Takes Reservations?** No. First-come, first-served.

**Number of Sites:** 92

**Bear Boxes?** Not needed in Death Valley.

### Campsites with the Most Privacy

**A1 Privacy Rating: A+**
**Reservable?** No. First-come, first-served.

Larger than other spots in the campground and shaded by a

grove of tall tamarisk trees, A1 is by far the most private campsite in any of the Furnace Creek campgrounds. That's why I've never been lucky enough to grab it and have been forced to stare at it longingly from afar. This site has no neighbors on the right. The thick trunks and leaves of the trees block from view the nearby neighbor on the left. Another campsite sits directly across the street, but since A1 is back in the trees, that's not an issue. The tent pad, under the trees, takes advantage of the shade. A1 also captures a good view of the Furnace Creek area and the Panamint Mountains beyond.

## #A12 Privacy Rating: B
**Reservable?** No. First-come, first-served.

A neighboring site nudges up close on the right, but a short tamarisk tree grows in between the two spaces, providing some privacy. The campground road passes by to the left, so there are no neighbors on that side. The road also runs in front of this site and campsite A1 is located directly across the street, but A1 doesn't interfere with A12's privacy. There are no campsites immediately behind this one. With only the one neighbor to contend with, A12 is a cut above many of other sites in this campground.

## #A9 Privacy Rating: B-
**Reservable?** No. First-come, first-served.

Even though #A9 is squeezed between two other campsites, it's tucked back from the road whereas the other two sites are closer to the pavement. Plus, there's a good amount of space between the three campsites. Pitch your tent next to a few tamarisk trees to take advantage of the shade and listen carefully for the sound of the small spring-fed creek gurgling past behind the campsite. Because #A9 is back from the road, the space across the street doesn't seem too intrusive. No other campsites exist behind #A9.

## #A25 Privacy Rating: A-
**Reservable?** No. First-come, first-served.

Even though #A25 is in full view of the road, it's surrounded on three sides by low-growing tamarisk trees. Through a gap in the trees to the left, you can see the neighbor, but that's the only neighbor visible. Across the street are the bathrooms. This site's biggest flaw is that it's lacking a good place to pitch the tent in the shade of the trees—the best spots for the tent bake in the sun, not as much of an issue in winter when the temperatures drop, but in early fall and spring, this could pose a problem. Even so, it's not easy to find campsites that have trees in Death Valley, so be grateful that this spot is at least surrounded by vegetation.

## #A26 Privacy Rating: A
**Reservable?** No. First-come, first-served.

A grove of tall tamarisk trees shade much of this campsite, which also has a view of the Furnace Creek area and the

Panamint Mountains beyond, although not quite as good of a view as A1. No other campsites intrude on the left or right. The one visible neighbor is behind the site and off to the right. From where you set up your tent in the trees, you won't see them at all, but from the picnic table and fire pit you'll have a clear view of them. Still, the two spaces are far enough apart and there are some low-growing tamarisk trees in between, so the neighbor's proximity doesn't ruin this site's privacy.

## Sunset Campground

**Directions:** From Lone Pine, turn left on Highway 136, which turns into Highway 190. Drive 103.5 miles to the campground on the left. The entrance to Sunset Campground is just past the main hub of Furnace Creek.

**What's It Like?**

This is more like a big RV parking lot. It's a privacy lover's nightmare.

**What's It Near?**

• Badwater, the lowest spot in North America at 282 feet below sea level, is a 17½-mile drive away.

• Zabriskie Point is a short drive away from the campground. Take the walk up the paved path to the lookout and admire the view of the badlands below the point, the salt flats beyond, and 11,049 Telescope Peak in the distance.

• Hikes to Natural Bridge (2 miles round trip), Golden Canyon/Gower Gulch Loop (6.5 mile loop), and Desolation Canyon (5.2 miles round trip). The Mosaic Canyon hike (3.6 miles round trip) is about a 25-minute drive from here, past Stovepipe Wells.

• Hike to the top of Mesquite Flat Sand Dunes, about a 20-minute drive away from the campground.

• The Salt Creek Interpretive Trail (1/2 mile total) wanders past a little stream filled with Salt Creek pupfish. You can spot hundreds of them swimming in the creek in spring. They're dormant the rest of the year.

• Follow the Artist's Drive past a display of colorful rocks.

• Travel the 25 miles to Dante's View, where you can look 5,755 feet straight down to the salt flats of Badwater. When it's hot at Furnace Creek, the cool temperatures up at Dante's View offer a respite.

• Dine at the elegant Inn at Furnace Creek for breakfast, lunch, or dinner. The dining room overlooks the salt flats and the Panamint Mountains. There's a "resort attire" dress code for dinner—no t-shirts or tank tops. The architecture of the Inn at Furnace Creek is stunning, with rock walls and terraces.

• A more casual dining option is the Ranch at Furnace Creek, which has a number of restaurants including The Wrangler, 49'er Café, Corkscrew Saloon, and The 19th Hole.

• Challenge the 18-hole Furnace Creek Golf Course, the world's lowest golf course at 214 feet below sea level.

**Elevation:** 196 feet below sea level

**Toilets:** Flush

**Verizon Cell Service?** Yes

**Takes Reservations?** No. First-come, first-served.

**Number of Sites:** 270

**Bear Boxes?** Not needed in Death Valley.

**Campsites with the Most Privacy**

None.

## Mesquite Springs Campground

**Directions:** From Lone Pine, turn left on Highway 136, which turns into Highway 190. Travel about 86 miles and turn left on Scotty's Castle Road past Stovepipe Wells and the sand dunes. Drive about 32 miles to the campground on the left.

**What's It Like?**

Thanks to the mesquite bushes and some nice spacing between many of the campsites, as a whole, this campground near Scotty's Castle seems more private than the ones in Furnace Creek. It's by no means perfect from a privacy perspective, but it has the largest choice of spaces with privacy of any campground in the park. It sits on the edge of Death Valley wash, and some of the campsites have a view of the interesting rock formations on the other side. In the spring, the fuchsia blooms of beavertail cacti add splashes of color to the campground. Because this campground is at 1,800 feet above sea level, it's 10 to 15 degrees cooler than Furnace Creek.

**What's It Near?**

• Circle around the Ubehebe Craters on a 1.5 mile loop hike that showcases the aftermath of the eruption that occurred only 3,000 years ago. More adventurous sorts can walk down to the bottom of the crater, but be warned it's a steep hike back up to the top.

• Take a guided tour of Scotty's Castle, with its dramatic architecture. The lawns in front of the castle are a peaceful spot to have a picnic lunch next to the spring-fed stream. The musical sound of water in Death Valley is a rare auditory treat.

• If you have a high-clearance 4WD vehicle, visit The Racetrack, with its rocks that leave trails on their mysterious journeys across the playa. The 6.2 mile round trip trail to Ubehebe Peak with its spectacular views of The Racetrack Playa, Saline Valley, and the Inyo Mountains, also departs from here.

• Walk up Death Valley wash. Lots of wildflowers here in the spring.

**Elevation:** 1,800 feet

**Toilets:** Flush

**Verizon Cell Service?** No

**Takes Reservations?** No. First-come, first-served.

**Number of Sites:** 30

**Bear Boxes:** Not needed in Death Valley.

**Campsites with the Most Privacy**

**#2 Privacy Rating: B-**
**Reservable?** No. First-come, first-served.

This site lacks the personality of some of the other spaces in the campground, with no spectacular views of the rock formation by the wash and a rather unspectacular location. However, it's well sheltered from its neighbors, at least as far as a desert campsite is concerned. On the left, there's a space about 15 feet away on the other side of some tall desert vegetation. The campground road runs to the right, so there are no neighbors on that side. The space behind the site is about 16 feet away with some mesquite filtering the view. It has no neighbors directly across the street.

### #4 Privacy Rating: B+
**Reservable?** No. First-come, first-served.

From this site, gaze at the mountains soaring up to the west beyond Death Valley Wash. The only close neighbor is to the right about 15 feet away, but tall mesquite in between the two sites mean they don't feel as if they're joined at the hip. It has no other nearby neighbors, giving it some nice separation.

### #9 Privacy Rating: A-
**Reservable?** No. First-come, first-served.

I camped here once and thanked my lucky campground stars that I found a campsite with a good amount of privacy on a Friday during wildflower season in spring. The site has no neighbors on two sides—to the right and behind. A space sits really close to #9 on the left but some mesquite hides a lot of the view. The site across the street is far enough away not to interfere with privacy. When I sat with my chair facing behind the campsite toward the mountains in that direction it was almost like I was alone in the desert.

### #10 Privacy Rating: B+
**Reservable?** No. First-come, first-served.

This site has a couple of neighbors about 18 feet away, one to the right and one behind, but mesquite filters out some of the view. No neighbors are to the left—only the campground road. For Death Valley, where most of the campsites are crammed together, this is a spot with some elbow room.

**#11 Privacy Rating: B-**
**Reservable?** No. First-come, first-served.

#11 features an expansive view toward the South thanks to the lack of campsites across the street. On three sides of #11, neighboring campsites sprout up between the mesquite and other desert vegetation. The campsite to the left is about 30 feet away, the space to the right about 24 feet, and the neighbor to the rear is about 18 feet away, give or take. There's enough space between that the neighbors don't feel as if they're closing in on you.

**#23 Privacy Rating: B**
**Reservable?** No. First-come, first-served.

With a view of an interesting rock formation on the other side of Death Valley Wash as well as a glimpse of the mountains beyond, #23 is typical of many of the sites in this campground, sprinkled with mesquite and out in the open. For Death Valley, where it's not easy to find a campsite that's not right in your neighbor's face, this isn't a bad spot. There's a neighbor a stone's throw away on the left, but there are no neighbors on the right or immediately across the street and the space behind is far away.

**#24 Privacy Rating: B+**
**Reservable?** No. First-come, first-served.

With no immediate neighbors to the left or right and the neighbor across the street a good distance away, you'll settle in among the mesquite without worrying about too much neighborly intrusion. The only close neighbor is the site behind, about 20 feet away. Like all the spots in this area of the campground, it has a good view of the sculpted cliffs on the other side of the wash. To me, the rocks look like side-by-side pointy cone head caps.

**#25 Privacy Rating: B-**
**Reservable?** No. First-come, first-served.

The biggest threat to your privacy while camping in this site is the neighbor to the left, about 15 feet away. But there are no spaces across the street and the other neighboring sites are far enough away to give you an acceptable cushion of privacy. The view of the cliffs on the other side of the wash will draw your gaze.

**#27 Privacy Rating: B+**
**Reservable?** No. First-come, first-served.

Mother Nature the artist sculpted the cliffs into an interesting rock formation that sits directly behind this campsite on the other side of Death Valley Wash.

Perched above the wash, the campsite will definitely have a good view of any flash flood that roars past. Even though this site is clearly visible from the road, it has no neighbors to the right and no neighbors across the campground road, either. Its only neighbor is to the left, about 15 feet away, but a ditch and some mesquite intervenes between the two spots, adding good separation.

**#39 Privacy Rating: A**
**Reservable?** No. First-come, first-served.

With no nearby neighbors on three sides, #39 is one of the best sites in the campground. It captures a nice view of the area's barren yet intriguing landscape and the layers of texture and color on the surrounding mountains. Its only neighbor is across the campground road

**#40 Privacy Rating: A-**
**Reservable?** No. First-come, first-served.

The campsite backs up to Death Valley Wash and has a fair amount of privacy thanks to its lack of neighbors on the left and behind. The neighbor to the right is about 20 feet away, so you'll have company, but still a good distance away. There's also a neighbor across the street. From this spacious spot gaze out toward the wash or at the ribbons of desert colors on the mountains to the east.

# 107 Campsites with Privacy Where Anglers Can Fish a Few Steps from the Picnic Table

| Campsite Number(s) | Campground |
| --- | --- |
| #9, #17 | Crystal Springs |
| #1, #7, #8, #17 | Lower Blue Lake Campground |
| #18, #22 | Middle Creek Campground |
| #58, #64, #65 | Upper Blue Lake Damsite Campground |
| #1, #5, #6 | Markleeville Campground |
| #15 | Silver Creek Campground |
| #13 | Chris Flat |
| #64 | Buckeye Campground |
| #3, #9 | Lower Honeymoon Flat, Twin Lakes Canyon |
| #9 | PAHA Campground, Twin Lakes Canyon |
| #1, #2, #3 | Green Creek Campground |
| #10 | Trumbull Lake Campground |
| #31, #32, #36 | Lundy Campground |
| #18 | Lower Lee Vining Campground |
| #3, #4, #15, #16 | Moraine Campground |

| | |
|---|---|
| #19, #24, #25, #44, #45, #46 | Aspen Grove Campground |
| #6 | Junction Campground |
| #12 | Sawmill Walk-in Campground |
| #A49 | Tuolumne Meadows Campground |
| #9, #11 | Gull Lake Campground |
| T-1, T-2 | June Lake Campground |
| #9 | Lower Deadman Campground |
| #19 | Big Springs |
| #75 | Sherwin Creek Campground |
| #25, #26, #28, #33 | Lower Twin Lakes Campground |
| #11, #23 | Minaret Falls |
| #B3 | Devil's Postpile National Park Service |
| #24, #31, #41, #57 (ADA Accessible) | Convict Lake |
| #26, #27 | McGee Creek |
| #30, #33 | Tuff |
| #68, #72 | French Camp |
| #6 | Iris Meadows |
| #9 | Big Meadow |

| | |
|---|---|
| #59, #62, #86, #99, #133 | East Fork |
| #25, #26, #21 | Rock Creek Lake |
| #27 | Bitterbrush |
| #1 | Lower Intake 2 |
| #4, #6, #15 | Bishop Park |
| #15, #18 | Sabrina |
| #2 | North Lake |
| #1 | Four Jeffrey |
| #2, #3, #25, #26, #27, #28 | Sage Flat |
| #8, #10, #11, #18 | Upper Sage Flat |
| #19, #21, #22 | Big Pine Creek |
| #10, #12, #33 | Upper Gray's Meadow |
| #40, #51 | Lower Gray's Meadow |
| #20, #21, #22 | Lone Pine Campground |
| #1, #22 | Whitney Portal |
| | |

## Acknowledgements

We struck up a lot of conversations with a lot of campers along the way. Some of them graciously allowed us into their campsites so we could get a feel for what it was like and so Patrick could take photos. We want to extend our sincerest of thanks to all of these people.

We also would like to thank all the camp hosts who took the time to answer our questions.

Finally, our deepest thanks go out to our talented graphic artist Teri Broad, who answered our call for help at the last minute to fix our book cover. Thanks to her, it looks great.

# About Kimberly and Patrick Wilkes

Kimberly is a freelance writer who has had more than 600 articles appear in publications such as *Sacramento Magazine, Alaska Airlines Magazine,* and the *San Jose Mercury News.* Under her maiden name of Kimberly Pryor, she authored *The Indestructible Relationship: Support and Understand Each Other Better During Grief, Illness, And All Life's Stressful Moments.* The Electronic Publishing Industry Coalition (EPIC) chose *The Indestructible Relationship* as the best non-fiction ebook of 2012.

Patrick is a professional photographer who earned acclaim for his exhibit *The Four Seasons of Pyramid Lake,* which was featured for a year at the Pyramid Lake Museum and Cultural Center. He spent two years living at Pyramid Lake capturing the beauty of the area and chronicling the lives of the Paiute Indians. He is known for his landscape photos, his black and white portraits, and his animal photos. He was the official photographer for Nevada's 150-year celebration and also is the official photographer for the annual Fort Ross Festival.

Kimberly and Patrick are a husband and wife team. The Eastern Sierra holds a special place in their hearts because Patrick proposed to Kimberly at The Restaurant at Convict Lake in September 2012. The first trip they ever took together was to Death Valley.

---

### Have You Enjoyed This Book? Write a Review on Amazon.com

Your input is important to us. We wrote this book to help you find peace and rejuvenation in the Eastern Sierra. Write a review on Amazon and let us know if we've succeeded in helping you find a peaceful campsite.

Made in the USA
San Bernardino, CA
16 June 2020

73437011R00257